# The Sad Citizen

# The Sad Citizen

*How Politics Is Depressing
and Why It Matters*

CHRISTOPHER OJEDA

THE UNIVERSITY OF CHICAGO PRESS     CHICAGO AND LONDON

The University of Chicago Press, Chicago 60637
The University of Chicago Press, Ltd., London
© 2025 by The University of Chicago
All rights reserved. No part of this book may be used or reproduced in any manner whatsoever without written permission, except in the case of brief quotations in critical articles and reviews. For more information, contact the University of Chicago Press, 1427 E. 60th St., Chicago, IL 60637.
Published 2025
Printed in the United States of America

34 33 32 31 30 29 28 27 26 25   1 2 3 4 5

ISBN-13: 978-0-226-84075-8 (cloth)
ISBN-13: 978-0-226-84076-5 (paper)
ISBN-13: 978-0-226-84077-2 (e-book)
DOI: https://doi.org/10.7208/chicago/9780226840772.001.0001

Library of Congress Cataloging-in-Publication Data

Names: Ojeda, Christopher, author.
Title: The sad citizen : how politics is depressing and why it matters / Christopher Ojeda.
Other titles: How politics is depressing and why it matters
Description: Chicago : The University of Chicago Press, 2025. | Includes bibliographical references and index.
Identifiers: LCCN 2024047416 | ISBN 9780226840758 (cloth) | ISBN 9780226840765 (paper) | ISBN 9780226840772 (e-book)
Subjects: LCSH: Political psychology. | Depression, Mental—Political aspects. | Political psychology—United States. | United States—Politics and government—Psychological aspects.
Classification: LCC JA74.5.O44 2025 | DDC 320.01/90973—dc23/eng/20241126
LC record available at https://lccn.loc.gov/2024047416

♾ This paper meets the requirements of ANSI/NISO Z39.48-1992 (Permanence of Paper).

# Contents

List of Tables and Figures   vii

CHAPTER 1.  A Sinking Feeling   1

CHAPTER 2.  When Politics Produces Loss   17

CHAPTER 3.  When Loss Becomes Depressing   32

CHAPTER 4.  When Depression Leads to Withdrawal   58

CHAPTER 5.  Election Blues   77

CHAPTER 6.  The Polarization of Private Life   96

CHAPTER 7.  The Pain of Public Policy   117

CHAPTER 8.  Democracy without Disruption   141

Acknowledgments   151

Appendix   153

Notes   195

References   203

Index   215

# Tables and Figures

TABLES

Table 1.1   Overview of Data Sources / 14
Table 2.1   Types and Examples of Stressors / 22
Table 2.2   The Components of Loss / 23
Table 3.1   The Appraisal Structure of Emotions / 40
Table 3.2   The Political Content of Poll Questions about Depression / 43
Table 4.1   Depressing Experiences in Politics and Personal Life / 67
Table 4.2   The Prevalence of Coping Strategies / 68
Table 4.3   Online Advice for Coping with Politics / 73
Table 5.1   The Prevalence of Depression in Election Poll Questions / 83
Table 5.2   The Scope of the Election-Depression Connection / 94
Table A.1   The Impact of Irrevocability as Solvability and Control / 157
Table A.2   The Impact of Irrevocability as Political Power / 158
Table A.3   The Impact of Electoral Loss in the United States / 161
Table A.4   The Impact of Losses and Gains / 166
Table A.5   The Impact of Irrevocable Losses and Gains / 167
Table A.6   The Impact of Repeated Loss / 168
Table A.7   The Categorization of Coping Strategies / 170
Table A.8   The Impact of Depression on Coping with Politics and Personal Life / 172
Table A.9   List of Psychology Websites and Pages / 174
Table A.10  Recommended Coping Strategies from Verywell Mind / 175

Table A.11  Recommendations on How to Manage Exposure to Politics / 175
Table A.12  The Impact of Obama's Election in 2008 / 178
Table A.13  The Impact of Obama's Election in 2012 / 179
Table A.14  The Impact of Harris's Election in 2020 / 180
Table A.15  The Impact of Palin's Loss in 2008 and Clinton's Loss in 2016 / 181
Table A.16  The Impact of the SCOTUS *Obergefell* Ruling / 182
Table A.17  The Categorization of Party Success in the 2006 Dutch Elections / 183
Table A.18  The Impact of Electoral Loss in the Netherlands / 185
Table A.19  The Impact of Ideology, Income, and Redistribution / 187
Table A.20  Items in the General Health Questinnaire-12 / 188
Table A.21  The Impact of Household Polarization on Overall Depression / 189
Table A.22  The Impact of Actual Political Differences with Parents / 192
Table A.23  The Impact of Perceived Political Differences with Parents / 192

FIGURES

Figure 1.1  The Stress-Appraisal-Coping Framework / 7
Figure 3.1  The Prevalence of Depression in Political Polls / 47
Figure 3.2  The Impact of Losses and Gains / 50
Figure 3.3  The Impact of Irrevocable Losses and Gains / 51
Figure 3.4  The Impact of Irrevocability as Solvability and Control / 54
Figure 3.5  The Impact of Irrevocability as Political Power / 55
Figure 4.1  The Four Coping Strategies / 61
Figure 4.2  The Impact of Depression on Coping with Politics and Personal Life / 69
Figure 5.1  The Impact of Electoral Loss in the United States / 85
Figure 5.2  Electoral Trends in Depression-Related Google Searches / 88
Figure 5.3  The Impact of Electoral Loss in the Netherlands / 93
Figure 6.1  The Impact of Household Polarization on Components of Depression / 106

Figure 6.2  The Impact of Household Polarization on Overall Depression / 107
Figure 6.3  The Impact of Perceived Political Differences with Parents / 109
Figure 7.1  The Impact of the SCOTUS *Obergefell* Ruling / 122
Figure 7.2  The Association between Inequality, Redistribution, and Depression in European Countries / 132
Figure 7.3  The Impact of Ideology, Income, and Redistribution / 133

CHAPTER ONE

# A Sinking Feeling

President Biden's ratings were low going into the midterm elections of 2022. He suffered from generic partisan negativity, the slow pandemic recovery, the botched withdrawal from Afghanistan, and the failed social spending bill. A CBS poll found that 49 percent of Americans were "disappointed" with Biden's performance. Ross Douthat at the *New York Times* dubbed 2021 "The Year of American Disappointment." Democrats seemed to be hit especially hard. The Cook Political Report described Democratic voters as disappointed, tired, and exhausted (Walter 2022). Nearly two years into the Biden presidency, it seemed like little had changed. Trumpism was alive and flourishing in the Republican Party, and the conservative majority on the Supreme Court continued, unimpeded, to reshape American law. This disappointment didn't bode well for Biden or the Democratic party. With only fifty seats in the Senate, Democrats couldn't afford any losses.

As the midterm election season got underway, Republican senator Rick Scott of Florida released an eleven-point plan for the Republican Party. Scott proposed finishing the wall on the Mexican border and naming it for former president Donald Trump, scrubbing questions about ethnicity from government forms, imposing term limits on federal employees and members of Congress, and making all Americans pay taxes regardless of income. Pundits were stunned. News outlets on the left and right reported that Scott had upended Senate minority leader Mitch McConnell and his plan to win back the Senate. One headline from the *Wall Street Journal* read, "Mitch McConnell Rebukes Rick Scott for Tax Proposal," while the *Washington Post* wrote, "Rick Scott walks away. Then McConnell dresses him down." McConnell claimed he opposed Scott's tax plan, telling reporters, "We will not have as part of our agenda a bill that raises taxes on half the American people" (Hounshell and Askarinam 2022).

No doubt McConnell was annoyed by the proposed tax hike, an idea that is eternally unpopular with Americans and antithetical to conservative values. However, I suspect he would have been annoyed with Scott's eleven-point plan even if it didn't include a tax hike. The key here is *disappointment*. Biden's poor performance was disappointing the left, so McConnell wanted to keep the spotlight on the president. McConnell's electoral strategy was to do and say as little as possible in the run-up to the midterm. When asked by a reporter what the Republican Party would do if it won the Senate, McConnell didn't talk about lowering taxes but instead quipped, "That is a very good question. And I'll let you know when we take it back" (C-SPAN 2022). McConnell understood that drawing attention to any policy priorities—whether he agreed with them or not—risked turning Democratic disappointment into anxiety over a Republican Congress, a feeling that would propel them to vote in the upcoming midterm election. In other words, his strategy was not to win voters with his ideas but to keep Democrats away from the voting booth by letting their disappointment fester.

In a surprising twist, however, Republicans underperformed in the midterm, barely eking out a win in the House and leaving Democrats in control of the Senate. Republicans were now the disappointed ones. Appearing on Fox News a few days after the election, Senator Scott told Sean Hannity, "Here's what happened to us. Election Day, our voters didn't show up. We didn't get enough voters. It was a complete disappointment." He went on to add, "I think we didn't have enough of a positive message. We said everything about how bad the Biden agenda was. It's bad, the Democrats are radical, but we have to have a plan of what we stand for" (Folmar 2022).

The performance of Biden, the maneuvering of McConnell, and the electoral loss of Republicans capture a certain truth about the political world: politics makes many people depressed, and depression is demobilizing. Emotions are central to politics, but depression hasn't received much attention from either political actors or political scientists. This omission may be surprising, particularly today, given that the country seems to be in the grip of a national malaise, but depression is usually less visible than other political emotions. Where anger draws new people into the political arena and fires them up (think of "Lock her up!" chants at early Donald Trump campaign rallies or "Not my president!" chants at the Women's March on Washington following Trump's election), depression leads to retreat rather than outward political expression.

The invisibility of depression doesn't make it any less important than emotions like anger, anxiety, or fear. Depression shapes the way citizens think about and engage with the political process, often with the consequence of exacerbating political and social inequality. Women, the poor, young people, and LGBTQ persons are both underrepresented in politics and, in many cases, more depressed. While anyone can feel depressed by politics, it's no coincidence that the most powerless groups in society are the ones who experience depression most intensely: politics is most depressing to those who lack power, and depression in turn creates barriers to exercising political power. This is what I think of as the political cycle of depression.

Depression also deserves attention in its own right. My home field of political science generally studies emotions as inputs into the political process, but I am just as interested in depression as an output, or product, of politics. Throughout the book, I take a broad and nonclinical view of depression, thinking of it as a family of emotions that include disappointment, sadness, despair, grief, and melancholy. These feelings vary in intensity and duration—ranging from mild disappointment to full-blown major depressive disorder—but they all meaningfully affect people's lives and their ability to engage in politics and other activities. By clarifying how politics produces depression, I hope to help ordinary citizens, psychologists, psychiatrists, and other mental health professionals better understand how to appropriately cope with these difficult and unpleasant feelings.

How politics shapes depression and how depression shapes politics are intertwined problems. I study them together in the context of modern Western democracies, and what I've found is that democracy and depression are sometimes at odds with one another. Elections are a staple of democracy but necessarily produce losses that can be depressing. Echo chambers can inflame polarization, spread misinformation, and undermine democracy but can also be a source of comfort. Following the news upholds norms of democratic citizenship but can be distressing. What should we do when what is good for democracy is bad for our mental well-being, and vice versa? This question recurs throughout the book, and while I don't have all the answers, I try to point us toward a "politics without disruption" in the conclusion. More importantly, however, my hope is to generate interest in this important topic, knowing that more smart people thinking about these problems will give us a better shot at solving them.

## What Is Depression?

Excessive feelings of sadness have been regarded as a disorder throughout much of history. As sociologists Allan Horwitz and Jerome Wakefield note, "From ancient Greek medical writings until the early twentieth century, what is now termed depressive disorder was generally referred to as melancholia, which literally means 'black bile disorder'" (2007, 54–55). Modern science has overturned the theory of black bile, but the pathologizing of excessive sadness has stuck around. The American Psychiatric Association now defines a depressive episode in the *Diagnostics and Statistics Manual V* as experiencing depressed mood or loss of interest along with at least four of the following additional symptoms for a period of two weeks or more: weight loss or gain, insomnia or hypersomnia, restlessness or being slowed down, fatigue, feelings of worthlessness or guilt, trouble concentrating, or thoughts of death or suicide. These symptoms must disrupt everyday life and should not be attributable to a medical condition, substance use, or a significant loss (e.g., the death of a loved one). Major depressive disorder occurs when major depressive episodes recur regularly.

Many people today think of major depressive disorder when they hear the word *depression*—an association that was bolstered by the spread of Prozac and the popularity of Elizabeth Wertzel's *Prozac Nation*—but depression doesn't have only one definition. How the term gets used varies from context to context and person to person. In fact, major depressive disorder is just one of several "mood disorders" in the *Diagnostic and Statistics Manual*. Persistent depressive disorder, which was formerly called dysthymia, refers to long-lasting low levels of depressed feelings that do not reach the threshold for major depressive disorder.[1] The term *depression* is also part of the vernacular. Today, we might use it colloquially for feelings that do not merit a clinical diagnosis or simply to describe something that seems pathetic (e.g., "this salad is depressing").

When academics, journalists, and politicians mention anxiety, anger, and fear, they don't mean generalized anxiety disorder, intermittent explosive disorder, or phobias. They are talking about feelings rather than disorders. I do the same with depression. I think of it as a "family" of feelings, which include disappointment, sadness, grief, despair, anguish, and more.[2] The core of the depression family is a *sinking feeling*. As the psychologist Josè Eduardo Rondòn Bernard writes, "The word depression comes from the Latin 'depressio' which means sinking. The person feels sunk with a weight on their existence" (2018, 6). Democrats had a sinking feeling going into the midterm because of Biden's poor performance, while Republicans had a sinking feeling coming out of the midterm because of their party's electoral misfortunes.

Defining depression as a family of feelings has advantages. While clinical terms like major depressive disorder are helpful to mental health professionals diagnosing patients, they are often too restrictive for academics studying the general public. For starters, many people experience feelings of depression that are not intense or prolonged enough to merit a clinical diagnosis. Defining depression as only a disorder would force me to overlook the experiences of these people. Major depressive disorder also conflates two ideas that I want to study separately: feelings and disruptions. One requirement for major depressive disorder is that it causes significant disruption to everyday life, such as relationships, work, or hobbies. This isn't a problem if the goal is to diagnose, but it is a problem if the goal is to examine disruption as a consequence of feeling depressed. I want to understand how politics produces feelings of depression *and* how these feelings in turn disrupt our social and political life. If I were limited to cases that involved significant disruptions to everyday life—in short, cases of major depressive disorder—then I would have to scrap any investigation into the disappointment of Democrats. This case is important, however, because it illustrates how feelings of depression that do not meet a clinical threshold can still be politically consequential.

It's often said that "to measure is to know." In other words, the meaning of depression ultimately comes down to how I measure it. I use two approaches that I call object-specific depression and generalized depression. Both rely on self-reported feelings, but in different ways. Object-specific depression means that feelings are reported in connection to something that happened in the world. For instance, the Associated Press asked Americans in 2010, "Thinking about American politics today, do any of the following words describe your own personal feelings about politics, or not? How about . . . depressed, does that describe your own personal feelings about politics, or not?" The feelings of depression are tied to a specific object—in this case, American politics today. This measurement approach can be modified to any object of interest (e.g., elections, political violence, the policymaking process, etc.) and any feeling of interest (e.g., depression, sadness, disappointment, etc.), which makes it highly adaptable to studying different areas of politics.

I am also interested in feelings that are not tied to any one object, which I refer to as generalized depression. Here, I draw on validated survey instruments developed by psychologists. For example, the Center for Epidemiologic Studies Depression Scale tells survey participants, "Below is a list of the ways you might have felt or behaved. Please tell me how often you have felt this way during the past week" and then displays twenty "symptoms" of depression, such as feeling depressed, feeling sad, feeling that everything is an effort, and feeling unable to shake off the blues. Each "symptom" can be reported rarely or none of the time (0–1 day), some or a little of the time (1–2 days), occasionally or a moderate amount of time (3–4 days), and most or all of the time (5–7 days). Although these instruments were developed as a way to identify survey respondents who may have major depressive disorder, I repurpose them as a way to capture the intensity of generalized depression felt by ordinary people, ranging from not at all to severe.

For all their resemblance, members of the depression family are distinct. It goes without saying that disappointment and despair are hardly the same thing. Family members are associated with a unique intensity, duration, cultural meaning, and affect type. Sadness is typically viewed as a short-lived emotion, while melancholia is thought of as a longer-lasting mood.[3] Disappointment is typically associated with dashed expectations, while grief is typically associated with loss.[4] These differences make it difficult to directly compare emotions to one another. Is it worse to feel intense disappointment for three weeks or intense despair for three days? What about one week of either intense disappointment or mild despair? There is no correct answer to these questions, because there is no standard unit of depression. Ultimately, the shared likeness of the depression family means I study a diverse set of feelings—such as disappointment, sadness, and depression—or symptoms—such as feeling blue, lonely, or fatigued. This diversity allows for a more comprehensive assessment of how politics is depressing, but their distinctiveness means I am cautious in making comparisons between them.[5]

## What Causes Depression?

We've learned a considerable amount about the origins of depression over the past century. Scholars in psychology, psychiatry, sociology, public health, medicine, and epidemiology have brought greater attention to

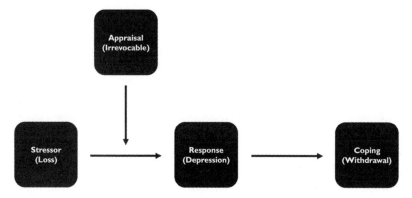

FIGURE 1.1. The Stress-Appraisal-Coping Framework

the role of genes, neurobiology, cognition, stress, gender, relationships, discrimination, poverty, income inequality, culture, and the healthcare system. This knowledge has contributed to the development of effective pharmacological and therapeutic treatments for the most severe feelings of depression, advances that have helped countless people. Yet around the world we continue to see depression persist and, by some accounts, worsen. The medical scientist Brandon Hidaka even dubbed depression the "disease of modernity," pointing out, "There has been much progress, but countless questions circling the concept of depression and its origins still remain unanswered. A better understanding of large-scale causes and the complex relationships between modern culture, chronic disease, and depression will be essential for systemic, population-based interventions to address a very common affliction" (2012, 211). It is the gap between what we've learned about depression and its stubborn persistence, if not increasing prevalence, that opens a space for new explanations, including politics.

So how might politics evoke depression? I begin answering this question by asking a broader one: How does anything evoke depression? And I begin answering this question with an even broader one: How does anything evoke any emotion? One answer comes from the stress-appraisal-coping framework, which was first proposed by the psychologists Richard Lazarus and Susan Folkman in their book *Stress, Appraisal, and Coping* (1984). The gist of this framework, which is displayed in figure 1.1, is that a change in our environment (stressor) that we perceive as important (appraisal) evokes neurological, psychological, and affective responses, which in turn influence our behavior (coping). The stressor is what happens, the appraisal is how we think about it, and the coping is what we do about it. For instance, you may recall a time you were stuck in traffic (stressor) and realized you would be late to an important meeting (appraisal). You may have felt anxious (response), which caused you to speed to avoid being late (coping).[6]

Different stressors evoke different responses. Threats make us anxious and fearful, while rewards bring us joy. Negative life events, such as the loss of a job or loved one, can make us depressed, while positive life events make us proud. Inequality can make us feel gratified if we have more and envious if we have less. Appraisals also shape how we respond. Changes appraised as irrelevant are unlikely to evoke any emotion, while unexpected changes may evoke surprise. We feel positive emotions when changes advance a goal and negative emotions when they hinder a goal. Coping is how we attempt to manage a situation. Anger makes us lash out, disgust leads us to avoid others, and fear can give rise to flight. I argue that *depression is a response to a loss (stressor) that is perceived as irrevocable (appraisal) and that leads to withdrawal (coping)*. The death of a loved one is the quintessential example of this pattern: it is an irrevocable loss, it generates feelings of depression, and it often leads the bereaved to withdraw from social life.

Armed with the stress-appraisal-coping framework, we can begin to see how politics is depressing. Stressors are inherent to politics because competition for scarce resources and conflict over political preferences creates winners and losers. Losing in politics can take a few forms. One type of loss is when our political preferences cease to be realized, such as when an election ousts a preferred politician from office, or a legislature enacts a policy we oppose. We preferred a different political outcome than the one we ended up with. Another type of loss is when politics takes away things of personal value. Often this occurs through the passage and implementation of policies, such as the tax collector taking away our income, or a court ruling taking away our rights. Yet another type of loss occurs when we pour resources into enacting change but ultimately fail to do so. Perhaps we donated to a candidate who lost an election or lobbied for legislation that failed to pass. What is lost in these cases is our time, energy, and resources.

These losses often feel irrevocable because the collective nature of politics makes it challenging—if not impossible—to personally control what happens. Coordinating with others is costly but often the only way to accomplish something in politics. Our sense of irrevocability—the idea that nothing can undo the loss—grows as coordination becomes more costly and our personal control over the situation diminishes. Those with fewer resources, who therefore cannot cover the cost of collective action or inoculate themselves from the harms of public policy, are especially likely to perceive loss as irrevocable. In short, politics is depressing when it creates losers who think the outcome is irrevocable.

How we cope has the potential to alleviate or deepen feelings. We commonly cope with depression by withdrawing, because depression signals to us that little can be done to resolve the problem. This is especially true in politics, where our behavior is less consequential to what happens. Whereas addressing problems in our personal life often makes them better, the collective nature of politics means our action (or inaction) by itself rarely improves (or worsens) the situation. If we can't solve the problem, we might as well ignore it so that it's not making us more depressed. This logic gives rise to what political scientists refer to as freeriding—we abstain from politics to reduce the stress we personally face, leaving it to others to tackle the problems facing the collective.

## What Is at Stake?

It may seem odd for a political scientist to write about depression, a subject that typically falls within the purview of psychology and psychiatry. Others may think the connection between politics and depression is obvious, in which case it may seem strange that political scientists aren't writing more about it. Either way, the connection between politics and depression has important implications. For starters, democracy should empower citizens rather than depress them. As the sociologist Gøsta Esping-Andersen points out, the ultimate goal of the democratic state is the "production and distribution of social well-being" (1990, 1). This idea motivates political scientists and sociologists to study economic outcomes, such as poverty and financial insecurity, as well as health outcomes, such as infant mortality and life expectancy. Considerable attention has also been devoted to happiness, or what is sometimes called life satisfaction or subjective well-being (Radcliff 2013). These metrics are important but tell only part of the story. There are good reasons to think that when politics makes one person wealthy, healthy, or happy, it makes another depressed. Depression should therefore be added to the list of outcomes for assessing the performance democracy.

However, depression is more than just a metric for evaluating the success of democracy. It can also help us better design democratic institutions. Institutions, such as electoral systems and legislatures, transform the ideals of democracy into the rules, roles, and norms that guide how political decisions are made. How should institutions be designed when the requirements of democracy come into conflict with the essentials of human well-being? For instance, elections are a core part of democracy, but electoral loss is a source of depression. Staying informed about current events and taking an active role in politics is an important part of being a responsible citizen, but being engaged is also sometimes depressing. Is there a way to design institutions so that they minimize depression as an unintended consequence of democracy? Answering this question is essential if we are to help democracy live up to its promise of empowerment.

Depression is also integral to understanding the political process. Whereas anger, anxiety, and fear are mobilizing emotions, depression is *demobilizing*. The depressed citizen doesn't go to the polls, take to the streets, run for office, attend meetings, or volunteer for campaigns (Landwehr and Ojeda 2021). This difference may explain why so little attention has been given to depression. Anger, anxiety, and fear attract our attention because they are displayed in public. In contrast, depression is an inconspicuous emotion and one that is produced quietly. Its invisibility leaves us with the impression that it doesn't share a connection with politics. However, if we are to understand why certain political outcomes occur, we need to account for who does and *who does not* participate.

The demobilizing effect of depression is important to political inequality. Less powerful people are disproportionately burdened by depression, a pattern that is itself concerning. Depression can further reinforce power imbalances by making it more difficult for the less powerful to express grievances, gain representation, or make decisions. That feelings of depression may be produced by the very system that is supposed to give the less powerful a voice presents a fundamental challenge to democracy. In short, the connection between politics and depression is important if we are to understand why some groups have more power, rights, and resources in society.

That depression demobilizes sufferers and entrenches political inequalities means it can be a tool for suppression. Political actors in a losing position want to expand the scope of conflict to gain an advantage (Schattschneider 1960). Expansion brings in new actors and changes the power dynamics of the situation. Anger, anxiety, and fearmongering are tactics commonly used by actors in a losing position, because appealing to these emotions mobilizes supporters and expands the scope of conflict. In contrast, political actors in the dominant position want to maintain power, so they seek to restrict the scope of conflict—to stop new actors from upending the political order. Just as losing actors seek to produce anger, anxiety, and fear among supporters, dominant actors have an incentive to produce depression among the opposition. Doing so demobilizes them and thus restricts the scope of conflict. It is what one of my friends dubbed "suppression through depression."

Is depression always bad? Is the goal to build a democracy free from depression? The assumption so far has been yes, but scholars also recognize that emotions have useful functions, so we should consider whether this is true for depression. When feelings of depression are tied to a specific irrevocable loss, they signal that the best course of action is to step away from the situation. Doing so can help avoid further loss, conserve resources that might be wasted trying to regain what cannot be regained, and create space to reappraise and restrategize (Nesse 1999). Nonparticipation in democracies is generally viewed as undesirable and something to be eradicated, but depression tells the sufferer that nonparticipation can sometimes be in their best interest. To sharpen this point, consider the cost of not feeling depressed—the loser doesn't know or doesn't want to step away from the situation, so they make matters worse by pouring resources into recovering their unrecoverable loss.

Depression, and its demobilizing effect, may sometimes help democracy work. For example, the peaceful transfer of power following an election depends on the consent of the losers (Anderson et al. 2007). That depression induces sufferers to step back from politics raises the possibility that it is somehow crucial to securing the losers' consent. The aftermath of elections is just one instance of demobilization helping facilitate democracy. Demobilization can also be useful when it de-escalates a tense situation or reduces the transaction costs of decision-making. In general, whenever democracy depends on demobilization to succeed, we have to consider whether some low-level depression is useful and whether democracy would be worse off without it.

Just as depression is invisible in politics, politics is largely invisible in depression. This is hardly surprising. Compared to relationships, family, school, and work, politics often seems too removed from everyday life to be relevant. Yet even if politics is not as crucial to depression as these other domains of life, overlooking it has hobbled our ability to describe, explain, predict, and change depression. Although we know a lot about depression, it continues to be a pervasive problem in society, it has worsened in recent years, and questions remain about its etiology (Hidaka 2012). We need to understand what causes depression if we want to combat it, and this includes politics.

While politics may be one item on the long list of depression's causes, it is also the pen used to write many other items on the list, such as discrimination, poverty, unemployment, income inequality, and poor healthcare. Some psychologists, psychiatrists, and medical scientists have turned their attention in recent years to studying how public policies, such as cash assistance, healthcare, food benefits, housing subsidies, and unemployment insurance, affect depression. Sorting out which policies relieve, exacerbate, or have no impact on depression is a good first step, but we ultimately need to examine the politics of the policymaking process if change is to occur. Public policies do not emerge out of thin air but are the result of a contentious and politicized policymaking process (Stone 2011). Investigating this process will help us understand why some localities, states, and countries have a full suite of policies that are known to reduce depression, while others have only policies known to make it worse.

Clarifying how and why politics is depressing is also essential to developing effective evidence-based therapies. Mental health professionals that I interviewed expressed uncertainty about how to help clients who were distressed by politics. Politics as a source of depression never came up in their training, so they often relied on basic principles, such as maintaining neutrality and avoiding self-disclosure, to navigate political conversations with clients. Yet many wondered if they had the right tools to help clients or whether these principles limited the support they could offer. As one therapist told me, "I'm honestly wondering about election week and like do I even want to—like I want to be there for my clients because I know they're going to be stressed; as you know, it's probably going to take days for us to get returns. But also, I'm also going to be stressed [chuckles] about the election and it taking days, but that's going to be very draining and hard to try and stay grounded and try to be, feel effective and helping them when I don't quite know how to help myself." Developing effective therapies isn't just about what mental health professionals say to clients with the most severe feelings of depression. Most people who feel depressed never see the inside of a therapy room; instead, they turn to family, friends, and the internet for support. What advice is doled out online or shared informally through social networks about coping with low-level depression? If we see a partner, family member, or friend who is depressed by politics, what should we do? Perhaps existing coping strategies are sufficient, but we can't know this for sure without directly studying politics.

Effective therapies can only be useful if used, and here politics matters too. The US surgeon general David Satcher made this argument two decades ago when he pointed out that "critical gaps exist between those who need service and those who receive service ... gaps also exist between optimally effective treatments and what many individuals receive in actual practice settings" (2000, 94). Although his view is narrowly focused on depression as a disorder, his argument that politics underpins issues of distribution and access resonates. It is not enough to develop effective treatments if politics hinders people from accessing them. The impact of politics can range from the public administration of healthcare systems that treat the most severe cases of depression to the politicization of coping strategies used by those with low-level depression.

Today, the need to incorporate politics into the study of depression feels especially urgent. Mass media has made politics visible and prominent, while polarization has made politics more vitriolic and high stakes. The result is that today we feel the intensity of politics in our everyday life more than in recent history. If there were ever a time to write about how politics is depressing, it is now.

## How Do I Study Politics and Depression?

Throughout the book, I study the relationship between politics and depression scientifically. I assert falsifiable claims about why, when, and how politics matters to depression (and why, when, and how it doesn't) and then subject these claims to empirical tests. I use surveys, experiments, polls, interviews, case studies, administrative data, and more. Mixing and matching research designs and data bolsters our confidence in the connection between politics and depression. This strategy—known as triangulation to social scientists—ensures that my conclusions are not simply artifacts of my tools. Table 1.1 provides an overview of the data sources and can hopefully serve as a guide to the reader as they make their way through the many results I report throughout the book.

The more boring details of the data, analytic strategy, and results are relegated to endnotes, appendices, and replication materials. As a general

TABLE I.I **Overview of Data Sources**

| Study | Chapters | Brief Description |
|---|---|---|
| Interviews of Therapists | 2, 6 | I interviewed mental health professionals in the United States to learn more about what clients say when they talk about politics in the therapy room. |
| Cooperative Election Study | 2, 3, 5 | The CES is a survey of Americans that occurs each election year and includes a preelection and postelection survey; I use special modules on the 2020 and 2022 surveys to illustrate political loss, to analyze appraisals of irrevocability, and to assess whether electoral loss is depressing. |
| Political Polls | 3, 5 | Searching Cornell University's Roper Center archives, I found over four hundred polls that ask Americans about feeling depressed about politics. I analyze the toplines and wording of these poll questions overall and as they relate specifically to elections. |
| Irrevocable Loss Experiment | 3 | I conducted a survey experiment of Americans that presented respondents with information about politics but included randomizations of loss and irrevocability so that I could assess the emotional impact of the information. |
| Coping Experiment | 4, 7 | I conducted a survey experiment of Americans that used an autobiographical recall task to randomize emotions across life domains, including politics, which allows me to assess how feelings of depression affected the selection of coping strategies. |
| Psychology Websites | 4 | I analyzed popular psychology websites to assess what kinds of recommendations are made by mental health professionals about how to cope with the stress of politics. |
| Google Trends | 5 | Google Trends provides information about the relative frequency with which different terms are searched on Google; I use this data to assess how electoral loss impacts online search behaviors related to depression. |
| Behavioral Risk Factor Surveillance Survey | 5, 7 | The BRFSS is an annual survey of hundreds of thousands of Americans conducted by the United States' Center for Disease Control; I use it to assess how social identities, such as gender and race, shape the impact of electoral winning and losing on depression. |
| European Social Survey | 5, 7 | The ESS is a biennial survey of tens of thousands of Europeans across thirty countries; the surveys in 2006 and 2012 include questions about depression. I use it to analyze the impact of electoral winning and losing on depression. I also use it (along with Standardized World Income Inequality Database) to analyze how cross-national differences in redistribution affect depression. |
| British Household Panel Study | 6 | The BHPS is a household-based longitudinal survey of Brits. The survey follows the sample, even as they may move from the initial household, and supplements with surveys of everyone residing in their house at the time of the interview. I use this survey to study how polarization in the home affects depression. |
| National Longitudinal Survey of Youth | 6 | The NLSY is a study of mother-child dyads. The children are mostly adults at the time of the survey, but I nevertheless use the survey to examine how political differences in parent-child relationships affect depression. |

rule, the main text contains a brief overview of the data as well as the results, the endnotes and appendix contain detailed information about the data and measures, and the supplemental information and replication materials posted on my website contain data, scripts, full results, robustness checks, and more. I take this approach to ensure that readers with a minimal knowledge of statistics can understand what I find without being overwhelmed by statistics. I believe a book about depression should be accessible to anyone who has ever felt depressed or knows someone who has. Since depression is not limited to academics with statistical training, it is important to me that I balance the rigor of the analyses with the readability of the findings.

Finally, I graft storytelling onto scientific analysis, because I believe personal experiences, current events, and anecdotes enrich what we can learn. Drawing on personal experiences—or what is sometimes called autoethnography—is unusual in political science. I use it occasionally throughout the book when I think doing so can enhance our understanding of how politics and depression are connected. Discussing my own personal experiences necessarily exposes some of my own political views. However, rather than compromising my scientific objectivity, I think this honesty enhances it by allowing the reader to assess how my arguments may be shaped by my perspective.

## What's Next?

The remainder of the book is dedicated to investigating how politics is depressing. The next three chapters break down the stress-appraisal-coping framework in detail. Chapter 2 focuses on stress and the politics of loss. Psychologists, evolutionary scientists, and sociologists have long recognized that loss is the type of stressor that causes depression, but what does this term mean, and how is it produced in politics? I argue that scarcity and competition in politics give rise to three types of losses: when our political preferences cease to be realized, when politics takes away personal objects of value, and when our efforts to enact political change fail.

In chapter 3, I turn to the appraisal component of the stress-appraisal-coping framework. Appraisals of irrevocability are what makes loss feel depressing rather than some other negative emotion, such as anger, anxiety, or fear. I explain how the appraisal process works in general and how it works specifically with respect to irrevocability and depression. I then analyze hundreds of political polls as well as a survey experiment and find that that losses in politics can be depressing, especially when appraised as irrevocable.

Coping is the third part of the framework and the subject of chapter 4. I break down the concept of coping and argue that coping with depression in politics is different than coping with it in our private life. The collective nature of politics makes us more likely to use withdrawal as a coping mechanism for depression. Experimental evidence bears out this idea: depression has a demobilizing effect, especially in politics. I then review professional advice about how to cope with the stress of politics. I analyze texts from popular psychology websites and find that there is underdeveloped and sometimes contradictory wisdom about what to do.

The next three chapters investigate how specific aspects of the political process can be depressing. Chapter 5 examines elections and electoral loss, chapter 6 examines polarization and political conflict in personal relationships, and chapter 7 offers four brief case studies on the politics of same-sex marriage, abortion, redistribution, and climate change. These chapters do not directly test the stress-appraisal-coping framework, but rather use it as a guide for thinking about why and how these aspects of politics may be depressing. Throughout, I provide extensive empirical evidence of politics' depressing effects, drawing on a range of data, including longitudinal surveys, election polls, Google Trends, interviews, and more.

Finally, in chapter 8, I conclude by proposing a few ways we can move forward. Politics will always be somewhat stressful and depressing, but can we lift its emotional burden for the public? Making visible the way in which politics is depressing is the first step in making depression an old political emotion, one of the past rather than future. However, much more work is required. I examine only a tiny sliver of politics, so much more remains to be learned about the connection between politics and depression.

CHAPTER TWO

# When Politics Produces Loss

The connection between politics and depression starts with *loss*: politics produces loss, and loss produces depression. Surprisingly, however, no one has systematically and clearly made this connection. The psychologist Richard Lazarus and epidemiologist Judith Blackfield Cohen came close when they asserted that "cataclysmic phenomena" are important causes of "sadness-depression." They argued that large-scale traumatic events, such as natural disasters, war, imprisonment, and relocation, could be a source of widespread depression because they affect "large numbers of people, are usually outside the control of individuals or groups, and are assumed to be more-or-less universally stressful" (1977, 91). Subsequent research would bear out this idea. Exposure to political violence, especially among children, has been linked to severe depression in places like Egypt, Indonesia, Ireland, and Palestine (Barber 2009). In the United States, veterans suffer from depression because of their exposure to war (Ginzburg et al. 2010), while many first responders and residents of New York City experienced depression in the aftermath of the 9/11 attacks (Galea et al. 2002).

Undoubtedly, politics can be widely depressing when it produces cataclysmic phenomena, but is this the only way politics is depressing? Most forms of stress increase our risk of depression, from daily hassles, such as a long commute or rainy weather, to more serious negative life events, such as a divorce or the death of a loved one. Some political psychologists have shown that more mundane forms of political stress can be depressing, too. One study found higher levels of depression among South African adolescents who reported more "political life events"—a portmanteau of politics and negative life events—such as conducting a security drill at school and attending a political demonstration (Slone et al.

2000). Another study of Polish citizens found that perceptions of politically related stress, such as the possibility of a foreign terrorist attack or increases in consumer prices, were correlated with lower life satisfaction and higher anomie, which is the breakdown of values in society (Kaniasty and Jakubowska 2014).

These findings show that politics can be depressing at least some of the time, but they are hardly a theory of *how* politics is depressing or even evidence that politics is *regularly* depressing. Research on cataclysmic phenomena focus on extreme cases of political violence and oppression (e.g., war, 9/11), while research on political life events tends to be idiosyncratic to the time and location of the study (e.g., adolescents in South Africa during apartheid, adults in Poland during the Great Recession). Does politics systematically produce the kinds of stress—ranging from the mundane to the traumatic—that leave us depressed? If so, how and why does this happen?

I argue that politics can be depressing because it routinely produces *irrevocable loss*. I focus on loss in this chapter and on irrevocability in the next chapter. I begin by synthesizing research from psychology, evolutionary sciences, and sociology to illustrate the importance of loss to depression. This is crucial because if we want to understand why we feel depressed by politics, we first need to understand why we would ever feel depressed. I then dig into the concept of loss, explaining what must happen before something can be considered a loss. Finally, I turn to politics and show three ways it produces loss: when a trade-off is made that goes against our preferences, when politics takes away something we value in our personal life, and when we are defeated in our attempt to achieve a desired political outcome.

## Why Do We Feel Depressed?

Depression has long been considered a response to loss, an idea rooted in the connection between death and grieving. Grieving is widely observed around the world and over time, dating back to ancient cultures such as Greece, India, and China. Modern psychology now attempts to explain the causes, purposes, and consequences of grief. Sigmund Freud argued that we engage in "grief work" after the death of a loved one—breaking our emotional tie to the deceased, adjusting to a life without them, and then forming new connections to fill their absence (1917). Grief work later morphed into the stages of grief—a concept popularized by Elisabeth Kübler-Ross in *On Death & Dying* (1969)—in which depression was consistently thought to be one of the stages.[1]

The study of death and grieving paved the way for scholars to consider how different types of loss might evoke different feelings in the depression family. Freud argued in *Mourning and Melancholia* that these feelings were rooted in different kinds of loss:

> Let us now apply to melancholia what we have learnt about mourning. In one set of cases it is evident that melancholia too may be the reaction to the loss of a loved object. Where the exciting causes are different one can recognize that there is a loss of a more ideal kind. The object has not perhaps actually died, but has been lost as an object of love (e.g., in the case of a betrothed girl who has been jilted). In yet other cases one feels justified in maintaining the belief that a loss of this kind has occurred, but one cannot see clearly what it is that has been lost, and it is all the more reasonable to suppose that the patient cannot consciously perceive what he has lost either.... This would suggest that melancholia is in some way related to an object-loss which is withdrawn from consciousness, in contradistinction to mourning, in which there is nothing about the loss that is unconscious. (1917, 245)

According to Freud, mourning and melancholia are responses to the *loss of a loved object* but differ from one another in terms of how we process the loss. Mourning occurs when we are aware of the loss—such as the death of a loved one—while melancholia occurs when we lack awareness of what has been lost—often an intangible object, such as confidence.

Loss is now a staple of psychological theories of depression. Building on the behavioral work of B. F. Skinner, some psychologists argued that the *loss of positive reinforcement* in a person's life gives rise to feelings of depression (Ferster 1974; Lewinsohn 1986). Another psychologist, Martin Seligman, developed the theory of learned helplessness after conducting a series of laboratory experiments in which dogs were exposed to repeated shocks (1972). Across several studies, Seligman and colleagues consistently found that the dogs who were not provided with a way to stop the shocks became depressed, a feeling which often persisted even after the shocks ended. They concluded that the *loss of personal control*—or what they call learned helplessness—was a source of depression.

Evolutionary theories of depression also emphasize loss. Darwin saw the evolutionary potential of emotions, including sadness, after observing their distinct behavioral and facial expressions across species (1872). This observation laid the groundwork for the "attachment" theory of depression. Pioneered by developmental psychologist John Bowlby, this theory holds that depression evolved as a response to a *loss in maternal care* (1980). He thought depression improved the chances of survival because crying helped infants reestablish contact with mothers. Others have since argued that infant cries are initially an expression of frustration; depression emerges only when contact is not eventually reestablished. The logic here is that drawing the attention of the mother also attracts predators, so crying out of frustration becomes increasingly risky over time. Depression, in contrast, leads the infant to quiet down, thereby improving its chances of survival when attempts to restore maternal care have failed (Watt and Panksepp 2009).

A multitude of evolutionary explanations for depression have emerged since this early work. Prominent among these is the "social competition" or "rank" (as in social rank) theory of depression, which arose from behavioral studies of animals. It argues that depression is a response to a *loss of status* (Price 1967). In this view, depression is an adaptive losing strategy because it signals submission, de-escalates conflict, and facilitates acceptance. As the biologist John Price and his colleagues write, "Depression can be seen as a ritual form of losing behaviour producing temporary psychological incapacity which signals submission to the winner but preserves the loser without physical damage. It performs the function which death performs in unritualised fighting, and which the referee performs in culturally ritualised competition" (1994, 310). Depression improves the chances of survival by helping avert the further loss of status, physical harm, or even death. In contrast, anger and frustration may worsen the situation by intensifying conflict.

When we encounter adversity, whether as a loss or merely the threat of a loss, we experience a *loss of social investment potential*. This loss is the focus of the social risk theory of depression, which attempts to integrate evolutionary theories. Social investment potential refers to our "ability to contribute adequate investments for the achievement of any socially implicated endeavor relevant to reproduction" (Allen and Badcock 2003, 892). When it becomes critically low, we find ourselves at risk of being excluded or ostracized from the group. Depression helps defend against this possibility by making us risk averse. We withdraw, take fewer chances, and avoid risky behaviors that could result in long-term expulsion, at least until our social investment potential has been rebuilt.[2]

Evolutionary theories of depression are ultimately more similar than different. At their core is the view that depression is an evolved response to loss. It signals that withdrawal is the best course of action and help is needed. The evolutionary psychiatrist Randolph Nesse elaborates on this idea by pointing out the many ways depression is useful: stopping further losses, recovering or replacing the lost object, abstaining from situations and actions associated with the loss, determining the causes of the loss, reassessing the need for life changes because of the loss, acquiring help from others, warning others about potential danger, and so on (1999). It is these adaptive functions that have led some psychologists to call sadness the "architect of cognitive change," noting how it helps in "facilitating adaptation to irrevocable loss by soliciting aid and restructuring expectations and goals" (Karnaze and Levine 2018, 46).

Unlike psychology and evolutionary science, stress research does not typically use the language of loss. Instead, terms such traumata, negative life events, chronic strains, and daily hassles are employed. Traumata are unusually intense experiences that involve sexual violence or the threat of bodily harm. They can be discrete experiences, such as being in a car accident, or ongoing conditions, such as living in a physically abusive relationship. Negative life events and chronic strains both describe dramatic and world-altering experiences but differ in their continuity, similar to sudden and chronic traumata. Events are discrete, such as a home burglary, while strains are ongoing, such as a bout of unemployment. Daily hassles describe low-intensity but regularly occurring experiences, such as traffic or bad weather.

Exposure to stress is typically measured using survey instruments, such as the Life Events Checklist for trauma (Gray et al. 2004), the Social Readjustment Rating Scale for negative life events (Holmes and Rahe 1967), and the Daily Stress Checklist for chronic strains and daily hassles (Bolger et al. 1989). These inventories ask respondents about stressors across life domains, such as the examples presented in table 2.1. Respondents then indicate which one they experienced over a fixed period of time, such as the past month or year. The stress burden of each respondent is then calculated as the total number of selected stressors and is correlated with depression.

We now know that "early, chronic, continuing, cumulative, and proximal acute stress" can have an especially strong impact on depression (Hammen 2015, 80).[3] To sum up both ends of the spectrum, numerous chronic traumata experienced recently by children tend to be the most

TABLE 2.1  **Types and Examples of Stressors**

|  | Chronic Strains | Life Events | Traumas |
|---|---|---|---|
| Work | Not getting along with coworkers | Being fired or permanently laid off | Serious workplace accident |
| Financial | Concerns about owing money | A financial downturn (short of bankruptcy) | Going bankrupt |
| Material | Rising prices of common goods | Having a car or furniture repossessed | Having a car totaled in an accident |
| Housing | Living next to troublesome neighbors | Needing major home renovations | Having a home destroyed |
| Family | Overburdened with family responsibilities | Getting divorced | Death of a child or partner |
| Crime | Living in a high-crime neighborhood | Having a home burglarized | Being sexually assaulted |
| Health | Declining physical abilities | Undergoing surgery | Being hospitalized for a severe illness |
| Caregiving | Having to care for aging parents | Child being suspended from school | Death of a child, partner, or parent |

depressing, while infrequent daily hassles experienced by adults long ago are the least depressing. In recent years, this conclusion has been bolstered by research designs that more effectively isolate the causal impact of stress on depression, such as twin studies and natural experiments.

Although the language of loss is not the *lingua franca* of stress research, its importance is still widely acknowledged. As the psychologist Carolyn Mazure notes, "A number of studies have investigated the role of loss or 'exit' events in depressive onset because psychological theories have implicated events that signify loss as important precipitants to depressive onset, and because studies of bereavement indicate increased risk for depression" (1998, 295). When loss is discussed explicitly, the focus is primarily interpersonal loss and secondarily job and property loss. As the psychologist Constance Hammen writes, "The most venerable and extensive line of research has focused on the unique significance for depression of interpersonal 'loss,' which may include bereavement, separations, endings—or threats of separation . . . such 'exit' events often precede depression, and may be more common in depressed samples than in other forms of psychopathology" (2005, 296–97). Indeed, loss is often the focus of stress research. A closer look at the examples in table 2.1 reveals that most involve loss. Not getting along with coworkers is the loss of collegiality, concerns about owing money is the loss of economic security, inflation in prices of common goods is the loss of affordability, declining physical ability is the loss of faculty, being fired is the loss of a job, getting divorced is the loss of a legal marriage, and so forth.

## What Is Loss?

Theories in psychology, evolutionary science, and stress research all recognize that depression is a response to loss. But what is loss? And does it matter what we lose? The answers to these questions may seem straightforward—perhaps even too obvious to be worth noting—but doing so will sharpen our understanding of the connection between loss and depression, and eventually why we think politics matters.

Loss occurs when we cease to have something of value, such as a loved object, personal control, maternal care, or social status. In his book *The Human Dimension of Depression*, the psychiatrist Martin Kantor put it this way: "Broadly speaking, the term 'loss' refers to any condition in which once there was more and now there is less" (1992, 137). I break down this definition into two components: it starts with the presence of something, and it ends with the absence of something. Table 2.2 plots the two components of loss and their inverses. Loss appears at the intersection of a past presence and a current absence. Identifying these components of loss helps us see what loss is *not*. However, what we deem the opposite of loss depends on which components are inverted. Gain occurs when the absence from a past state becomes a presence in the current state—an inversion of two components. In contrast, maintenance and lack each invert one component. Maintenance shares a starting point with loss but differs in its outcome—it occurs when we keep what we have. Lack shares the same outcome but differs in its starting point—it occurs when we had and continue to have nothing.

This definition of loss implies that it occurs anytime we have something at one point but don't have it at a later point. This may be technically true, but it doesn't capture the social meaning of loss. A person might lose five pounds, but if their goal was to do so, then this isn't a loss at all. In fact, it is a gain—these five pounds turned the absence of their preferred weight into its presence. In short, they gained something of value (i.e., the

TABLE 2.2 **The Components of Loss**

| Current State | Past State | |
|---|---|---|
| | *Presence* | *Absence* |
| *Presence* | Maintenance | Gain |
| *Absence* | Loss | Lack |

fulfillment of a goal). If the person is indifferent to their weight, then the five pounds isn't a loss or gain but merely a subtraction—a mathematical fact of no personal significance. The importance of value is a shared assumption in the major theories of depression. Freud didn't argue that mourning and melancholia are responses to the loss of any object, but rather to the loss of a *loved* object. The loss of maternal care, personal control, and social status are not just any kind of loss—they are losses of things we value. As Kantor puts it, "The symbolic meaning of loss makes every loss at least partly in the eye of the beholder" (1992, 137).

Loss occurs when we cease to have something of value, but the value of something often depends on how much we already have. Consider the loss of $1,000. This loss becomes more severe if it prohibits you from paying rent and leads to an eviction. In this case, it is not just a loss of money but also a loss of shelter. Now consider an example from politics. Imagine your preferred political party loses seats in Congress. If they become the minority party as a result, it is not merely a loss of seats but also a loss of majority power. The loss of an object in these cases—whether money or Congressional seats—crosses a threshold that triggers additional losses—such as shelter or majority power—making the initial loss more severe. This occurs when our goals depend on a specific value of an object. Paying rent requires a fixed sum of money, and securing a majority in Congress requires a fixed number of seats. This distinction is important because theories of depression are ultimately about losses of significant value (e.g., the ability to meet a goal) rather than marginal value (e.g., a quantity of a valued object that is too small to affect a goal).

Goals are also essential to understanding maintenance and lack. Imagine three scenarios that result in $1,000: after either gaining $500, losing $500, or not experiencing any change. Is this last scenario—where we continue to have the same amount of money—lack or maintenance? It depends on our goals. Maintenance occurs when a goal continues to be met (e.g., paying rent) even if there are underlying changes to the object we need for our goal (e.g., money). In contrast, lack occurs when a goal continues to go unmet. In this way, we can experience marginal loss or gains at the same time we experience significant maintenance or lack. For instance, our preferred party may win a seat in Congress following a special election (marginal gain) but still not hold majority power (significant lack).

Value also depends on how much we already have because of what economists refer to as diminishing marginal utility. The economist Herman Gossen first observed this law in 1854, writing, "The magnitude of one and the same satisfaction, when we continue to enjoy it without interruption continually decreases until satisfaction is reached" (1983). The implication is that an object is most valuable when we have none of it and diminishes as we gain more of it. For instance, my partner and I agree that the first bite of a dish is the best bite and that each additional bite brings less enjoyment (i.e., diminishing marginal utility). So when we go out to eat, we maximize our first bites by ordering many small dishes instead of two entrees. More commonly, the concept is applied to money. For instance, an increase from $10,000 to $30,000 is of greater value than an increase from $110,000 to $130,000, even though the dollar differences are numerically equal (Pacheco and Plutzer 2008).

There is a saying that losses loom larger than gains. This idea is often referred to as loss aversion and is another reason the value of something can vary. First pioneered by psychologists Daniel Kahneman and Amos Tversky (1979), loss aversion is the tendency to feel more pain from the loss of something than we feel pleasure from an equivalent gain. For instance, we associate a greater change in value to the loss of $1,000 than to the gain of $1,000. This asymmetry means that losses may create depression more than gains alleviate it. Put another way, the depression we feel may not be fully overcome by simply replacing the lost object.

## How Does Politics Produce Loss?

Depression occurs when we experience loss, which is to say we cease to have something of value. Not all losses are the same, however. Significant loss matters more than marginal loss (goals), starting with less amplifies loss (diminishing marginal utility), and loss is more deleterious than gain is beneficial (loss aversion). Having laid out the importance of loss and clarified its meaning, I now explain how it is produced by politics. I describe three types of loss—when political preferences cease to be fulfilled, when politics takes away objects of personal value, and when efforts at collective action fail.

I illustrate each type of loss with stories I heard while interviewing mental health professionals. I also draw on responses from the 2020 and 2022 Cooperative Election Study. I included a series of questions on these surveys that allowed me to identify which respondents attended therapy, and, among those who did, which ones talked about politics. I then asked this subset of respondents about which aspects of politics they discussed with their therapists. These stories are useful because they offer diverse and real-life examples of political loss.

*When Preferences Cease to Be Fulfilled*

The first type of political loss is *when preferences cease to be fulfilled*. In politics, we have preferences about a range of issues.[4] One set of preferences, known as process preferences, concern how collective decisions are made and enforced. Democracy, for example, is a widely held process preference. Most people prefer having free and fair elections, freedom of the press, and the rule of law to not having these elements of democracy. Beyond these core elements, however, people may hold diverging preferences about how democracy should operate, such as whether it should be majoritarian, deliberative, technocratic, or something else (Landwehr and Steiner 2017). A second set of preferences, known as substantive preferences, concerns political outcomes. For instance, many people care about representation as an outcome and not just a process. We want representatives who have a particular background (identity, values) or way of thinking (ideology, partisanship). We also want specific economic and social policy outcomes. Some people prefer more redistribution and regulation of markets; others prefer less. Some people prefer more social freedoms, liberties, and rights; others prefer less.

If the fulfillment of our preferences is what we lose, *scarcity* is why we lose it. Scarcity is when the demand for something exceeds its supply. Any allocation of a scarce resource—even one that is perfectly equal—leaves someone, somewhere, getting less than they prefer.[5] Scarcity in politics can be found wherever there are limits on participation, agenda space, or outcomes. Consider the US Congress as an example. The demand for a seat in Congress exceeds the number of seats. The demand for speaking time on the floor of Congress exceeds the amount of time available. The demand for leadership roles or committee assignments among members of Congress exceeds their supply. The demand for legislation to be put to a vote exceeds the capacity of Congress to cast votes. Scarcity forces us to make trade-offs, or situations where we must choose between two or more options, and this is especially true in politics. As the political scientists Todd Landman and Hans-Joachim Lauth note, "It is often not possible to accomplish all beneficial political goals at the same time. Trade-offs are inevitable: Achieving the benefit of one political goal comes necessarily at the expense of another political goal, challenging the rather simple and linear views of 'the more the better' or 'all good things go together'" (239). Going back to the example of Congress, we make trade-offs about whom to send to Capitol Hill, what positions representatives hold when they get there, when and how much they speak during debate, which bills they can introduce and vote on, and so on.

If preferences are what we lose and scarcity is why we lose, *competition* is *how* we lose. Competition occurs when individuals or groups in society strive to resolve trade-offs in favor of their preferences. Just as competition in economics is driven by the profit motive, we might say that competition in politics is driven by the *preference* motive. Individuals and groups want to maximize the fulfillment of their preferences, so they engage in activities that help them achieve this goal. Often individuals work together to enhance the chances of fulfilling their preferences. Groups may form around a shared preference or set of preferences or as coalitions of individuals who have different preferences but nevertheless benefit from cooperation. Whatever the case, groups are often useful because they can more efficiently and effectively deploy resources to bring about their preferences.

Preferences, scarcity, and competition allow us to understand how politics produces this type of loss. *When competition changes how a trade-off is resolved, some people start getting what they prefer, while others stop getting what they prefer.* We lose when our preferred representative is ousted from office, when our preferred policy is repealed, when our preferred issue is taken off the agenda, when our preferred government benefit is taken away, or when our preferred right is disenfranchised. Sometimes our preferences are negative rather than positive—we don't want a particular policy passed, candidate elected, issue discussed, benefit provided, or right given. Since loss is indifferent to whether our preferences are about wanting or not wanting something, loss can occur in these cases too.

To better see how preferences, scarcity, and competition create the conditions for loss, consider what happens when each is missing. A lack of preferences means we are indifferent to how trade-offs are resolved. No degree of change can make us a political loser or winner. A lack of scarcity means everyone's preferences can be fulfilled, and competition becomes obsolete. Loss is impossible since we are not at risk of having our preferences unfulfilled. A lack of competition means there are no changes in how trade-offs are resolved, so no one risks becoming a political winner or loser. In this scenario, everyone is in a perpetual state of maintenance (preferences fulfilled) or lack (preferences unfulfilled). Only when preferences, scarcity, and competition are all present can loss become possible.[6]

I often heard about this type of loss when interviewing mental health professionals. One therapist told me about a client who struggled with the gap between his preferences and what the government was doing. He told me, "I basically get all my news updates from him, like, what happened with the confirmation of the new Supreme Court justice, and what it is that the Trump administration is trying to do to suppress voting in various swing States." I also saw this type of loss expressed in a survey. When asked about a time they talked about politics with their therapist, one survey respondent wrote, "I talked about the position of the United States on the war between Russia and Ukraine." Another respondent wrote, "My anxiety with the rights of Whites disappearing and my disappointment with all this LGBTQ and transgender nonsense that is ruining the traditional American family model." The concerns expressed here are about political preferences that cease to be fulfilled.

## When Politics Takes Objects of Personal Value

The major theories of depression highlighted the loss of loved objects, maternal care, positive reinforcement, personal control, and social status. Research on stress pointed to the loss of financial well-being, adequate and stable housing, a happy family life, good health, a fulfilling work life, and more. These "personal objects" have economic and social value, and their loss can be depressing. The second type of loss is thus *when politics takes away objects of personal value*. Whereas the first type of loss was purely political—what we lost (the fulfillment of preferences) and how we lost it (scarcity and competition) were fully contained by the political domain—this loss is only partly political because it occurs only when politics reaches into our personal lives.

There are a few ways this can happen. The most obvious way is through public policy. Personal objects, like our political preferences, are subject to the dynamics of political scarcity and competition. Politics produces policies, and it is ultimately these policies that determine "who gets what, when, and how" (Lasswell 1936). Many policies impose economic, political, or social costs on at least some citizens by taking property and restricting freedoms. We lose income when the state raises taxes or slashes benefits. We lose our good health when government fails to provide clean drinking water. We lose loved ones when the government decides to go to war.

Several of the mental health professionals I interviewed talked about clients dealing with this kind of loss. I heard about a client who, in the run-up to the 2020 presidential election, was stressed about the possibility of Trump being reelected because of how his presidency had impacted their personal life. He told me, "Where like a few years ago it was like, 'Well, I don't believe in supply-side economics. I don't think it works,' now it's just like, 'He [Trump] is going to get us all killed, and he already is.' So it's very personal now. It's not just a theoretical political argument." Another mental health professional told me about a client who was stressed about Obamacare, saying their clients had brought up politics in the therapy "because their insurance is not good. Um, their deductibles are higher, and their premiums are higher and like . . . one person was paying I think $300 or $400, and when Obamacare came in, they had to pay $1,000 for their deductible." One survey respondent expressed this type of loss very straightforwardly by writing, "Cutbacks in social services because they affect me."

The politicization of social life is another way this loss can occur. Our relationships with partners, family, friends, and coworkers are often the plane through which political competition unfolds—just recall a difficult political conversation you've had at the dinner table—and this competition puts us at risk of losing social support, self-confidence, or a sense of belonging, especially when it becomes conflictual. In extreme cases, it can lead to a loss of financial support, housing, or employment. Social life was frequently mentioned by the mental health professionals and survey respondents. One mental health professional told me about a client who experienced this type of loss, "She had to argue a point on the debate team that she really was struggling with, and the kids started making fun of her because of her political views." She elaborated, "It made her depressed and withdrawn. Um, she is a straight-A student. She does a lot of AP classes. She does a lot of dual enrollment for college and everything, and really is just like, 'I hate high school and I can't wait to get out of here.'" One survey respondent wrote, "Different political beliefs between myself, spouse, other family members. Rifts it causes." Another wrote, "How isolated I feel in my neighborhood as the only household with our political values and beliefs." Whether in school, home, or the neighborhood, it is clear that politics can be depressing when it creates conflict in our relationships.

Memory is another pathway for this type of loss. In these cases, politics evokes painful memories of a past loss, which may or may not have been caused by politics, but whose recall can be depressing. As one mental health professional told me, "Another example could be a woman who hates Trump, who is transplanted from New York to Florida, and lives here and is disabled and comments on all the news. What is said, what was not said by Trump, his followers, and Democrats, with a view of agreeing with the Democrats. Because of her strong PTSD diagnosis, she retraumatizes herself as she sees a battle of—though she doesn't use these words—good and evil being played out in the American political arena." This mental health professional was only one of two who talked about memory, and none of the survey respondents mentioned it explicitly. The two cases where memory was relevant involved clients who experienced trauma in the past, and, in the words of their therapists, found themselves "retraumatized" by what was happening in politics. This suggests that memory, while a valid pathway, is limited to cases where the past loss was highly traumatic.

*When Costly Collective Action Fails*

A third type of political loss is *when costly collective action is unsuccessful*. Groups who want to change or defend the status quo must organize and act, which requires time, energy, and resources. Simply paying the transaction costs to coordinate and carry out a plan does not guarantee success, however. Groups are often defeated in their attempts to change or enshrine how a trade-off is resolved. What group members lose in these circumstances are the *costs* of the failed effort and, potentially, the window of opportunity for action and a sense of hope that the group will eventually succeed.

Not everyone is affected by the loss of the cost of action. Whereas the first type of loss can be experienced by anyone with the relevant preference, this type of loss is limited to only those who pay the transaction costs of organizing and acting. People who share the preferences of the group but do not contribute their time, energy, or resources to its efforts are free riders. They know that if the group succeeds, their preferences will be fulfilled at no cost to themselves, and if the group fails, they will at least be inoculated from paying any of the costs associated with competition. This type of loss did not come up in any of the interviews or survey responses, which suggests it may be a fairly uncommon way that politics is depressing. However, a case study of climate change activists, which I report on later in the book, shows that this is a real phenomenon, although one that is perhaps limited to only the most politically active citizens.

Notably, the three types of political loss can, and often do, co-occur. We may prefer a policy because it provides some personal benefit, so when the policy gets overturned, our preferences cease to be fulfilled, and we lose the benefits we previously enjoyed. Groups who seek to defend the status quo but fail to do so are likewise hit by multiple types of loss: their preferences are no longer fulfilled because the status quo has now changed, and they've paid the costs of organizing to unsuccessfully keep the status quo in place.

## What's Next?

Theories of depression have long pointed to the importance of loss. Whether it is losing a loved one, control over a situation, or social standing, this type of stress can be depressing. It is through the concept of loss that I showed how politics might be depressing. I explained how politics can lead to three types of loss: when preferences cease to be fulfilled, when politics takes away objects of personal value, and when costly collective action is unsuccessful. The political production of loss creates the *potential* for politics to be depressing, but loss by itself is not enough to conclude that politics *is* depressing. Depression starts with loss, but not all loss leads to depression. Loss can also lead to anger, anxiety, or fear. Before we conclude that politics is in fact depressing, let's examine some other possibilities in the second part of my framework — appraisal and irrevocability — which are the subjects of the next chapter.

CHAPTER THREE

# When Loss Becomes Depressing

Depression is probably not the first emotion that comes to mind when thinking about politics. Instead, the political landscape might seem to be dominated by anger, an emotion that likes to make itself known. Anger was front and center in the emergence of the Tea Party, reflected in protest signs that read "Proud Members of the Angry Mob" and "We are Tea'd Off." One political commentator proclaimed the twenty-first century to be the age of anger (Mishra 2017), while others point to the ubiquity of "angertainment" on partisan talk shows and talk radio. Today anger has reached such a feverish pitch that the term no longer seems to adequately describe the intense emotions felt by many Americans. Though its pages once questioned whether "the angry American" was so bad for democracy, the *Atlantic* now runs headlines like "America Descends into the Politics of Rage" and "The Real Roots of American Rage."

Anxiety and fear have a long history in politics and now seem to be kindled regularly during election season. Lyndon Johnson's "Daisy" campaign ad famously showed a young girl dying in a nuclear explosion. A voice-over by Johnson told citizens, "These are the stakes . . . we must love each other, or we must die." This type of emotional appeal is regularly used on both sides of the aisle, whether it is Clinton's "3:00 a.m. Phone Call" ad or Trump's speech proclaiming, "When Mexico sends its people, they're not sending their best. . . . They're bringing drugs. They're bringing crime. They're rapists." Fear and anxiety may be the *lingua franca* of electoral politics, but it doesn't stop there. Whether they're thinking of the surveillance state or the deep state, domestic terrorists or international terrorists, the police or antifa, immigrants or vigilantes, many Americans feel fear and anxiety when they think about politics. Indeed, a range of issues now come with their own *anxiety* labels: climate anxiety, economic anxiety, racial anxiety, and democratic anxiety.

Compared to anger, anxiety, and fear, depression is rare in politics. Aside from glib stories about former Speaker of the House John Boehner crying on the floor of Congress ("Why Does John Boehner Cry So Much?" in *Politico Magazine*) or solemn occasions marked by tragedy (9/11, Sandy Hook), depression has never been a hallmark of politics, or at least not the politics reported in the news. Pundits don't talk about climate, economic, or racial depression in the way they pair those issues with anxiety. Protesters don't march with signs that declare themselves "Proud Members of the Depressed Mob." Journalists don't write long-form essays titled "America Descends into the Politics of Depression." And candidates don't appeal to depression in their campaign advertisements.

The dearth of attention to depression contrasted with the prominence of anger, anxiety, and fear in politics raises an important question: When, if ever, does political loss lead to depression rather than other negative emotions? Depression begins with loss, but not all loss leads to depression, and so it is possible that politics is rarely depressing, even though it frequently produces loss. In this chapter, I tackle this issue by unpacking the *appraisal* part of my framework. I describe the concept of appraisal and explain its importance. I argue that appraisals of *irrevocability* — the belief that there is little to no chance of restoring what has been lost — are what cause depression rather than anger, anxiety, or fear. I then offer a theory of when and why politics leads citizens to appraise loss as irrevocable. Finally, I analyze polls, an original survey experiment, and the Cooperative Election Study to show that politics is regularly and systematically depressing, especially when it produces irrevocable loss.

## What Are Appraisals?

Imagine you've been asked to participate in a study. You go to a laboratory and are greeted by a scientist, asked to take a questionnaire, and then hooked up to skin conductance and blood pressure machines. The scientist then instructs you to count backward from 18,652 in increments of seven for one minute. After you finish, the scientist reports with some annoyance that the data is useless because you fidgeted too much and spoke too quietly. You are instructed to complete the task again, this time counting backward from 27,809 in increments of thirteen. The scientist once again berates your performance but with more intensity. After a third attempt and even more intense negative feedback, the scientist asks you to complete a questionnaire, and the study ends. How would you feel in this scenario?

This exact study was conducted by psychologists Matthias Siemer, Iris Mauss, and James Gross, resulting in the publication "Same Situation—Different Emotions: How Appraisals Shape Our Emotions" in the journal *Emotions* (2007). They found that participants reported a wide variety of emotions. Some felt anger, others guilt, shame, sadness, amusement, or even pleasure. Their conclusion: "It is the way a person interprets a situation—rather than the situation itself—that gives rise to one emotion rather than another emotion" (Siemer et al. 2007, 599). I would argue that both the situation and our interpretation of it are important—this situation evoked far more negative emotions than positive ones, but the reverse would probably be true if the scientist had praised the participants rather than berated them. Even so, this study nicely illustrates the concept of emotional appraisal—that how we *think* about a situation profoundly shapes how we *feel* about it.

Psychologist Richard Lazarus fielded one of the earliest theories of emotional appraisal in his groundbreaking article "Progress on a Cognitive-Motivational-Relational Theory of Emotion" (1991). He argued that we appraised situations in two steps. The first step, the primary appraisal, is an assessment of "the stakes one has in the outcomes of an encounter" (1991, 827). These stakes are defined by our perceptions of the relevance, congruence, and content of a situation. Is the situation relevant to our goals? Only when we perceive a situation as relevant is there any possibility of an emotional response. Is the situation congruent with our goals? Congruent situations create positive emotions; incongruent situations create negative ones. Finally, what is the content of the situation? If a relevant and incongruent situation leads to negative emotions, the content determines which negative emotion will result; the same is true of positive emotions in congruent situations.

Next is a secondary appraisal in which we assess our "options and prospects for coping" (Lazarus 1991, 827). Here we consider three aspects of the situation: blame or credit, coping potential, and future expectations. It matters who we think created and controls the situation—and the potential harm or benefit that comes along with it. We feel pride when we credit ourselves for a good situation but gratitude when we credit someone else. How much we can alter a situation—or our relationship to it—is our coping potential and can affect the type and intensity of our response. For instance, we feel less anxious about a bad situation when we have resources to cope with it. Finally, our future expectations matter, too. We may feel dread when we expect a bad situation to worsen but relief if we think the situation will improve.

Which appraisals lead to which emotions—the appraisal structure—continues to be debated and refined. There is widespread agreement that relevance and goal congruence are key aspects of the appraisal structure, but there is disagreement about what other appraisals matter (content, credit/blame, and others.) A variety of dimensions and structures have been proposed and studied (Ellsworth and Smith 1985). Psychologist Ira Roseman, for instance, argues that five dimensions interact to explain thirteen discrete emotions (1991). These five dimensions are whether we seek to attain a reward or avoid a punishment (motivational state), whether the reward or punishment is present or absent (situational state), whether the outcome is certain or uncertain (probability), whether a positive or negative outcome is deserved (legitimacy), and whether the outcome is caused by ourselves, someone else, or impersonal circumstances (agency).

Other scholars study the way our brain processes sensory information in order to generate appraisals—what is commonly referred to as the appraisal *process*. For instance, psychologists Craig Smith and Leslie Kirby highlight three parallel processes at work in our brain when we form an appraisal: perceptual stimuli (such as pain or looming objects), associative processing (that is, our mind automatically and subconsciously making associations between our current environment and our memories), and reasoning (our conscious mind deliberately assessing the environment). These processes feed information to "appraisal detectors," which determine whether an emotional response is appropriate.

Smith and Kirby offer the following example of how this process unfolds:

> You are attending a conference in an unfamiliar city. It is late in the afternoon and you and a colleague are walking around town intensely discussing the implications of an intriguing presentation you both have just heard. The two of you are so engrossed in conversation that you are not paying close attention to where you are going. This continues for a while, until, suddenly, you realize that you are feeling rather anxious. Looking around, you quickly realize why: You have wandered off the beaten path, it is starting to get dark, the buildings around you look run down, and seedy-looking characters are wandering about. You stop your conversation to point out the situation to your companion, and the two of you turn around and head back to the touristic part of town without incident. (2000, 96–97)

In this scenario, the engrossing conversation diverted your attention away from potential problems. Nevertheless, you automatically and subconsciously continued to process your surroundings, drawing connections to memories of similar situations. Once your "appraisal detectors" accumulated enough information, they set off an anxious feeling that drew your attention away from the conversation. Alerted by this anxiety, your reasoning kicked in, and you decided to turn around.

Emotions are a response to the world around us, but what emotion we feel—or whether we feel any emotion at all—depends on how we *appraise* our situation. So what appraisal gives rise to depression?

## When Is Loss Depressing?

Depression begins with loss, but not all loss leads to depression. It might instead evoke feelings of anger, embarrassment, or guilt. How we feel about loss ultimately depends on how we appraise it. It is now believed that depression occurs when we appraise loss as *irrevocable*. This idea has been a key element in theories of depression for a long time, although often only implicitly. Scholars like Sigmund Freud, Melanie Klein, and Elisabeth Kübler-Ross did not use the term, because losses such as the death of a loved one or the dissolution of a romantic relationship were understood to be irrevocable, so there wasn't a need to explicate this aspect of loss. Today, however, the term *irrevocable loss* is widely used in the study of depression.

Importantly, when it comes to depression, whether a loss is revocable or irrevocable is not inherent to the loss itself but is instead determined by the loser. Even if outsiders deem a loss as irrevocable, it can be depressing only if the loser sees it this way, too. This distinction is important because some scholars question the connection between irrevocable loss and depression by pointing out that people often respond to irrevocable loss with feelings other than depression (e.g., Wortman and Silver 1989). However astute this observation may be, it overlooks the importance of appraisal and the fact that not everyone may deem a seemingly irrevocable loss as irrevocable.

So how do we appraise loss, and when do we conclude that it is irrevocable? Psychologist Magna Arnold pioneered the study of appraisal and offered one of the first answers to this question (1960). She distinguished among three sets of depression family members—sorrow and sadness, dejection, and hopelessness and despair. She argued that sorrow and sadness resulted from the presence of something harmful that was easy to overcome, dejection from the presence of something harmful that was too difficult to overcome, and hopelessness and despair from the absence of something beneficial that was too difficult to overcome. That something might be "too difficult to overcome" suggests irrevocability, or a low coping potential as Lazarus put it. To Arnold, we feel more intense depression (e.g., despair) as we perceive a bad situation to be increasingly difficult to overcome.

The idea of a bad situation that is "too difficult to overcome" continues to shape how scholars think about the types of appraisals that evoke depression, even if other aspects of Arnold's theory, such as her view of sadness, were ultimately left behind. For instance, consider what Lazarus said about sadness:

> The goal relevance in sadness is not content specific, as it is with anger, anxiety, guilt, and shame, but consists of any commitment of importance to the individual—for example, one's social role, job, public reputation, or loved one. An irrevocable loss of this commitment, which implies helplessness or lack of control, is the goal incongruent event that produces sadness. When sadness is experienced, the person believes there is no way to restore the loss. And as in the case of anxiety, no agent is held accountable, hence blameable, for the loss. If the person locates an external agent, the emotion will be anger, or perhaps anxiety, rather than sadness. If it is internalized, the emotion will be guilt or shame. It is possible for attributions of accountability and control, therefore appraisals of blame, to change from moment to moment as the person grieves over the loss, and the emotion will also be transformed thereby from sadness to anger, anxiety, guilt, or shame. (1991, 829–30)

In Lazarus's explanation, loss is depressing when it is *irrevocable*, and a situation is irrevocable when we make three appraisals about it: we lack control, there is not an "external agent" who caused the loss, and we did not personally cause the loss.

Now consider how psychologist Ira Roseman defines the appraisal structure of depression. He argues that sorrow—or what he later referred to as sadness—can be explained by five appraisals dimensions: when the *broader circumstances* cause the *certain* and *legitimate absence* of a *reward* (1984). He would later replace the "legitimacy" dimension with a "power" dimension, in which a person feels depressed if they perceive themselves to be weak in a situation (Roseman et al. 1990). This appraisal structure of depression is one part of Roseman's groundbreaking effort to define the appraisal structure of thirteen discrete emotions using only five dimensions. Notably, however, what he says more or less aligns with Lazarus's view. The certain absence of a benefit corresponds to loss, and the role of broader circumstances and the lack of power correspond to a lack of control.

Psychologist Klaus Scherer offers another assessment of depression, focusing on the roles of goal-conduciveness and coping ability (1997). Ultimately, however, these two appraisal dimensions are not substantively different from what Lazarus and Roseman propose: we feel depressed when a situation hindered a personal goal (loss), and we lack the power or control to cope with it (irrevocability). For instance, coping ability is measured by asking study participants, "How did you evaluate your ability to act on or to cope with the event and its consequences when you were first confronted with this situation?" Potential answers ranged from feeling powerless to feeling like they could positively influence events and change consequences.

In one of the more unusual proposals, psychologist Nico Frijda argued that how we localize a problem in space is relevant to depression (1987). He thought depression and unhappiness had a global focus, while sadness and misery had a local focus. However, his analysis revealed that this dimension was marginal at best. Moreover, this dimension is not especially relevant at explaining when loss would evoke the depression family versus some other negative emotion—either a global or local focus might evoke feelings in the depression family.

Another line of thinking holds that depression—especially when it is more severe and chronic—often stems from emotions like guilt or shame. As psychologists Andrew Ortony, Gerald Clore, and Allan Collins note,

> The attribution of the cause of undesirable events to one's own agency and the resulting feelings of blameworthiness can be the occasion for further emotional reactions . . . to the extent that we commonly blame ourselves, such blameworthiness may become part of our schema for ourselves and hence a basis for dispositional dislike. Indeed, depressives often report being disgusted with themselves and often view themselves as thoroughly unappealing. . . . Depressed people, by this analysis, dislike themselves for being dislikable, blame themselves for being blameworthy, and are depressed about being depressed (2022, 201–2).

From this perspective, people who blame themselves for something bad may come to feel depressed over time, even if their initial reaction is guilt, shame, or regret. Nevertheless, this theory could be interpreted as cohering with the other appraisal theories. The depression here is not about the initial negative event, but about the loss of self-respect and the perceived inability to recover it (Burgo 2018). Guilt, shame, and regret are merely the feelings that precipitate a sense of irrevocable loss.

There is now consensus that the irrevocability of loss makes us feel depressed rather than feel angry, anxious, or afraid. Psychologists Heather Lench, Thomas Tibbett, and Shane Bench sum up this view nicely, writing that "sadness" comes from "the perception that a goal has been lost, without the possibility of restoration given one's current abilities" (2016, 13). The perception that a loss is impossible to restore is rooted in the appraisal of how our capabilities stack up against the situation. Restoring a loss will seem difficult, perhaps even impossible, if we lack control or power over the situation—or when the broader circumstances, rather than a particular person, caused the loss.

## How Does Politics Produce Irrevocability?

The concept of appraisal influences how we think about emotions in politics. In their landmark book *Affective Intelligence and Political Judgment*, political scientists George Marcus, W. Russell Neuman, and Michael MacKuen argue that we possess "surveillance" and "disposition" systems that process information about the political world and help us respond appropriately. The disposition system allows us to "rely on learned routines to manage the buzzing and blooming reality of political choice and judgment" while the surveillance system signals "the need to break from routine and pay close attention to the external world" (2001, 127). When the disposition system evokes enthusiasm, for instance, it signals that all is well—we can rely on learned habits, such as choosing a candidate on the basis of their party identification. In contrast, when the surveillance system evokes feelings of anxiety, it signals that something is wrong—we shouldn't rely on learned behaviors, but instead should stop, look, and listen, perhaps collecting more information about the past performance or proposed policies of candidates before deciding whom to support.

The work of Marcus and colleagues renewed interest in political emotions and ushered in a more appraisal-oriented approach to how they're

TABLE 3.1 **The Appraisal Structure of Emotions**

| Emotion | Stressor & Appraisal Structure | Coping Strategies | Example |
|---|---|---|---|
| Anger | A losing situation with a clear source and a sense of control | Anger increases action and partisan loyalty (Webster 2020) | Trump supporters were angry about Biden's win and started "Stop the Steal" |
| Anxiety | A threatening situation where we lack certainty and control | Anxiety increases information seeking and trust during crises (Albertson and Gadarian 2015) | About 87% of Americans in 2018 worried about whether leaders in Washington could solve the country's biggest problems (Parker et al. 2019) |
| Disgust | A situation that presents something offensive or unpleasant | Disgust arouses our prejudice and amplifies our moral judgments (Peterson et al. 2020) | The idea of a welfare queen evoked disgust among white Americans, making reform palatable (Hancock 2004) |
| Enthusiasm | A situation that is familiar and rewarding | Enthusiasm keeps us engaged in the hopes of replicating success (Marcus et al. 2001) | Rallies generate enthusiasm, which turns into donations, volunteers, and votes |
| Envy | A situation where someone else has something we want | Envy shapes attitudes on fairness and redistribution and motivates us to enhance our group's standing (McClendon 2018) | Rural conservatives resent urban liberals who take more than they deserve (Cramer 2016); on the left, Occupy Wall Street and slogans like "Eat the Rich" |
| Fear | A threatening situation that presents a specific and immediate danger | Fear activates flight or fight (Valentino et al. 2009) and shifts attitudes to the right (Jost et al. 2017) | Many Americans live in fear of being attacked by a terrorist, shot by a police officer, gunned down at school, or robbed by an immigrant |
| Hope | A situation where a preferred outcome is possible but uncertain | Hope makes us more open to persuasion and politically active (Just et al. 2007) | Slogans like Obama's "Yes We Can" and Trump's "Make America Great Again" create and harness hope |

studied. Political scientists have since investigated a wide range of emotions (Neuman et al. 2007), including anger (Phoenix 2019), fear (Pearlman 2016), and resentment (Cramer 2016). Table 3.1 highlights seven of the many emotions that have been studied along with their distinctive appraisal structure and behavioral consequences. For example, anxiety is a response to a threatening situation (stressor) where we lack certainty and control (appraisal), so it leads us to search for information and look for ways to neutralize the threat (coping). In their book *Anxious Politics*, political scientists Bethany Albertson and Shana Gadarian show how political elites use anxiety in their messaging to make the public more receptive to their views (2014).

I argue that politics *distinctly* and *systematically* produces appraisals of irrevocability. Let's first consider the distinctive part. Appraisal theorists typically define irrevocability as a lack of control in a situation, or when the broader circumstances, rather than any one person, caused a loss. These definitions are fitting for losses that occur in our private lives but make less sense when it comes to politics. The collective nature of politics means that, by definition, we lack control over what happens. That doesn't mean we lack agency—we are still free to participate, learn, make our voice heard, and so on—but the ultimate outcome of a political situation is generally outside the control of any one person. For the same reason that we lack control, it's often difficult to attribute what happens in politics to any one person. In a way, politics *is* the broader circumstances that appraisal theorists were writing about.

In politics, the traditional definitions of irrevocability work better if we think in terms of *groups* rather than individuals. I may lack personal control over what happens in politics, but I align and identify with *groups* who have varying degrees of control. Likewise, no one person may be responsible for political losses, but groups or a coalition can be. Groups include political parties (e.g., Democrats), interest groups (e.g., the National Organization for Women), identity groups (e.g., women), professional associations (e.g., the American Medical Association), civic groups (e.g., the League of Women Voters), and others. In short, whether a loss is irrevocable depends on our appraisal of whether the groups to which we belong lack control or power in the situation or whether a specific group or set of groups caused the loss. Groups are what makes the political production of irrevocability distinct.

Next is the systematic part. I argue that irrevocability is systematically produced in two ways. The first is from inequality between groups. Interest group scholars have long recognized that groups vary in their political power. Some groups have more resources, decision-making roles, and public support, while others have less. As political scientist E. E. Schattschneider famously wrote, "The flaw in the pluralist heaven is that the heavenly chorus sings with a strong upper-class accent" (1960, 34). As inequality between groups grows, losses will feel more irrevocable to the losing group, because the gap between their abilities and those of the winning group will feel too vast. Appraisals of irrevocability are also systematically produced by political institutions—the rules, norms, and practices that guide political decision-making. Institutions can make losses seem more or less irrevocable by making change more difficult through high transaction costs or long time horizons. For instance, requiring a supermajority creates a higher transaction cost to passing legislation than a simple majority, so undoing a loss in the institution that requires a supermajority becomes more difficult. Elected positions with longer terms cause electoral losers to see the outcome as more irrevocable, or rather irrevocable for a longer time, than positions with shorter terms.

## What Is the Evidence?

So far, I've argued that politics is depressing whenever it produces irrevocable loss. We lose when our preferences cease to fulfilled, when politics takes away objects of personal value, and when our efforts at collective action fail. These losses can seem irrevocable when the groups we belong to lack control or power, or when broader circumstances, rather than an identifiable political group or coalition, are responsible for the loss. Does political depression actually work this way? Is there evidence that people feel depressed when confronted with irrevocable losses in politics? I turn to three sources of evidence to answer these questions. I first analyze polls in the United States to provide evidence that people report feeling depressed by a wide variety of political topics. This analysis establishes that depression is a widespread and recurring feature of politics. I then turn to a survey experiment that provides stronger causal evidence that politics is depressing due to irrevocable loss. Finally, I analyze data from the Cooperative Election Study to better elucidate the importance of irrevocability. Together, these three studies provide firm evidence in support of my framework. While they do not test every aspect of my theory, they form a base from which to more deeply explore the connection between politics, irrevocable loss, and depression.

### *Evidence from Polls*

Political polling has proliferated in the United States over the past few decades, and polls contain a wealth of information on how Americans think and feel about politics over time. I searched the digital polling repository at Cornell University's Roper Center to identify every poll in the United States that asked a question about feeling disappointed, sad,

TABLE 3.2 **The Political Content of Poll Questions about Depression**

| Topic | Total | Question is about feeling... | | |
| --- | --- | --- | --- | --- |
| | | Disappointed | Sad | Depressed |
| Campaigns & Elections | 112 | 93 | 3 | 16 |
| | 27.1% | 31.1% | 3.9% | 31.4% |
| Political Violence | 77 | 18 | 37 | 23 |
| | 18.6% | 6.0% | 48.1% | 45.1% |
| Evaluation of Elected Officials | 66 | 60 | 1 | 5 |
| | 15.9% | 20.1% | 1.3% | 9.8% |
| Policymaking by Legislatures | 45 | 45 | 0 | 0 |
| | 10.9% | 15.1% | 0.0% | 0.0% |
| General Impressions | 31 | 24 | 6 | 6 |
| | 7.5% | 8.0% | 7.8% | 11.8% |
| Scandal & Death | 28 | 10 | 21 | 0 |
| | 6.8% | 3.3% | 27.3% | 0.0% |
| Performance of Political Parties | 22 | 22 | 2 | 0 |
| | 5.3% | 7.4% | 2.6% | 0.0% |
| Miscellaneous | 13 | 7 | 7 | 1 |
| | 3.1% | 2.3% | 9.1% | 2.0% |
| Decision-Making by Courts | 12 | 12 | 0 | 0 |
| | 2.9% | 4.0% | 0.0% | 0.0% |
| Cabinet Appointments | 8 | 8 | 0 | 0 |
| | 1.9% | 2.7% | 0.0% | 0.0% |
| *Total* | *414* | *299* | *77* | *51* |
| | *100%* | *100%* | *100%* | *100%* |

*Note*: Some questions ask about multiple emotions, so the total number of questions may be less than the sum across the three emotions within a category. The top number in a cell is the absolute number of questions for the given topic and emotion, while the bottom number is the column percentage.

or depressed about some political object, such as an institution (e.g., legislatures or courts), a group or actor (such as Democrats or Lyndon Johnson), an aspect of the policymaking process (e.g., pending legislation), or an event or outcome (e.g., 9/11). This search produced 414 relevant poll questions asked of Americans between 1943 and 2022.

I begin by analyzing which aspects of politics pollsters think evoke feelings of depression. To do so, I categorize questions by political topic, then analyze which topics appear and whether some topics are more strongly associated with disappointment, sadness, or depression. This descriptive analysis does not establish that politics is depressing, but it provides some initial insights into the connection between the two. Table 3.2 shows the frequency with which pollsters asked questions about emotions related to a range of political topics. Disappointment is the most commonly occurring emotion in poll questions, asked about in roughly 70 percent of the questions. Sadness and depression appear less frequently.

There are several notable topic-emotion pairings. Nearly 77 percent of the depression questions are about elections and political violence, even though these categories only comprise about 46 percent of the total questions. Sadness is especially overrepresented in questions about political violence as well as scandals around political actors or their deaths. Disappointment dominates in categories relating to the actions of actors or institutions, including the evaluation of elected officials, policymaking by legislatures, the performance of political parties, decision-making by courts, and cabinet appointments.

Campaigns and elections were the most commonly asked-about political topic, constituting over a quarter of the total questions. This topic was especially prominent among the questions on disappointment and depression. Roughly 92 percent of these questions inquired about the *outcome* of an election. Questions asked before the election were generally phrased in terms of hypothetical results. For example, a Fox News polled asked registered voters in 2004, "How disappointed would you be if the (2000) presidential candidate you are planning to vote for . . . (George W.) Bush loses the election?" However, some questions were not about irrevocable loss, or at least not *only* about it. Six questions mixed the outcome of the election with an assessment of the future. For instance, a Democracy Corp poll from 1999 asked, "Imagine for a minute that you wake up the morning after the election in 2000 and Al Gore has been elected President and the Democrats have taken control of the Congress. On television, the Democratic leaders have committed to enacting their agenda for the country. Which two of these words best capture your own reaction to this news? . . . Concerned, hopeful, disappointed, upset, uncertain, positive, excited, optimistic, angry." This question is about both the outcome of the election and the promise or peril of a Democrat-controlled Congress. Only one question in this category has an exclusive focus on the future. A poll by *Fusion* in 2016 asked young adults, "What one word best describes how you feel about the possibility of Donald Trump as president?" The remaining 17 percent of questions focus on the evaluation of nominees or general feelings about an election.

Political violence is the next most common category and the focus of nearly half the sadness and depression questions. These questions cover a range of issues, including the Vietnam War; the Gulf War; the war in Iraq; the attacks of September 11, 2001; the insurrection on January 6, 2021; police brutality; and more. About 5 percent of these questions are clearly *not* about irrevocable loss. For instance, Pew Research asked Americans in 2001, "In the past few days, have you yourself felt depressed because of your concerns about terrorist attacks or the war against terrorism?" Another question from CNN/*Time Magazine* in 2003 asked, "When you think about the possibility of a war with Iraq, please tell me whether you sometimes feel each of the following." One of the possible emotions listed was "depressed." These questions draw attention to the future and the possibility of loss due to political violence, but they are not about loss themselves.

The remaining 95 percent of the questions about political violence are phrased in a way that allows respondents to appraise the subject matter through the prism of irrevocable loss. Most often, these questions are about the event having occurred in the past or as it unfolds in the present, but a few focus on hypothetical future outcomes. For instance, *USA Today* asked Americans in 1991, "Will you be disappointed if Saddam Hussein is still alive when the war (with Iraq) ends?" Other questions asked how the respondent's life changed because of the event. These questions are not explicitly or exclusively about irrevocable loss but allow for this kind of appraisal. For instance, when asked about 9/11, some respondents might focus on the loss of life, the injustice of the attacks, the threat of terrorism, or something else entirely.

The third most common subject is the evaluation of elected officials. This category is part of a quintet of topics—along with policymaking by legislatures, the performance of political parties, decision-making by courts, and cabinet appointments—that focuses almost exclusively on disappointment. Some questions focus on general evaluations of elected official and political parties, but the overwhelming majority are about real or hypothetical actions of elected officials, legislatures, political parties, courts, and presidents. For instance, an NBC News/*WSJ* poll in 1993 asked, "Are you generally pleased or disappointed with the people Bill Clinton has appointed to posts in his administration?" Given that these questions focus on past changes, they allow respondents to make appraisals of irrevocable loss, such as a lost opportunity for a more preferable decision or lost confidence in the political actor. However, it does not appear that pollsters view these losses as intense or irrevocable enough to merit asking about sadness or depression.

General impressions of American politics is the fourth most common topic, and it features all three emotions to some degree. These questions ask respondents to broadly evaluate American politics rather than a specific actor, event, or outcome. For instance, the *Associated Press* asked in 2010, "Thinking about American politics today, do any of the following words describe your own personal feelings about politics, or not? How about . . . depressed?" Most of these questions present American politics as an ongoing endeavor, leaving it open to respondents to choose how to appraise the subject matter, potentially including as an irrevocable loss. Five questions, however, focus exclusively on the future, asking respondents to "look ahead." These questions are open ended, so in their answers, it was respondents who volunteered the term "disappointed"—pollsters had not built it into the response options.

Of the remaining categories, depression appears in only one miscellaneous question. In 2019, *USA Today* asked Americans, "How have destructive partisan disagreements and divisiveness affected your life?" Sadness also appears with some frequency in this category, which includes topics like political polarization, campaign finance, stay-at-home orders during the pandemic, international relations, political knowledge, and others. All questions in this category are phrased in terms of the past or present, rather than the future, which opens a space for respondents to appraise the subject matter in terms of irrevocable loss.

The final category is the scandals and deaths of political figures. Questions about scandal cover Bill Clinton's affair with Monica Lewinsky and the subsequent impeachment trial, Democratic candidate Gary Hart's extramarital affair, Elliot Spitzer's resignation as governor of New York, the investigation into President George Bush's advisor Scooter Libby over the leaking of CIA information, and the Mueller investigation into potential election interference by President Donald Trump. Questions about death cover the assassinations of Martin Luther King Jr., Malcolm X, Robert Kennedy, John F. Kennedy, Medgar Evers, and George Lincoln Rockwell, as well as the unexpected deaths of Princess Diana, John F. Kennedy Jr., Carolyn Bessette-Kennedy, and her sister Lauren Bessette. Notably, questions about death are always linked to sadness, while the questions about scandal are mixed in their focus on sadness and disappointment.

Just because pollsters ask about disappointment, sadness, and depression doesn't mean Americans feel these emotions, so I now examine the responses to these questions. I count a respondent as having felt disappointed, sad, or depressed if they answered yes (for yes/no questions), volunteered one of these emotions (for open-ended questions), or choose the most intense option (for ordinal questions). Figure 3.1 displays the prevalence of these feelings across the hundreds of poll questions. On average, 32 percent of respondents report disappointment, 26 percent re-

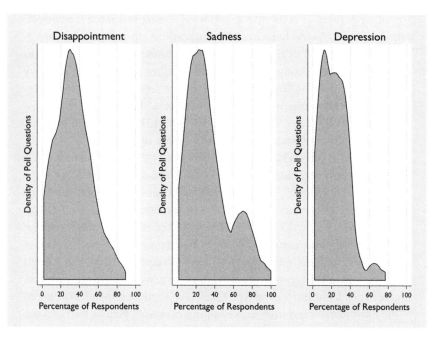

FIGURE 3.1. The Prevalence of Depression in Political Polls
*Note*: I use the poll's topline information to determine the percentage of respondents reporting each emotion. For questions with ordinal response options, I calculate the percentage of respondents as those who select the most emotional response option (e.g., very depressed vs. somewhat, a little, or not at all depressed). More information about the analyses can be found in the appendix.

port sadness, and 20 percent report depression. Given that respondents could have said no, volunteered a different feeling, or chose a different emotion, it is striking just how many Americans report feeling disappointed, sad, and depressed about politics.

Notably, the prevalence of these feelings varies considerably from question to question. Sometimes very few respondents report feelings of depression. For example, only 1 percent of respondents said they were disappointed when Gallup asked in 2006, "Next, we'd like to learn about your impressions of some of the leading Republicans who might run for president in 2008. What comes to your mind when you think about John McCain?" No one volunteered that they felt sad or depressed about a McCain candidacy. Questions that are open-ended or do not explicitly ask about irrevocable loss typically yield the lowest prevalence. In contrast, some questions garner a near-universal prevalence of these feelings.

About 93 percent of respondents reported feeling sad when CNN/ORC asked in 2011, "Now here are some questions about the (January 8, 2011) shootings that occurred in Tucson, Arizona in which Jared Loughner allegedly shot a congresswoman and 18 other people. . . . (Please say whether you, personally, have felt each of the following emotions in response to the shootings in Arizona.) . . . Sadness." High prevalence questions are typically ones with a yes/no format or that ask about political violence, electoral outcomes, or the general state of politics.

While these polls do not provide conclusive evidence that depression is a response to irrevocable loss, they enrich our understanding in a few ways. A substantial number of Americans report feelings of disappointment, sadness, and depression when asked about a wide range of political topics. This finding provides a broad base of support for the idea that politics can be depressing. Whereas any one poll might be characterized as an outlier or anomaly, taken collectively, they make it hard to deny that depression is felt by many Americans across many areas of politics. We can also see a connection between topic and feeling type. Questions about depression are limited to the most intense and irrevocable of political losses, such as the outcome of a presidential election or a war, while questions about disappointment are more prominent for outcomes that could be broadly characterized as less intense, consequential, or long lasting, such as the appointment of a cabinet member or the passage of a piece of legislation. Finally, pollsters do not focus questions about disappointment, sadness, and depression on the future. By making the *past*—such as a real or hypothetical outcome, action, or decision—the subject of the question, pollsters create a window for respondents to make appraisals of irrevocable loss. This question construction is compatible (or at least not incompatible) with my framework.

*Evidence from a Survey Experiment*

The polls reveal that depression is a regular response to politics. However, one potential objection to the polls is that they only look for depression where it is most likely to appear—after an election, during a war, amid a scandal—and so the polls may give the impression that politics is more depressing than it really is. So I devised a survey experiment to more rigorously test my arguments. The experiment exposes respondents to recent trends in American politics through the presentation of dry, boring statistics. If this kind of information can evoke feelings of depression, we would have even stronger evidence that politics matters.

In my experiment, I asked respondents to read about a political trend that was randomly selected from among nine topics: corruption, democracy, trust in government, abortion, guns, taxes, same-sex marriage, government healthcare, or immigration. After reading about the trend, respondents were asked about their emotional response to it. Specifically, I asked them whether the trend made them feel depressed, sad, disappointed, angry, anxious, afraid, happy, or hopeful. They could select not at all, a little, somewhat, moderately, or very for each emotion. This part of the experiment was repeated twice more, so each respondent evaluated a total of three trends. Finally, the survey wrapped up by asking respondents how they feel about politics in general and how they feel about life in general, as well as some standard demographic and political questions.

Importantly, I randomized two components of each trend. The first randomization was whether the trend indicated a loss, a gain, or no change. For example, the text of the trends about corruption were:

- **<u>Loss Trend</u>: Corruption in the United States has *increased* in recent years.** The most recent corruption score from Transparency International shows the United States at a 31 on a scale from 0 (very clean) to 100 (very corrupt). This is an increase compared with the score of 24 in 2015.
- **<u>No Change Trend</u>: Corruption in the United States has *not changed* in recent years.** The most recent corruption score from Transparency International shows the United States at a 31 on a scale from 0 (very clean) to 100 (very corrupt). This is no change compared with the score of 31 in 2019.
- **<u>Gain Trend</u>: Corruption in the United States has *decreased* in recent years.** The most recent corruption score from Transparency International shows the United States at a 31 on a scale from 0 (very clean) to 100 (very corrupt). This is a decrease compared with the score of 33 in 2020.

Each trend was based on real data, but the reference year was strategically selected to give the appearance of loss, gain, or no change. The trends for corruption and democracy in the United States come from expert estimates. The trends on trust in government, abortion, guns, taxes, same-sex marriage, government healthcare, and immigration are based on Gallup surveys of Americans. These latter trends highlight trust/distrust in government or support/opposition for various policy positions. This randomization allows me to analyze whether loss trends evoke stronger feelings of depression compared to no-change trends, and vice versa for gain trends.

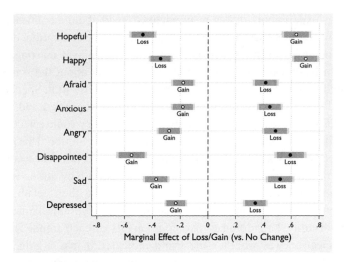

FIGURE 3.2. The Impact of Losses and Gains
*Note*: The results are based on regressions of each emotion on the loss/gain treatment (with "no change" as the omitted category). The model clusters standard errors by respondent and includes task and topic fixed effects. More information about the analyses can be found in the appendix.

Whether a trend is perceived as a loss or gain depends on our preferences. In the abstract, we generally prefer less corruption, stronger democracy, and a more trustworthy government, so we lose when there is more corruption and less democracy and trust. The trends for the policy issues are more difficult to categorize because Americans have conflicting preferences. I classify these trends by matching left and right shifts in public opinion to the party identification of respondents.[1] Leftward shifts in public opinion are gains for Democrats and losses for Republicans, and vice versa for rightward shifts.[2]

The second randomization is the irrevocability of the trend. In addition to the loss and gain trends, I randomized whether respondents were given no additional information, a statement that analysts thought the change was permanent, or a statement that analysts thought the change was temporary. This randomization allows me to assess whether irrevocable losses (or gains) are more (or less) depressing than revocable ones. Notably, a validity test reveals that respondents were persuaded by the irrevocability treatment but not the revocability one, which affects how we interpret the results of this analysis.[3]

I begin by examining the emotional impact of losses and gains. Figure 3.2 shows the predicted change to each emotion. Compared to respondents who saw trends showing no change, those who saw a loss trend reported increased depression, sadness, disappointment, anger, anxiety, and fear, and decreased happiness and hopefulness. Gain trends had the opposite effect on emotions. Notably, members of the depression family, including their "cousins" happiness and hope, are affected by politics trends as much as anger, anxiety, and fear, and in some cases more. Within the depression family, these trends have the biggest effects on disappointment and the smallest effects on depression, a pattern that is consistent with the earlier polls.

I now want to turn to the *irrevocability* of loss and gain. Figure 3.3 reports the results of this analysis for loss trends on the left and gain trends on the right. The results show how information about the permanence (that is, irrevocability) or temporariness (revocability) of the trend, compared to no additional information, changed the emotional impact of the

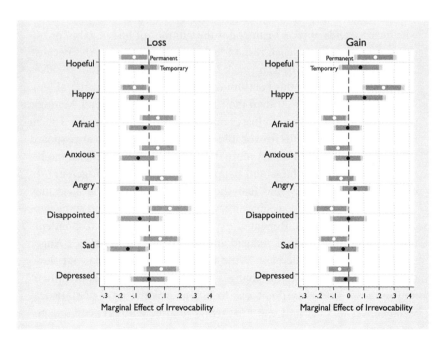

FIGURE 3.3. The Impact of Irrevocable Losses and Gains
*Note*: The results are based on regressions of each emotion on the loss/gain treatment (with "no change" as the omitted category), the irrevocability treatment (with "no information" as the omitted category), and their interaction. The model clusters standard errors by respondent and includes task and topic fixed effects. More information about the analyses can be found in the appendix.

loss or gain. Respondents who read about irrevocable losses experienced more disappointment and less hope and happiness. In contrast, respondents who read about revocable losses experienced less sadness. In terms of gains, irrevocability decreased sadness, disappointment, and fear, and increased hopefulness and happiness.

The findings in figure 3.3 are a bit messy but generally support my argument about irrevocable loss. The irrevocability treatments are largely limited to members of the depression family—disappointment and sadness—as well as their close cousins—happiness and hope. Depression is the one emotion in this family that seems to be unaffected by the irrevocability treatment, but a closer examination reveals that the effects of irrevocable losses and gains lean in the expected direction and fall just shy of a conventional level of statistical significance. In contrast, anger, anxiety, and fear are generally unaffected by whether a loss is irrevocable or revocable.

I now want to leverage a "hidden" aspect of the experiment to provide another test of my argument. Since respondents were presented with three trends apiece, I can count the number of losses, gains, or no-change trends seen by each respondent during the survey. And because I randomized the type of trend each time, the overall pattern of trends is also randomized. I use this measure to predict respondents' general feelings toward politics rather than their feelings about each trend. My logic is that repeated exposure to losses makes the problems of politics seem more intractable and thus irrevocable. If so, respondents who are exposed to repeated loss should report more depression, sadness, and disappointment, and less hopefulness and happiness, about politics in general. In contrast, anger, anxiety, and fear should be less affected because they tend to be responses to specific situations or problems. I find some support for this argument. Repeated exposures to loss caused respondents to feel more disappointed and sad and less happy about politics. Anger and depression also increase, while hopefulness takes a hit, but these changes are smaller than the changes to the emotions of disappointment and sadness—and they don't rise to a conventional level of statistical significance. Anxiety and fear are largely unaffected by repeated exposure to loss.

These results provide the strongest causal evidence we have right now that political loss is disappointing, saddening, and depressing—feelings that can be amplified or quieted by the irrevocability of the loss. Reading about trends in American politics mimics the kind of information citizens encounter in the news, lending external validity to this experiment. Moreover, statistics are boring and therefore not well suited for evoking emotions, especially compared to other ways we experience politics. The boringness of the task (reading statistics) means that the experimental treatment is not an especially effective way to garner an emotional response; that it did should ultimately bolster our confidence in the findings.

*Evidence from the Cooperative Election Study*

I now want to dig deeper into the role of irrevocability. In the survey experiment, I defined irrevocability as the permanence or temporariness of the trend (as evaluated by fictitious "analysts") and as exposure to repeated loss. This approach allowed me to make causal claims about the emotional impact of irrevocability, because I could randomize which respondents were exposed to irrevocable and revocable losses and gains. However, by prioritizing causal identification in the experiment, I ended up operationalizing irrevocability in somewhat narrow and unusual ways. There are two issues here. First, appraisal theorists traditionally define irrevocability as a lack of personal control over a situation and/or whether a loss was caused by the broader circumstances. Building on these ideas, I argued that *political power* shapes appraisals of irrevocability when it comes to political loss—people who occupy less powerful positions in politics, such as women, people of color, youth, and the economically disadvantaged, will be more likely to appraise political loss as irrevocable than those in more powerful positions. The second issue is that the experiment lacked any actual appraisals. At its core, appraisal is how we *think* about a situation. Yet, rather than ask respondents in the experiment to appraise the trends, I simply imposed irrevocability on them through its design.

I use the Cooperative Election Study (CES) to remedy these issues and to expand our understanding of how irrevocable loss can be depressing. The CES is a recurring election-year survey in the United States. I made use of a special module that was administered to one thousand respondents in the 2022 CES. This module began by asking respondents to recall and describe "an *unpleasant political experience* from the past year." Following this exercise, respondents appraised whether the experience was important, unpleasant, unfair, solvable, and within their control. I operationalize irrevocability using the ratings of solvability and control. Next, respondents rated whether the experience made them feel depressed, disappointed, happy, hopeful, angry, anxious, and/or afraid. For

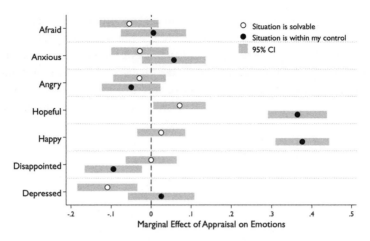

FIGURE 3.4. The Impact of Irrevocability as Solvability and Control
*Note*: The results are based on regressions of each emotion on appraisals of solvability and control. I control for appraisals of importance, unpleasantness, unfairness, gender, race, ethnicity, education, age, income, political interest, party identification, and the cause of the recalled experience. More information about the analyses can be found in the appendix.

both the appraisal and emotion questions, respondents could select from a scale ranging from "not at all" (1) to "a great deal" (11) with the midpoint labeled as "somewhat."

Irrevocability may be the reason loss evokes depression rather than anger, anxiety, or fear. If this is true, appraisals of solvability and control should influence feelings of depression, but not other negative emotions. Examining the results, I find this is exactly the case. Figure 3.4 shows the impact of solvability and control appraisals on each emotion. The results show that appraising a situation as solvable decreases depression, while appraising it as controllable decreases disappointment and increases happiness and hopefulness. In contrast, these appraisals have no impact on anger, anxiety, or fear. Irrevocability thus seems to be an important component of why political loss leads to depression rather than some other emotion.

I also argued that our position in the political system shapes our appraisals of irrevocability. To test this argument, I analyze whether members of less powerful groups report more depression and disappointment than members of more powerful groups. Figure 3.5 displays the results, which show the predicted level of depression and disappointment across key demographic groups. I find that women and younger people report higher levels of depression and disappointment than men and older people. Income is associated with less depression and more disappointment, which raises the possibility that the depression family is economically stratified—the wealthiest members of society may be shielded from the most intense members of the depression family, while the poorest members of society leapfrog over disappointment and right into depression. Notably, there aren't any differences when it comes to education and race, except for the fact that Black Americans report *less* depression than White Americans.

These findings provide further support for my argument that irrevocability is a defining feature of what makes political loss depressing. When a loss seems within our control or solvable, we feel less depressed and disappointed, but neither more nor less angry, anxious, or afraid. Likewise, being a member of a less politically powerful group is generally associated with more depression and disappointment. Women, younger people, and the poor were hit harder by feelings of depression than their more privileged counterparts. The few caveats to this pattern, such as with race and education, merit exploration in future research. Other important political groups, such LGBTQ persons, other racial and ethnic groups, and immigrants, should also be studied in the future.

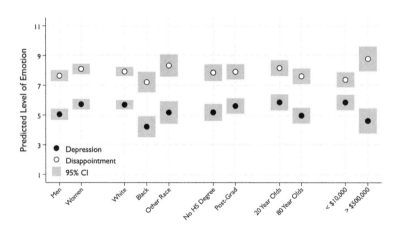

FIGURE 3.5. The Impact of Irrevocability as Political Power
*Note*: The results are based on regression models of depression and disappointment on gender, race and ethnicity, education, age, income, political interest, party identification, and the cause of the recalled experience. More information about the analyses can be found in the appendix.

## What's Next?

We can now say with confidence that disappointment, sadness, and depression, like anger, anxiety, and fear, are regular political emotions, not exceptions. Moreover, irrevocable loss helps us make sense of depression as a political emotion. Competition for scarce resources and conflicting preferences make loss an unavoidable part of the political process, and this loss can often seem irrevocable because the collective nature of politics makes it difficult to enact change, especially for groups who lack power. In short, politics produces irrevocable loss, and irrevocable loss leaves us feeling depressed.

Analyses of hundreds of polls, an original survey experiment, and the Cooperative Election Study provided the strongest evidence to date that politics is systematically depressing. First, the polls provided some initial indication that politics can actually be depressing. Americans reported feeling disappointed, sad, and depressed about a wide variety of political events, actors, and issues, even though they had the option to say otherwise. Then, the survey experiment gave us *causal* evidence that political loss can be depressing, especially when it is characterized as irrevocable. Finally, the Cooperative Election Study supplemented our understanding of irrevocability by digging into appraisals of solvability and control as well as political power.

While it is now undeniable that politics can be depressing, some questions may linger about this evidence. One issue concerns the measurement of depression. The studies all directly tied depression to political trends, issues, actors, events, and outcomes—are you depressed *about X*? This measurement approach isn't a problem per se, but it is limiting. It tells us that politics can give rise to *object-specific* feelings of depression, but it doesn't tell us whether politics shapes *generalized* feelings of depression. I overcome this limitation in later chapters in connection with electoral loss and political polarization. A second issue relates to types of political loss. Earlier, I argued that we lose when our political preferences cease to be realized, when politics takes away an object of personal value, or when we face repeated defeats in our efforts to enact political change. The three studies here focus primarily on the first type of loss, which means we still lack evidence that these other losses are depressing. I address this issue in a later chapter on public policy.

We now know that politics can be depressing, but how do we behave when we feel this way? What do we do to mitigate these feelings? Does coping with depression have consequences for our political engagement? And what do mental health professionals say we should do when we feel depressed by politics? In the next chapter, I answer these questions by turning to the third part of my framework: coping.

CHAPTER FOUR

# When Depression Leads to Withdrawal

Kevin Carter, a White South African, was born on September 13, 1960, in Johannesburg. After considering several career options—including as a pharmacist, air force serviceman, and radio DJ—Carter took up photography at the age of twenty-three. He initially worked in sports but soon took a position covering the news for Johannesburg's largest newspaper, the *Star*. Over the next twenty years, he would go on to hold positions at the *Sunday Tribune*, where he was head of photography; the *Daily Mail*, where he started the photography department; and Reuters. Apartheid defined the political landscape of South Africa at the time, and it quickly became Carter's most prominent subject. He was one of the first to photograph an apartheid-related execution, the killing of Maki Skosana, a Black woman who antiapartheid activists suspected was an informant because of her relationship with a police officer. Carter would later say of this incident, "I was appalled at what they were doing. I was appalled at what I was doing. But then people started talking about those pictures... then I felt that maybe my actions hadn't been at all bad. Being a witness to something this horrible wasn't necessarily such a bad thing to do" (Porter 2003).

In 1993, the United Nations paid for Carter and his colleague João Silva to travel to South Sudan to cover the famine. It is here that Carter captured the now-infamous photograph of a starving Sudanese boy being stalked by a vulture. Silva would later write about the shock Carter felt in that moment, especially as the boy, who was thought at the time to be a girl, reminded Carter of his own young daughter (Marinovich and Silva 2000). The *New York Times* purchased the photo and ran it on March 26,

1993, sparking such an intense demand from readers to know the fate of the child that the *Times* clarified a week later, "She recovered enough to resume her trek after the vulture was chased away." The photo would win the Pulitzer Prize a year later. The child's father would report decades later that the boy, whose name was Kong Nyong, survived the famine but died in young adulthood due to illness.

Witnessing the execution of Maki Skosana, the hunger of Kong Nyong, and untold other political traumas weighed on Carter, leading him to feel deep despair. A few months after returning from South Sudan, he died by suicide. An excerpt from a note he left behind reads, "I'm really, really sorry. The pain of life overrides the joy to the point that joy does not exist . . . depressed . . . I am haunted by the vivid memories of killings & corpses & anger & pain . . . of starving or wounded children, of trigger-happy madmen, often police, of killer executioners." Shortly after his death, his father told the South African Press Association, "Kevin always carried around the horror of the work he did." The life of Kevin Carter reveals how the darkest side of politics—violence, starvation, war, destruction—can evoke despair and anguish, the most intense feelings of depression. His suicide offers a tragic and rare example of how depression leads to a complete *withdrawal* from politics.

In this chapter, I argue that we cope with feelings of depression by withdrawing from politics. Most of the time, withdrawal is less severe than in the case of Kevin Carter. For instance, Democrats who were disappointed in the performance of President Biden "withdrew" from politics by expressing disinterest in the 2018 midterm election. These two cases represent the mildest and severest forms of withdrawal, bookending a myriad of forms it can take. Below, I build my argument by explaining the concept of coping, how we cope with feelings of depression specifically, and how coping strategies are affected by politics. I then report the results of a novel survey experiment that shows we are more likely to withdraw when we experience depression than when we experience anger, anxiety, or fear—especially in politics where free riding, which is letting others bear the cost of collective problem-solving, is a more feasible strategy for dealing with irrevocable loss. I then dig into what mental health professionals say about coping with politics and find somewhat mixed advice. I conclude by exploring the tension between what mental health professionals recommend as effective coping strategies for political stress and what democratic theorists identify as the behaviors of good citizenship.

## What Is Coping?

Imagine that you don't want to feel depressed, but a friend has invited you to watch the movie *Schindler's List*. What can you do? You might decline the invitation or propose an alternative movie. If you end up watching *Schindler's List*, you might leave the lights on and turn down the volume so the viewing experience is less intense. Other options are to avoid the saddest scenes by scrolling on your phone or covering your face, or to remind yourself that the movie isn't real; the people on screen are just actors. Once you feel sad, you might close your eyes, take deep breaths, or even walk outside for fresh air in order to calm your feelings.

The behaviors in this movie-watching scenario reflect some of the ways we cope with difficult situations. Coping broadly refers to the "process of attempting to manage the demands created by stressful events that are appraised as taxing or exceeding a person's resources" (Taylor and Stanton 2007, 378). Any time we attempt to regulate affect—that is, emotions, mood, personality, or mental health—we are coping. The example of *Schindler's List* draws specifically on the idea of emotion regulation (Gross 2001) in order to highlight how we adjust our thoughts and actions, often unintentionally and subconsciously, in order to up- and down-regulate positive and negative *emotions*. We select into or out of situations (watch the movie or not), modify the situation as needed (leave on the lights), change our thoughts (tell ourselves they are just actors), deploy our attention (scroll on our phone), and then modulate our response (take deep breaths).[1]

To date, psychologists have identified hundreds of coping behaviors and arranged them into countless classification schemes, such as approach versus avoidance or cognitive versus behavioral. One team of researchers reviewed over four hundred coping behaviors from one hundred schemes and distilled them into twelve coping families (Skinner et al. 2003). Each family is comprised of numerous strategies that serve an adaptive process: self-reliance, support seeking, delegation, and isolation (coping families) help coordinate social resources (adaptive process); problem-solving, information-seeking, helplessness, and escape help coordinate actions and contingencies in the environment; and accommodation, negotiation, submission, and opposition help coordinate preferences and options. I divide coping behaviors into four strategies—problem-focused, appraisal-focused, emotion-focused, and attention-focused—that are commonly

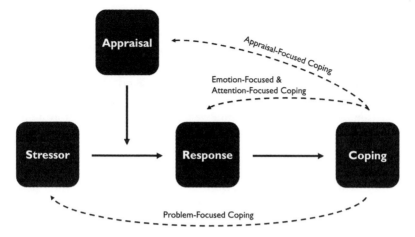

FIGURE 4.1. The Four Coping Strategies

found in the study of coping and that fit with my framework, as seen in figure 4.1.

Problem-focused coping refers to any behavior "directed at managing or altering the problem causing the distress" (Lazarus and Folkman 1984, 150). It includes gathering information about the problem, creating a plan of action, securing the resources needed to execute the plan, and enlisting support from others. In clinical settings, therapists often employ behavioral therapy to help clients develop and execute these types of strategies. Appraisal-focused coping, or what is sometimes called meaning-focused coping, "draws on values, beliefs, and goals to modify the meaning of a stressful transaction" (Folkman and Moskowitz 2004, 752). It includes behaviors such as identifying the upsides of a bad situation, adjusting our priorities, and updating our goals. This approach is especially helpful when problem-focused coping is not viable, either because it is too costly or because the situation cannot be altered. In clinical settings, cognitive therapies emphasize the development and execution of these strategies, including skills such as restructuring, approximation, and mindfulness. Perhaps the most well-known therapeutic approach is cognitive-behavioral therapy, which melds problem-focused and appraisal-focused coping.

Emotion-focused coping is "directed at regulating emotional response to the problem" (Lazarus and Folkman 1984, 150) and can include behaviors such as meditation, substance use, or seeking emotional support. Strategies such as pharmacological treatments, journaling, and meditation are often deployed in conjunction with cognitive-behavioral therapies in clinical settings. Attention-focused coping occurs when we fixate on something other than the problem, how we think about it, or how it makes us feel. Although the purpose of this strategy is to ignore all aspects of the situation, including the stressor, appraisal, and response, the goal is nevertheless to change how we feel (emotion-focused) rather than the situation itself (problem-focused) or how we think about it (appraisal-focused). For this reason, attention-focused coping behaviors, such as distraction or avoidance, are often classified as a subset of emotion-focused coping.

One long-standing question about coping is its effectiveness. Are some strategies and behaviors more effective than others? The answer is both yes and no. As the psychologists Susan Folkman and Judith Tedlie Moskowitz write, "An important motivation for studying coping is the belief that within a given culture certain ways of coping are more and less effective in promoting emotional well-being and addressing problems causing distress, and that such information can be used to design interventions to help people cope more effectively with the stress in their lives. Despite the reasonableness of this expectation, the issue of determining coping effectiveness remains one of the most perplexing" (2004, 753). This isn't to say that we know nothing about effective coping, only that the best way to cope is often highly contingent on the situation, person, and coping behavior. For instance, emotion-focused strategies have long had a reputation as ineffective, or at least less effective, but researchers have begun to revise their view in recent years. Some behaviors such as substance use are generally ineffective and may even make things worse in the long run. Other behaviors that help in "actively identifying, processing, and expressing one's emotions" may be useful because they provide "information about one's goal status" (Baker and Berenbaum 2007, 96). The effectiveness of attention-focused strategies can likewise vary. Distraction can be a useful short-term strategy because it provides us with distance from the problem and thus allows us to eventually think more critically about the situation. However, refusing to think about or confront the underlying problem—a strategy known as avoidance—is generally considered ineffective in the long term. In short, there is no one-size-fits-all solution when it comes to coping.

The effectiveness of coping strategies also relies on our emotions. Emotions provide us with information about the best way to navigate a situation, which is what psychologists refer to as their adaptive function (Keltner and Gross 1999). My framework reflects this idea by showing how our response to stress influences how we cope. At the same time, how we cope has the potential to amplify or diminish how we feel or to create new feelings altogether (Folkman and Lazarus 1988). The reciprocal relationship between emotions and coping can be seen in how coping strategies can influence the underlying problem, how we appraise it, and ultimately how we feel about it. This adaptive function makes coping with depression different from coping with anger, fear, or some other emotion. So how do we cope with depression?

## How Do We Cope with Depression?

The Pixar film *Inside Out* achieved smashing success in 2015. It made many year-end lists and would go on to win an Oscar for Best Animated Feature. The movie tells the story of a young girl, Riley, as she moves from Minnesota to San Francisco with her family. Her emotions are anthropomorphized into characters, including Joy, Sadness, Anger, Fear, and Disgust, and the plot centers on how these emotions jostle for control over Riley's thoughts and behaviors. Despite their best efforts, Anger, Fear, and Disgust struggle to help Riley cope with her life in a new city. Anger even convinces Riley to run away to Minnesota at one point, thinking this will make her happy again. Ultimately, it is Sadness who saves the day by telling Riley to take a deep breath, reassess the situation, and seek emotional support from her parents. Riley learns that her parents also miss Minnesota, and together they strive to turn San Francisco into a place they can call home.

Feelings of depression can signal to us the appropriate way to cope with irrevocable loss, just as Sadness helped Riley come to terms with the loss of her friends, community, and routines when she moved across the country. Evolutionary psychiatrist Randolph Nesse points out that depression helps us abstain from situations associated with the loss, determine the causes of the loss, reassess the need for change because of the loss, acquire support from others, warn others about potential danger, and withdraw when the loss is one of social status (1999). In short, depression directs us to place less emphasis on problem-focused strategies (e.g., abstain from the situation, withdraw) and more emphasis on appraisal-focused strategies (e.g., determine cause, reassess goals) and emotion-focused strategies (e.g., acquire emotional support). It is these adaptive functions that have led some psychologists to call sadness the "architect of cognitive change," noting how it helps in "facilitating adaptation to irrevocable loss by soliciting aid and restructuring expectations and goals" (Karnaze and Levine 2018, 46).

Not all attempts at coping are adaptive or effective, and this is especially true when it comes to depression. Intense depression can lead us to conclude that nothing will make us feel better, which can in turn deepen our feelings and affirm our belief that nothing can help. This maladaptive response creates what psychologist John Teasdale refers to as a "vicious cycle" (1983, 14). In her groundbreaking work on coping with depression, psychologist Susan Nolen-Hoeksema elaborates how this cycle might take hold: "People who engage in ruminative responses to depression, focusing on their symptoms and the possible causes and consequences of their symptoms, will show longer depressions than people who take action to distract themselves from their symptoms. Ruminative responses prolong depression because they allow the depressed mood to negatively bias thinking and interfere with instrumental behavior and problem-solving" (1991, 569). When our ability to cope with this vicious cycle breaks down, routine feelings of depression can be prolonged, and in more extreme circumstances transformed into a mental health problem. As psychologists James Gross and Ricardo Munoz point out, "Usually, transient increases in depressive mood are countered by adaptive emotion regulatory efforts, which permit a return to normal mood states. In vulnerable individuals, however, increases in depressed mood are not met by successful regulatory measures. When this happens, the person may cross the diagnostic threshold into an episode of major depressive disorder" (1995, 156).

## How Do We Cope with Politics?

Historically there has been little crossover between the study of coping and the study of politics. This has been slowly changing in recent years. The role of emotion regulation has now been studied in political conflict (Halperin et al. 2013), rally-around-the-flag effects (Porat et al. 2019), White fragility (Ford et al. 2022), and more. Beyond these studies—which focus only on emotion regulation—there has been little attention to coping in the study of political science or attention to politics in the study of coping. This may be due to the fact that in many ways, coping with a political problem is like coping with any other problem. Consciously or not, we make decisions about how to act based on expected costs and benefits of our available coping strategies. Costs include time, money, effort, social capital, and whatever other resources may be required to implement a strategy; the benefits are the extent to which a strategy ultimately upregulates or downregulates the desired feeling and for how long. All other conditions being equal, we tend to choose strategies that are less costly and more beneficial, whether the problem is political or personal.

Still, coping with politics is unique in at least two ways. The first is how it shapes our "cost-benefit" analysis when selecting a coping strategy. Politics is about making and enforcing decisions in society, which means it is a *collective* process and therefore requires coordination. Coordination is costly, and it becomes more so as the number of people who need to be coordinated grows. It is this coordination that transforms how we cope, because it changes the costs of some coping strategies but not others. Problem-focused strategies emphasize removing or modifying the underlying problem, something that often cannot be accomplished alone. This is especially true when it comes to addressing political problems—perhaps repealing an undesirable policy or unseating an undesirable representative—which can be accomplished only through large-scale coordination.

In contrast, reappraising the situation, diverting our attention, and modifying our emotions are strategies we can typically pursue on our own. They require less coordination than problem-focused strategies and no more coordination when coping with politics than when coping with other aspects of life. Put another way, the costs of these strategies are unaffected by the collective nature of politics because they don't require coordination in the first place. For instance, exploring our feelings about a situation—an emotion-focused coping strategy—can be done alone, regardless of whether the underlying problem is political or otherwise. These strategies should therefore be more common in politics than in our personal life—not because they are necessarily more effective but because they are relatively less costly than problem-focused strategies.

The second unique aspect is the availability of political participation as a "political" coping behavior. We can vote, donate money, and volunteer in elections when we are angry with elected officials and want them ousted. If we're anxious about the impact of a policy, we can contact an official, petition, vote, or protest to have it changed. The goal of participation in these cases is the removal or modification of a problem; in short, participation often functions as a problem-focused coping strategy in the political arena. Negative emotions like anxiety, anger, disgust, or envy spur participation by drawing our attention to a grievance that needs to be remedied or a threat that needs to be neutralized. In contrast, depression signals to us that the best way to cope with the irrevocability of our loss is to withdraw, reappraise the situation, and/or refocus our attention elsewhere, at least temporarily. Feeling depressed about politics should therefore reduce our reliance on participation.[2]

## What Is the Evidence?

The third part of my framework proposes that depression shapes our coping behavior. It signals to us that something has been irrevocably lost and the appropriate way forward is to withdraw from the situation, direct attention elsewhere, and/or change how we appraise what has happened. We would expect these patterns to be accentuated when it comes to politics, where coordination amplifies the cost of problem-solving. We'd also anticipate that depression in politics would make us less reliant on problem-focused coping strategies, including political participation, compared to depression in our personal life.

There is already some evidence in support of this argument. In a study I conducted with political scientist Claudia Landwehr, we found that depression was consistently and negatively associated with political participation, interest, and internal efficacy in the United States, Israel, and dozens of European countries (Landwehr and Ojeda 2021). As we note in our conclusion, "Our findings provide compelling evidence for the negative effect of depressive symptoms on political participation. Apart from education and age, depressive symptoms in fact constitute the only other variable that has a consistent and significant effect on both electoral turnout and political motivation across the studies" (329). I bolster this evidence by conducting a novel survey experiment, in which I better isolate the causal effect of depression on participation, examine a broader array of coping strategies, assess whether politics changes how we cope, and compare the impact of depression to the standard political emotions.

Here's how the experiment worked. Each respondent was randomly assigned to an emotion (depressed, afraid, angry, anxious) and domain (politics, personal life) and then asked, "Please recall a time when you felt [emotion] because of something that happened in [domain]. This may be something recently, a few months ago, or even a few years ago. If noth-

TABLE 4.1  **Depressing Experiences in Politics and Personal Life**

|            | Politics | Personal Life |
|------------|----------|---------------|
| Anger | "Because my candidate did not win the election." | "Being stuck and hungry in the heat with my kids." |
|       | "Such an easy question. I usually feel this way every time Trump gets on TV and starts to spout." | "I remember when an ex-housemate keyed my car . . . after a huge fight . . . I was incredibly angry that she'd done that and gotten away with it." |
| Anxiety | "When Biden was elected because he would hurt our country, which he has." | "I felt anxious last time I had a job interview and I was waiting in the lobby" |
|         | "I feel anxious when I see politicians lie" | "Getting my first job and thinking what it would be like." |
| Depression | "I am bisexual, and seeing how some laws might get past [sic] that could hurt me makes me sad." | "Father was neglected at nursing home in 2020. Then passed away shortly after." |
|            | "The madness happening in Ukraine. This specifically was showing a school building that was bombed and just seeing all of this loss of innocent life was very sad." | "I was criticized for using my phone too much even though I was only looking up answers to important questions that the criticizer had been asking! The blatant hypocrisy . . . left me super depressed." |
| Fear | "When *Roe vs Wade* was overturned. I was afraid for my daughters and my granddaughters . . . I cried when I found out." | "I was physically abused by a previous spouse" |
|      | "World Trade Center—definitely it was scary." | "Assault—unable to get away from my attacker—felt helpless." |

*Note*: Two responses for each condition were randomly selected for inclusion. Some responses were lightly edited and shortened for the purposes of presentation.

ing comes to mind immediately, please give yourself a few moments to think carefully. Can you think of a time you felt [emotion] about something in [domain]?" Respondents then wrote a brief description of what happened and why they felt the way they did. This procedure is known as an autobiographical recall task, and it has been successfully deployed by psychologists to study depression and other emotions (Siedlecka and Denson 2019). Table 4.1 presents examples of the open-ended responses across the emotion and domain conditions.

Respondents were then asked questions about how they appraised the situation, how intensely they felt various emotions, and what coping strategies they employed at the time. These coping strategies are listed in table 4.2. For each strategy, respondents indicated whether they did it a lot, a medium amount, a little, or not at all. I calculate the percentage of each respondent's overall coping strategy that is focused on the emotion,

TABLE 4.2 **The Prevalence of Coping Strategies**

| Focus | Coping Behavior | Average Percent of Overall Strategy |
|---|---|---|
| Emotion | I got upset and let my emotions out | 8.5% |
| | I laughed about the situation | 4.0% |
| | I discussed my feelings with someone | 9.7% |
| | I used alcohol or drugs to make myself feel better | 3.7% |
| | *Average* | 25.9% |
| Attention | I turned to other activities to take my mind off things | 8.8% |
| | I kept myself from getting distracted [reversed] | 12.1% |
| | I daydreamed about other things | 6.5% |
| | *Average* | 27.5% |
| Appraisal | I tried to grow as a person as a result | 8.2% |
| | I said to myself, "This isn't real" | 8.1% |
| | I got used to the idea that it happened | 8.8% |
| | *Average* | 25.0% |
| Problem | I tried to get advice from someone about what to do | 6.4% |
| | I concentrated on doing something about it | 7.7% |
| | I talked to someone to find out more | 7.5% |
| | *Average* | 21.6% |

attention, appraisal, and problem. For example, imagine a hypothetical respondent who selects "a lot" for discussing their feelings, concentrating on doing something about it and making a plan of action, and selects "not at all" for the remaining coping strategies. This respondent's overall approach would be two-thirds problem focused and one-third emotion focused. Their dominant strategy is to try to solve the problem, rather than to reappraise the situation, divert their attention, or manage their emotions. The percentages in table 4.2 indicate how much each coping behavior contributes to the overall strategy of respondents on average.

I first examine how depression and politics influence coping strategies. Does depression lead to fewer problem-focused coping behaviors than anger, anxiety, and fear? What about politics compared to personal life? And what happens when we feel *depressed about politics*? Figure 4.2 answers these questions by plotting how often each coping strategy is used on average across the emotions and domains. The results generally support my argument. Fewer problem-focused coping strategies are reported by respondents in the depression condition (regardless of domain) and in the politics condition (regardless of emotion). The alternative strategies used by respondents in the depression condition—in place of problem-focused coping strategies—varied across politics and personal life. Emotion-focused strategies were more common in personal life, while attention-focused strategies were more common in politics.

Next, I examine political participation as one type of problem-focused coping strategy. Respondents were asked, "Thinking about the situation you described, what actions do you think you would take if a similar situation occurred today?" They were allowed to select from the following actions:

1. Attend a political meeting
2. Give money to a political organization
3. Attend a protest march, rally, or demonstration
4. Try to persuade others to vote one way or another
5. Wear a campaign button, put a sticker on your car, or display a sign at your home
6. Give money to a candidate, political party, or any other group involved in elections

This question presents a low barrier to political participation. Respondents need not have undertaken the action or even considered it at the time of

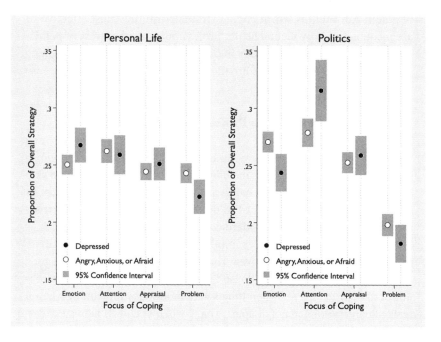

FIGURE 4.2. The Impact of Depression on Coping with Politics and Personal Life
*Note*: The results are predicted proportions based on fractional logistic regressions of each type of coping strategy on the depression treatment (vs. anger, anxiety, and fear treatments), the politics treatment (vs. the personal life treatment), and their interaction. More information about the analyses can be found in the appendix.

the situation. They are merely asked whether they *think* they would take such actions if a similar situation occurred today. If feelings of depression impede even this kind of response, it suggests depression is a substantial barrier to political participation. In fact, the results show this very pattern. Respondents in the depression condition selected about 1.12 actions on average, while respondents in the anger, anxiety, and fear conditions selected about 1.34 actions on average, a difference that is statistically significant. For respondents who are *not* in the politics condition, depression has no substantive or statistical effect on political participation—respondents in the depression condition reported 0.68 acts on average, while respondents in the anger, anxiety, and fear conditions reported 0.77 acts on average.[3]

The survey experiment provides causal evidence of how people cope with political stress. It reveals that depression in politics leads us to withdraw and refocus our attention elsewhere, while anger, anxiety, and fear lead to more problem-focused coping and political participation. These patterns provide support for my argument and bolster the existing evidence that depression is demobilizing. At the same time, the survey experiment can't tell us which coping strategies are the most effective or are recommended by mental health professionals. As the stress of politics increasingly permeates everyday life, more and more people are seeking professional help. What advice are they getting?

## What Coping Strategies Do Professionals Recommend?

I listen to several political news podcasts each week and have done so for many years. Most podcasts include advertisements, which I try to skip but sometimes hear when my hands are tied up with cooking, laundry, or driving, which is typically what I'm doing while listening. The advertisements are usually about a standard consumer product or service, such as bed sheets, a phone app, or even another podcast, but lately I hear advertisements for *therapy*. On the *New York Times' The Daily*, one pitch goes, "Unfortunately being human doesn't come with a user's manual. There is no set of instructions for when things get emotionally difficult or when it feels like everything may fall apart. That's when you need help to understand what's causing difficult emotions and how to cope with them." It goes on to describe a database where potential clients can find the right therapist, noting that "it's convenient, accessible, and entirely online." Although politics is not explicitly mentioned, we know too much about how advertisers target their messages to imagine their appearance on political news podcasts is coincidental.

Seeking out therapy to cope with politics may not seem surprising today, but this hasn't always been the case. For decades, the field of psychiatry distanced itself from politics. The American Psychiatric Association created the "Goldwater Rule" in 1973, which barred licensed psychiatrists from using their professional position to comment on political leaders and candidates. The rule stemmed from widespread commentary on then-candidate Barry Goldwater's mental state. At the time, *Fact Magazine* conducted a survey of over twelve thousand psychiatrists, asking, "Do you believe Barry Goldwater is psychologically fit to serve as President of the United States?" Several mental health professionals penned op-eds offering their own assessments. One commentator wrote, "I believe Goldwater to be suffering from a chronic psychosis." Others took stronger views, with one arguing, "Goldwater has the same pathological makeup as Hitler, Castro, Stalin, and other known schizophrenic leaders" (Levin 2016).

Despite the Goldwater Rule, questions about the mental health of presidential candidates recently resurfaced—this time about Donald Trump during the 2016 election season. A group of mental health professionals published a book, *The Dangerous Case of Donald Trump: 27 Psychiatrists and Mental Health Experts Assess a President*, warning the public about the dangers of electing Trump (Lee 2017). This commentary divided the field of psychiatry. Jeffrey Lieberman, former president of the American Psychiatric Association, said the book was "not a serious, scholarly, civic-minded work, but simply tawdry, indulgent, fatuous tabloid psychiatry" (2017). Other psychiatrists were torn about commenting on the mental health of Donald Trump and the value of the Goldwater Rule in general.

The cases of Goldwater and Trump highlight how the mental health profession has struggled and continues to struggle with its relationship to politics. Even as Americans increasingly seek information about how to cope with depression and anxiety from politics, the American Psychiatric Association has not proposed, much less formalized, guidelines for how therapists should handle political conversations in professional settings. As one team of psychiatrists wrote in the *Psychotherapy Bulletin*, "Few training programs address political affiliation as a component of culture or identity or how it may inform treatment or affect the therapy relationship. When clients bring differing political views into the therapy room, it can cause us unease, a sense of not knowing the way forward" (Spangler et al. 2017).

The absence of guidelines doesn't mean mental health professionals are indifferent to politics, however. While individuals in the field might disagree about commenting on candidates, increasing numbers recognize that the profession should help its clients cope with the stress of politics and the way it makes them depressed, anxious, angry, and afraid. In an essay for the *New York Times*, aptly called "Why Therapists Should Talk Politics," the psychotherapist Richard Brouillette argued, "Typically, therapists avoid discussing social and political issues in sessions. If the patient raises them, the therapist will direct the conversation toward a discussion of symptoms, coping skills, the relevant issues in a patient's childhood and family life. But I am growing more and more convinced that this is inadequate. Psychotherapy, as a field, is not prepared to respond to the major social issues affecting our patients' lives" (2016). The increased attention to politics within the mental health profession seems to be driven by demand. In one survey, researchers found that roughly two-thirds of the Democrats and Republicans who recently attended therapy had talked to their therapist about politics (Solomovo and Barber 2018).

So what advice is given out by mental health professionals about how to cope with politics? I offer a preliminary answer to this question by analyzing psychology websites. Not everyone who is depressed by politics needs to see a therapist or can afford one, so many people turn to the internet. One study found that 80 percent of young adults conducted an internet search when looking for help with their mental health, and nearly 60 percent consulted a psychology website (Pretorious et al. 2019). Today these websites routinely, although not universally, offer guidance from mental health professionals about how to cope with politics. Some sites have a single page on the issue, while others have several pages on subtopics, such as the news, postelection stress, or political conflict with family and friends. These pages offer a glimpse into the kind of advice that the mental health profession provides and that ordinary people see.

I reviewed, categorized, and counted the recommendations from eleven of the most commonly viewed psychology websites. Table 4.3 summarizes the results of my analysis. In many ways, these recommendations reflect the four types of coping strategies—emotion-focused (self-care, seek social support, take medication), attention-focused (manage exposure), appraisal-focused (rework the discussion, go to therapy, self-reflect,

TABLE 4.3  **Online Advice for Coping with Politics**

| Strategy | Summary of Advice | Frequency |
| --- | --- | --- |
| Manage Exposure | Reduce political news intake and/or change the medium through which news is consumed (e.g., read rather than watch) | 9/11 |
| Self-Care | Activities such as meditation, exercise, and eating healthy can be calming; "the idea is to forget about things like politics and anything else that is upsetting you" (Better Health) | 8/11 |
| Become Engaged | Get involved in politics, whether voting, volunteering, contacting an official, or something else; engagement can be empowering | 7/11 |
| Seek Social Support | Seek support from family, friends, religious groups, or community organizations, especially ones that have shared values | 5/11 |
| Change the Discussion | Try to avoid persuading others to your point of view; instead learn about others' views, find common ground, embrace differences when disagreement ensues, and set boundaries around what to discuss, when, and with whom | 5/11 |
| Go to Therapy | Therapists can provide a safe space to discuss politics and can provide assistance in developing effective coping strategies | 4/11 |
| Self-Reflect | Understand which aspects of politics are most stressful to you; monitor your mood to know when coping with politics will be necessary | 3/11 |
| Learn about Politics | Educate yourself about how the political system works and what aspects of it are within your control | 2/11 |
| Take Medication | Antidepressants can help; discuss this option with your doctor | 1/11 |

learn about politics), and problem-focused (become engaged) — although several recommendations cut across strategies. Seeking social support may simultaneously target how we feel and think about the situation. Becoming engaged may attempt to solve the problem and/or change how we perceive it. Some recommendations also appear contradictory at first glance, such as managing exposure to politics and becoming more politically engaged. In theory it is possible to do both, although becoming engaged may make managing exposure a more difficult task — engagement takes us closer to, not further away from, political conflict.

The most frequent advice was to manage exposure, with nearly all the websites recommending this attention-focused strategy. This advice may be grounded in the fact that nearly all of our political experiences are mediated — rarely are we firsthand witnesses to the political events that make us upset. We're not in Congress when a policy is passed or at an inauguration when a president takes the oath of office. Sometimes we witness these events in real time *on the news*, but more often we find out about them after the fact *through the media*. Exposure management means controlling the channels through which politics is communicated to us.

Self-care was the second most frequent recommendation. These activities are typically considered emotion-focused coping because of their soothing function. However, they may simultaneously count as attention-focused coping because of how they distract from politics. When we focus on exercising, meditating, eating healthy, or some other self-care activity, we become less attentive to politics. So whereas managing exposure is negative advice ("don't watch the news"), self-care is positive advice ("go exercise") that ends up being functionally equivalent because it has exposure management as a byproduct.

The third most frequent advice is to become engaged. While ostensibly a problem-focused strategy, the logic behind this advice tends to be appraisal focused. The idea is that engagement has the potential to transform how we *think* about politics rather than transform politics itself. This advice might be grounded in the recognition that politics is a collective enterprise, and so a person cannot bring about desired outcomes on their own except in perhaps the rarest circumstances. Put another way, engagement can never yield the changes we want to see, so we should think about its benefits in terms of its potential to reorient our thinking about the political process.

The next two pieces of advice—seek social support and rework the discussion—are found on about half the websites. In some ways, these recommendations are in tension. Seeking social support is about retreating to a space where exposure to politics is not stressful—what many would describe as an echo chamber. Reworking the discussion is about adjusting how a conversation unfolds when there is disagreement, either by trying to find common ground, by focusing on understanding rather than persuasion, or setting boundaries around what can be discussed. In short, reworking the discussion is about how to manage life outside the echo chamber so as to avoid retreating back to it. In other ways, these recommendations dovetail. Both view politics as an interpersonal endeavor—one that happens when we engage with others, even if those others are talking heads on a television screen. Since it's inevitable that we'll find ourselves sometimes in the echo chamber and other times out of it, both pieces of advice can be useful, even if they don't tell us *how much* time should be spent in and out of the echo chamber.

The remaining recommendations, including going to therapy, self-reflecting, learning about politics, and taking medication, are found on roughly one-third or fewer of the websites. It is surprising that so few websites run by mental health professionals promote therapy. Perhaps the idea is that the stress of politics is not so intense or widespread that it generally requires a therapist or medication. The other two recommendations are like two sides of a stress-reducing coin. Self-reflecting addresses how politics can fit into our lives, while learning about politics addresses how we can fit into the political process.

These websites offer a snapshot into how mental health professionals think about coping with the stress of politics. Nearly all the websites with pages devoted to politics recommended managing exposure (an attention-focused coping strategy), while large numbers also endorsed self-care (emotion-focused) and becoming engaged (problem-focused). Once we got beyond this consensus, however, substantial differences emerged. Websites varied in what they recommended or whether they recommended anything at all. In fact, ten highly popular websites did not have a single page devoted to politics. The pages analyzed here came from ten other websites, which means that exactly half of the websites I consulted were silent about how to cope with politics. This variation may reflect a lack of evidence-based research, training, or professional guidelines about how best to cope with politics. Or it may indicate that some mental health professionals do not think politics is stressful enough to merit their attention. Either way, it signals the need for more research on what can be done to manage depression caused by politics.

## What's Next?

In this chapter, I offer the first experimental evidence that depression shapes the political thoughts and actions of citizens. I also found that problem-focused coping strategies were generally less common in politics than in personal life—which may reflect the greater capacity to free ride in politics. This was especially true when coping with depression. Compared to feelings like anger, anxiety, and fear, feeling depressed about politics reduced reliance on emotion-focused and problem-focused coping strategies and increased the use of attention-focused strategies. It also reduced interest in political participation, such as voting, contacting an elected official, protesting, or even posting online about politics. As politics increasingly permeates everyday life, more and more people seek professional help to deal with the depression (and anxiety, anger, and fear) it causes. The advice from mental health professionals seems to be that citizens who feel this way need to reconfigure how they engage with politics. They say that exposure should be reduced in general and more carefully managed when it happens. Echo chambers should serve as safe spaces, and we should erect boundaries around how we engage with crosscutting ideas.

These findings raise normative concerns about how we reconcile what is good for democracy with what is good for mental well-being when the two come into conflict. As psychologists Brett Ford and Matthew Feinberg write, "Although politics often resembles a chronic stressor, people have the tools to regulate that stress. Successfully managing this stress, however, can come with a crucial trade-off: Commonly-used forms of emotion regulation can protect individual well-being, but can also come at a cost to collective political action that challenges the status quo. Only by understanding the complex interplay between emotion, emotion regulation, and political action can we hope to optimize both well-being and productive political action" (2020, 127). This important point highlights a potential conflict between effective coping—which might entail stepping away from politics—and responsible democratic citizenship—which entails participation in and knowledge of politics (Barber 1994). Figuring out how to balance the demands of democracy with the mental health of the public is a difficult undertaking and one that will require sustained collaboration between scholars and practitioners of both politics and psychology.

By demonstrating the depressing consequences of politics and the political consequences of depression, I've now provided evidence for each component of the stress-appraisal-coping framework. The experience of irrevocable loss in politics is depressing, and we cope with these feelings by withdrawing. So what's next? In the chapters that follow, I show how this framework can be applied to topics like elections and political polarization, as well as issues such as climate change, abortion, same-sex marriage, and wealth redistribution. Not every component of the framework is applied to every topic. Sometimes I focus on only one component, while other times the framework serves as only a backdrop. With this in mind, let's turn now to elections and electoral loss.

CHAPTER FIVE

# Election Blues

The Associated Press called Ohio for Donald Trump at 10:39 p.m. on November 8, 2016. I was sitting on my friend's couch when this first bit of news came in. Every four years since 1964, the winner of the presidency had also won Ohio. Trump won Florida fifteen minutes later. My friends, who supported Hillary Clinton, turned to me for reassurance. Was this the beginning of the end? I still felt confident that Hillary Clinton would win — after all, piles of polling data, prediction models, and political scientists told me she would prevail. Nate Silver at FiveThirtyEight had given Clinton a 71.4 percent chance of winning the election. The *New York Times* had put it at 85 percent, noting, "Mrs. Clinton's chance of losing is about the same as the probability that an N.F.L. kicker misses a 37-yard field goal." It felt unimaginable that she would lose.

The unopened champagne bottles on the coffee table started to sweat. At 11:14 p.m. the AP called North Carolina for Trump. On CNN, Wolf Blitzer ticked off Clinton's remaining pathways to victory. Mostly this consisted of Clinton's blue firewall — Pennsylvania, Michigan, and Wisconsin — and either Nevada or Arizona. Over at *FiveThirtyEight*, Nate Silver pointed out that Clinton might win an electoral vote from Nebraska's Second Congressional District. I explained to my friends that Nebraska isn't a winner-take-all state.

In continuing attempts to soothe the rising anxiety among my friends, I told them Clinton had a healthy lead in the popular vote, and the winner of the popular vote only rarely lost the Electoral College. I told them about a recent study that used a new, cool "list" experiment and found that the "shy Trump supporter" was a myth. This meant that the election results should line up with the polls once all votes were counted, I said. I explained that random error in prediction models meant that some breaks—the ones we'd seen so far—would go to Trump, while other breaks—the ones then yet to come—could still go to Clinton. I'm not sure anyone was convinced, but it lightened the mood.

The last polling station in Hawaii shut down at 1:03 a.m. Trump clinched Pennsylvania about thirty minutes later, breaking the blue firewall. All he needed to win was either Michigan, Wisconsin, or Arizona. My friends and I, on the West Coast, kept watching the news. Pundits began talking about faithless electors, weak political parties, and spoiler candidates. I tried to elaborate on these talking points, but the conversation had grown quiet. What was there to say? The watch party ended around 2:00 a.m. I told my friends that it can sometimes take a day or two to process absentee and mail-in ballots. If they couldn't celebrate with champagne, they might as well sleep while the final votes were tallied. They clearly felt dejected and ready to go home, so we said our goodbyes.

The major media outlets declared Trump the winner by the next morning. I sat at my desk on campus and watched Clinton concede. Afterward, I texted a friend from the watch party to check in, and we agreed to meet at a nearby coffee shop. As we sat sipping our coffee, we recounted Clinton's concession speech. *We must accept this result . . . Donald Trump is going to be our president . . . we owe him an open mind and a chance to lead.* My friend started to tear up. Clinton had lost, and there was nothing anyone could do about it. As I watched my friend cry, I began to wonder: Can elections make us depressed?

In this chapter, I take a look at the "election-depression connection." I explain how elections produce irrevocable loss and then dig into what we already know about their depressing effects. Although there is some anecdotal and scholarly evidence of electoral blues, many questions remain about the scope of the election-depression connection. I outline five scope conditions—the type of election, the timing of the election, the rules of the election, who is affected, and which feelings are evoked—and then present evidence from five studies that begin to address these scope conditions. I conclude by discussing the importance of the loser's consent, whether feelings of depression help secure it, and what this might mean for democracy and the design of electoral institutions.

## How Depressing Is Electoral Loss?

Elections are one of the most visible aspects of politics for citizens in a democracy, so they give us a natural starting point for exploring how politics is depressing. Loss is inherent to any competitive election whenever at least one person prefers a different result from what was produced—so almost always. Power is lost when an incumbent candidate or party suffers defeat, and the opportunity to gain power is lost when a challenger loses an election. The outcome of elections are not generally contested in stable democracies, so they carry a sense of irrevocability. Elites and the public usually accept that the winner has the right to keep their position (if an incumbent) or to ascend to power (if a challenger) until the next election.

We saw the depressing consequences of electoral loss for my friend following the election of Trump, but testimony from candidates and their advisors provides further evidence of the election-depression connection. In the run-up to the 2000 election, *Los Angeles Times* reporter Maria La Ganga talked to former presidential candidates about losing (2000). George McGovern, who lost to Nixon in 1972, told her, "Where did all those voters go? Where were those huge crowds on election day? You have a huge sense that the country deserted you and left you alone." John Anderson, who ran as an independent in 1980, also talked about loneliness, feeling as if he had been "thrown over a cliff." Donna Brazile, who advised the Gore campaign in 2000, shared a "Letter to the Losers" on CNN following the 2008 election, in which she wrote, "Just thinking back to 2000 still gets me upset . . . I remember feeling lost and disillusioned. I was empty inside as if someone had used a vacuum cleaner and sucked out every bit of my passion for politics and public service."

There is growing evidence that the public finds electoral loss depressing. As *Psychology Today* wrote recently on their website, electoral loss "feels similarly to other sorts of losses that lead to grief (e.g., loss of a meaningful job, the end of a romantic relationship) and there are similar sorts of emotions at play" (Martin 2016). Like *Psychology Today*, many popular psychology websites now offer advice on how to cope with electoral loss. News outlets have also started featuring stories about the election-depression connection. A few days after the 2016 election, Business Insider ran the headline, "Your Post-Election Sadness Is Real Grief—Here's the Best Way to Move Forward." The article began by noting that "supporters of Hillary Clinton . . . woke up on November 9 with a range of emotions, including shock, sadness, anger, confusion, anxiety, and fear." These websites and stories indicate that there was a public appetite for this content, a kind of indirect evidence for the election-depression connection.

The strongest evidence to date comes from two academic studies. Psychologist Linda Levine surveyed Perot supporters after his withdrawal from the 1992 presidential election. Disappointment was the most common emotion, but some supporters reported feeling sad, angry, betrayed, or even hopeful (1996). Also, political scientists Lamar Pierce, Todd Rogers, and Jason Snyder found the unhappiness of Romney supports after the 2012 election was as intense as the unhappiness of Bostonians after the Boston Marathon bombing (Pierce et al. 2016).

The anecdote from my friend, the testimony of losing candidates, and the results of scientific studies tell us that electoral loss is depressing—at least in some elections and for some people. But just how strong is the election-depression connection? The evidence so far generally focuses on presidential elections in the United States during highly polarized times in American history. Would we see similar results if we looked elsewhere? To begin answering this question, I outline five scope conditions—the set of cases to which a theory applies—that will help us assess the extent to which electoral loss is depressing.

The first condition is *which* elections matter. Does a parent feel depressed after their sixth grader loses an election for elementary school government? Probably not. Would that same parent feel depressed if they personally lost an election for the local parent-teacher association? Perhaps. I don't examine school elections, but I bring them up to illustrate the breadth of elections we encounter in democracies. I highlighted anecdotal and systematic evidence from the 1992, 2012, and 2016 presidential elections, but knowing that some presidential elections are depressing is not the same as knowing all presidential elections—or even some nonpresidential ones—are depressing. Whether an election is depressing depends on its salience and what is at stake. Presidential elections are prominent and feel highly consequential, but local elections, especially for downballot offices, often are not perceived to carry the same weight. For which elections are the stakes and salience big enough that losing is depressing?

The second condition is *when* elections matter. When candidates, parties, and the public are highly polarized, the stakes of elections feel higher. This is important because periods of intense polarization can amplify how we feel about winning or losing. The Obama-Romney presidential election in 2012 was not especially contentious, at least compared to the Clinton-Trump presidential election in 2016, but it still took place during a polarized period in America history. As Pew Research wrote at the time, "As Americans head to the polls this November, their values and basic beliefs are more polarized along partisan lines than at any point in the past 25 years. Unlike in 1987, when this series of surveys began, the values gap between Republicans and Democrats is now greater than gender, age, race or class divides" (2012). The study of Perot supporters in 1992 suggests we can be disappointed and sad in less polarized times, but this study is also idiosyncratic in its focus on a third-party candidate. Is losing an election in less polarized times also depressing?

The third condition is the *design* of electoral and party systems. Elections look different from one locality, state, or country to another. The Electoral College in the United States is unique. It is winner-take-all and functions in a two-party system that often pits very different candidates against one another. This system makes choices appear stark and stakes feel high, so citizens may be primed to feel depressed when they lose. Other countries have multiparty systems where the loss of a partisan friend may not mean the win of a partisan foe. Counting votes proportionally, as other systems do, may also help losers feel like their voice was heard, potentially dampening the depressing consequences of loss. Do the structures of our electoral and party systems shape how much losing hurts?

The fourth condition is *who* is affected by elections. The study of Perot defined losers in terms of active support—someone who donated to or volunteered for the Perot campaign—while the study of Romney defined losers in terms of copartisans. These are reasonable decisions, but it's not hard to imagine alternative definitions of winning and losing. For instance, among copartisans, is someone who leans toward a party as affected by electoral loss as someone who has a strong attachment to the party? What about a copartisan who donates to the campaign compared to a copartisan who reluctantly supports the party's candidate? Winning and losing may not always be simply about partisanship either. Recent studies show that Black men became less emotionally distressed after the election of Barack Obama (Brown et al. 2020), while White women in Democratic states became more distressed after the loss of Hillary Clinton (Yan et al. 2021). These studies highlight how winning or losing can also be defined in terms of race and gender. More generally, which aspects of ourselves determine whether we feel like winners or losers?

The fifth condition is which *feelings* are evoked by electoral loss. The study of Romney supporters focused on happiness, specifically whether respondents reported feeling "happy or very happy." However, the absence of feeling happy is not the same as feeling depressed. Some respondents who did not report being "happy or very happy" may have felt angry, anxious, or disgusted. The study of Perot supporters shows us that unhappiness can take different shapes, including disappointment and sadness. The extent to which members of the depression feeling family are affected by electoral winning and losing remains unclear. So what are the range and intensity of depressed feelings we experience after losing an election? And does winning reduce feelings of depression as much as losing increases them, or are the emotional consequences of winning and losing asymmetrical?

## What Is the Evidence?

I analyze four studies to deepen our understanding of the connection between electoral loss and depression. The results build on what we know, even if they do not fully define its scope. Each study speaks to multiple scope conditions—the type of election, the timing of the election, the design of the electoral and party system, the position of the loser, and the type and intensity of the depressed feeling—so they cannot be easily organized in this way. Instead, I arrange the studies from roughly the least to most methodologically complex: election polls, the Cooperative Election Study, the Behavioral Risk Factor Surveillance Survey, and the European Social Survey.

### A Simple Test: Election Polls

Sometimes the most straightforward way to learn how a person feels about an election is to ask them directly. Many pollsters do exactly this, so I begin my analysis by returning to political polls I found in the archives of Cornell University's Roper Center, a nonpartisan, nonprofit digital repository for public opinion datasets. I focus here on the sixteen questions between 2004 and 2016 that asked about depression in response to (1) the potential election of a candidate, (2) the actual election of a candidate, or (3) the inauguration of a candidate. Only two polls asked about feelings of depression in connection to a midterm election. An example of a typical question comes from Pew Research, which asked respondents in 2004, "How do you feel about George W. Bush winning the 2004 presidential election? Do you feel depressed or not?" Respondents were then given the option of saying yes or no. For questions that presented a range of response options (e.g., thrilled, happy, don't care, unhappy, depressed), I focus only on the depressed/not depressed dichotomy.

Table 5.1 reports the percentages of the samples who felt depressed. I break down these numbers by Republicans and Democrats when pos-

ELECTION BLUES 83

TABLE 5.1 **The Prevalence of Depression in Election Poll Questions**

| Year | Candidate | Timing | Depressed Feelings | | |
|---|---|---|---|---|---|
| | | | Overall | Dems | Reps |
| 2004 | John Kerry | Preelection | 7% | | |
| 2004 | George Bush | Preelection | 11% | | |
| 2004 | | Postelection | 27% | 49% | 4% |
| 2004 | | Postelection | 26% | 30% | 9% |
| 2004 | | Postelection | 15% | 31% | 1% |
| 2005 | | Inauguration | 10% | 21% | 2% |
| 2008 | John McCain | Preelection | 33% | 35% | 14% |
| 2008 | Barack Obama | Preelection | 18% | 13% | 19% |
| 2008 | | Postelection | 12% | | |
| 2008 | | Inauguration | 4% | 0% | 10% |
| 2010 | Midterm News | Preelection | 36% | 37% | 33% |
| 2010 | Midterm Results | Postelection | 16% | | |
| 2013 | Barack Obama | Inauguration | 14% | 4% | 27% |
| 2016 | Donald Trump | Postelection | 6% | 10% | 1% |
| 2016 | Donald Trump | Postelection | 16% | 27% | 5% |

sible. Since preelection questions ask about hypothetical loss (e.g., "Now thinking ahead to the election in November, which two of these words best describe how you would feel if John Kerry were elected President?") I indicate which candidate is "losing" in the question. These results make several contributions to our understanding of the election-depression connection. First, it is useful to know people voluntarily report feeling depressed when they have the option to say otherwise, such as reporting "no" if asked directly or choosing "angry" if given the option. Second, these results suggest the election-depression connection is not a new phenomenon or limited to especially polarized times. Ordinary citizens reported these feelings in all elections for which there are polls. The country was well on its way to current levels of polarization in 2004 (Jacobson 2005)—the year of the earliest poll—but it was still less polarized than it is today (Pew Research 2014). So these results provide preliminary evidence that midterm elections can be depressing.

One potential problem with these polls is that pollsters may only ask about depression, sadness, or disappointment in especially contentious elections, where they expect a significant number of respondents to report these feelings. This would make depression seem more common than if pollsters included these questions in all elections, including those where such feelings may be less likely. However, this potential source of bias is also a potential source of information about what kinds of elections are depressing. Questions almost always pertain to presidential elections, only rarely to midterm elections, and never to downballot races. This pattern *suggests* that feelings of depression are more widespread and intense when elections are more important and/or salient.

### Generalized Depression: The Cooperative Election Study

The polls tell us that people report feeling depressed about electoral loss, but does electoral loss lead to *generalized* feelings of depression, feelings that aren't directly tied to the election? To answer this question, I analyze data from the Cooperative Election Study (CES). The CES surveys the same Americans before and after each presidential and midterm election. I included a standard battery of depression questions on the pre- and postelection surveys in 2020, so I can assess whether and for whom depression increases, decreases, or stays the same. Respondents were asked how often over the past week they felt depressed, felt like everything was an effort, felt lonely or remote from other people, felt hopeful about the future, could not shake off the blues even with help from family and friends, and had restless sleep. For each item, they could select rarely or none of the time, some or a little of the time, a moderate amount of time, and most or all of the time. I reverse-code the positively worded items and take the average of the six to generate a preelection and postelection depression score. I then calculate the change from before and after the election; positive values indicate an increase in depression.

I measure winning and losing in terms of partisanship and presidential candidate preference. Partisanship is measured as a seven-point scale ranging from strong Democrat to strong Republican. Candidate preference is measured using the preelection survey based on whom respondents voted for (if they voted early), whom they would vote for (if they had not yet voted), or whom they preferred to win (if they did not plan to vote). Because Donald Trump, the Republican candidate, lost the presidential election in 2020, I expect respondents who more strongly identify with the Republican party to exhibit an increase in depression. Because Joe Biden won the election, I expect respondents who did not prefer Biden to exhibit an increase in depression. The difference in partisanship and candidate preference isn't just semantic. About 16 percent of respondents did not express support for either Trump or Biden, so the analysis of partisanship may overlook them. These respondents either preferred a third-party candidate, were unsure of who they preferred, or refused to

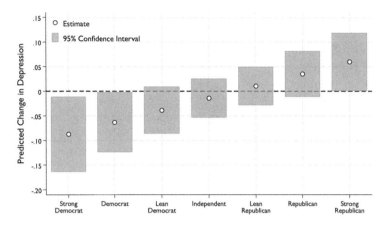

FIGURE 5.1. The Impact of Electoral Loss in the United States
*Note*: The results are based on an ordinary least squares regression of change in depression on partisanship. The model includes survey weights and control variables for gender, race, age, education, income, and marital status. More information about the analyses can be found in the appendix.

give a preference because they did not plan to vote. They are therefore either explicitly losers (prefer a third-party candidate) or decidedly not winners (unsure, no preference).

Figure 5.1 plots the predicted change in depression based on partisanship. Respondents who identify as strong Republicans became *more* depressed following the election, which affirms the connection between electoral loss and depression. Losers aren't just telling pollsters they feel depressed; they are in fact exhibiting symptoms of depression. Respondents who identify as strong and not-so-strong Democrats become *less* depressed, a pattern we couldn't see in the polls. We feel more depressed when we lose and less depressed when we win. Even so, a large chunk of Americans—those who identify as independents and partisan leaners—remains unaffected by winning or losing. It is possible this group felt disappointed or sad but were not so intensely affected as to feel depressed. When I analyze candidate preference rather than partisanship, I find a similar pattern—depression decreased for respondents who preferred Biden and increased for those who didn't.

The aftermath of the 2020 presidential election was unique in modern American history. Even after all major media outlets called the election for Biden, Trump refused to concede and began telling supporters the election had been stolen by Democrats, an idea he foreshadowed before the election by refusing to say he would concede. This falsehood eventually became known as "the big lie" and got Trump kicked off Twitter (the platform now known as X). It also evoked a deep anger among Trump supporters, giving rise to the "Stop the Steal" movement and the January 6, 2021, attack on the US Capitol. If many Trump supporters responded to his loss with anger rather than depression, these results may *underestimate* the election-depression connection. In other words, we might see larger changes in generalized depression if we had analyzed a different election using this same research design.

*Behavioral Impact: Google Trends*

One potential concern with the election polls and the Cooperative Election Study is that respondents may misreport feelings of depression. If respondents fall prey to acquiescence bias, which is the tendency to agree on surveys, or social desirability bias, which here may be the belief that "good" copartisans feel depressed when their candidate loses, then the results may be overstated. Results could also be understated if stigma around depression cause respondents to be reluctant to report these feelings.

Whatever the case, I turn to Google Trends for *behavioral* evidence of the election-depression connection. Google Trends provides data on Google searches over time, allowing me to use it examine trends in depression-related searches. The output from Google Trends is normalized between 0 and 100 for each query. The unit of time (e.g., week, month) with the most searches gets a score of 100, and all other units are scored in relation to it. So a unit with a score of 50 indicates half as many searches as the top week, a score of 25 a quarter as many searches, and so forth.

I analyze Google Trends in two ways. First, I look at monthly searches for the term *post-election depression* between 2004 (the first year for which data are available) and 2020. This sets a low threshold for evaluating whether elections matter, because it specifies "election" in the search term. Second, I conduct a difference-in-differences test based on weekly searches for *disappointment*, *sadness*, and *depression* for each year between 2004 and 2021. I calculate the ratio between the score in the week following the first Tuesday in November (postelection) and the score in the preceding week (preelection) and then convert this value into a percentage change. I use percentage change instead of a simple difference because of the normalization of Google Trends data. If elections matter, we should see more positive values—that is, increased searches for these terms after an election—in election years when compared to nonelection years.

Figure 5.2 reports the results. The left panel shows how often Americans searched post-election depression each month from 2004 to 2020. The spikes around presidential elections confirm the results from the election polls. The occasional small spikes around midterm elections suggest that they too can be depressing, but much less than presidential elections. Results of the difference-in-differences analysis are reported in the right panel. The bars show the percentage change in searches with higher values, indicating more searches in the week after the first Tuesday of November. In nonelection years, there is no real change in searches for disappointment or sadness and a small uptick in searches for depression. Relative to this baseline, midterm elections see a small uptick in disappointment and sadness and a small downtick in depression. Presidential election years see a huge uptick in disappointment, a small uptick in sadness, and a small downtick in depression.

Election polls showed that many people *say* they feel depressed by electoral loss. Google Trends reveals that this isn't just cheap talk — people *act* depressed too. Searches for post-election depression spike following presidential elections and, to a lesser extent, midterms, while searches for disappointment, and to a lesser extent sadness, grow in the aftermath of elections. These findings reveal that election blues are prevalent and strong enough to shape citizens' online searches. At the same time, we did not see an uptick in searches for depression, which suggests limits to the election-depression connection — the hue of electoral blues may be cerulean rather than navy.

## *Beyond Partisanship: The Behavioral Risk Factor Surveillance Survey*

I now want to consider definitions of electoral winning and losing that go beyond partisanship. Earlier, I cited two studies that connected social identity to election blues. The first study found that Black men became less emotionally distressed following Obama's election in 2008 (Brown et al. 2021). The second study found that Clinton's loss in 2016 lead to an uptick in emotional distress among women living in states that voted for Clinton (Yan et al. 2021). I replicate and extend these studies in a few important ways. I use the same Behavioral Risk Factor Surveillance Survey (BRFSS) data that these studies used. The BRFSS is administered by the United States Center for Disease Control and has surveyed more than four hundred thousand American adults in all fifty states, the District of Columbia, and three territories every year since 1984. The survey focuses

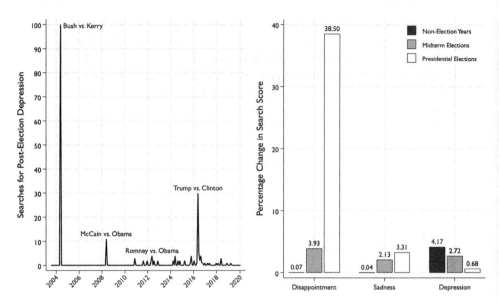

FIGURE 5.2. Electoral Trends in Depression-Related Google Searches

on health-related behaviors, conditions, and service utilization, making it one of the richest health surveys in the world.

Unfortunately, the BRFSS does not collect information about politics. However, the structure of data collection process means it can still be useful here. Interviews are randomly spread out over the entire year, so there are hundreds of data points each day, allowing me to leverage the randomization of the interview day in my analysis. Theoretically, respondents interviewed just before and just after the election are identical except for the election outcome. So if there was a difference in feelings between respondents interviewed right *before* the election and respondents interviewed right *after* the election, we would have evidence that the outcome of elections shapes how we feel. This regression discontinuity design was used in the other studies I mentioned, and I also use it in my analysis here.

I build on prior research by bringing greater clarity to the emotional impact of electoral winning and losing. Existing studies use a measure of psychological distress, which asks respondents, "Now thinking about your mental health, which includes stress, depression, and problems with emotions, for how many days during the past thirty days was your mental health not good?"[1] The advantage of this question is that it is asked of all respondents each year because it is part of the core questionnaire.

The disadvantage is that it taps into any type of negative emotional response rather than depression specifically. I therefore examine two questions that ask narrowly about feelings of depression and anxiety, which together allow me to better isolate the impact of electoral outcomes by showing that depression is affected, but anxiety is not.[2]

I also include a wider set of elections and identities in my analyses. The election of Barack Obama in 2008 was a watershed moment for Black Americans in the United States. As historian Penial E. Joseph wrote in the *Guardian* at the end of Obama's presidency, "Black America's conception of ourselves was forever changed by Barack Obama's presidency. For African Americans, the first family helped to unlock the transformational potential that always existed in democracy's beating heart, but which too often excluded black Americans" (2017). Clinton's 2016 loss was also a momentous occasion. As Julia Azari wrote in *Vox*, "For many women who began the day with high hopes of a shattered glass ceiling, it was a devastating disappointment" (2017). Since these cases involve high-profile candidates from traditionally underrepresented groups, they offer a good starting point — if we can't see an impact of descriptive representation here, it seems unlikely we will see it elsewhere. However, other candidates can be easily plugged into the same research design — Sarah Palin in 2008 (for women), Obama in 2012 (for Black Americans), and Kamala Harris in 2020 (for women and Black and Asian Americans). Analyzing these other candidates' elections will contribute to determining whether the Obama and Clinton effects, like their historic candidacies, are exceptional.

I begin by replicating research that found Obama's victory in 2008 reduced psychological distress among Black men and extending it to also look at depression and anxiety.[3] Consistent with prior research, I find that the number of distressed days reported by Black men declines following the election. However, I also find that there is also a reduction in the number of depressed days, a pattern that persisted for the duration of the calendar year. The number of anxious days is also reduced, but the reduction does not persist, nor is it statistically significant. Together, these patterns support the idea that the distress effect found in prior research is due in part to the impact on *depression* among Black men.[4]

I now turn to the impact of Obama's reelection in 2012. Unlike in 2008, Obama's success in 2012 does not seem to affect the psyche of Black Americans except for a small *uptick* in distressed days among Black men. This pattern is a reversal from 2008 and may reflect a wearing off of Obama's honeymoon period and/or a reflection of how Obama's historic presidency was met with more, rather than less, racism among much of the public (e.g., birtherism). Put into this context, it is understandable that Black men might be mildly stressed by the continuation of Obama's presidency, even if they supported him politically.

Next I want to jump ahead to 2020 and the historic vice-presidential election of Kamala Harris. As the *New York Times* wrote shortly after the election, "With her ascension to the vice presidency, Ms. Harris will become the first woman and first woman of color to hold that office, a milestone for a nation in upheaval, grappling with a damaging history of racial injustice exposed, yet again, in a divisive election" (Lerer and Ember 2020). Did her election do the same thing for women of color that Obama's election did for Black men? The answer is a cautious yes. Women of color reported fewer distressed days, but only after the inauguration in January, rather than the election in November. The refusal of Trump to concede, and the subsequent conflict that culminated in the insurrection on January 6, 2021, may have inhibited women of color and Democrats more generally from celebrating until after the inauguration. Unfortunately, measures of depressed and anxious days were not included by any states in that year's questionnaire, so I am limited to analyzing distressed days.

Finally, let's turn to the candidacies of Clinton and Palin and their impact on women. Given that women are split in their support for the Republican and Democratic party, it seems unlikely that all women will feel equally depressed by their losses. So, consistent with prior research, I split the analyses based on whether respondents reside in a state that voted for Clinton or Palin. Women living in states that voted for these candidates should be more depressed after their electoral loss on average than women living in states that voted for the opposing candidates. In fact, we see exactly this pattern with Clinton in 2016—there is not an uptick in distressed days when analyzing all women, but there is an uptick when analyzing women in states that voted for Clinton. This pattern is accentuated when analyzing depression days but absent when it comes to anxious days. In contrast to Clinton, Palin's loss did not seem to have any impact on the psyche of women or even White women in states that voted for the McCain-Palin ticket.

Altogether, these analyses support the idea that winning and losing, and their impact on depression, are sometimes tied to our social identity. There were substantial changes in feelings of depression and/or psychological distress for Black men in 2008, women in states that voted for

Clinton in 2016, and women of color in 2020, but not for Obama's election in 2012 or Palin's loss in 2008.

*Electoral Systems: The European Social Survey*

One scope condition that has not yet been analyzed is whether electoral loss is depressing in different electoral systems. I illuminate this issue using data from the Netherlands. Many countries have substantially different systems than the United States, and this is especially true of the Netherlands, which makes it a useful case for studying the election-depression connection. To understand why, we first need to compare and contrast the electoral systems of these two countries. In the United States, citizens elect representatives to Congress using two-party, plurality, single-member districts—two candidates compete against one another in each of the 435 Congressional districts, and a candidate only needs more votes than the other candidate, rather than a majority of votes, to win. Third-party candidates sometimes run but are not typically competitive enough to win or to even siphon enough votes from other candidates to alter the outcome. This electoral system can lead to extreme outcomes, in theory. If all Democratic candidates won their district with 49 percent of the vote, while each Republican candidate won 48 percent and another 3 percent went to Independent and write-in candidates, then the Democratic party would end up with 100 percent of the seats in Congress even though they failed to win a majority of the vote in any one district or overall.

The Netherlands is the exact opposite. They elect representatives using a multiparty, proportional, at-large system. Every candidate "competes" with every other candidate in the country via party lists, and seats are allocated to political parties in proportion to the popular vote. If Party A wins 36 percent of the popular vote, they are allocated roughly 36 percent of the seats in the legislative body. There is no winner-take-all feature like there is in the United States. The differences between these two countries makes them "most-different" cases with respect to the design of their electoral systems. I leverage this difference to better understand the election-depression connection. If electoral loss is also depressing in a system as different as the Netherlands, then it suggests it can be depressing in most electoral systems. If it is not depressing, on the other hand, then we have evidence that elections can operate without depressing voters.

I use the European Social Survey to assess electoral loss and depression in the Netherlands. The 2006 elections for the Tweede Kamer, which is the Dutch House of Representatives, occurred at the same time the European Social Survey was fielded. Some Dutch respondents therefore took the survey before the election, while others took it after. This wave of the European Social Survey included ten questions about depression—such as feeling depressed, lonely, sad, that everything is an effort, and more—allowing me to analyze how feelings change for winners and losers before and after the election.[5]

Defining winning and losing is easy in the United States because we can simply look at which of the two parties captured the presidency. This task is more difficult in a multiparty, proportional, parliamentary system like the Netherlands. There are some clear winners and losers, but there are also parties whose win or loss status is less clear. Even if we could definitely classify parties as winners and losers, there remains the issue of how these parties map onto the electorate, since the European Social Survey asks respondents whether they are members, voters, and/or supporters of the various political parties. I classify respondents as clear winners if they supported the Christian Democratic Appeal, which was the major party in the postelection ruling coalition. I classify respondents as clear losers if they supported a party that lost seats, including the Labour Party (lost nine seats), the People's Party for Freedom and Democracy (lost six seats), Democrats 66 (lost three seats), Pim Fortuyn List (lost eight seats), and GroenLinks (lost one seat). I classify respondents as neither winners nor losers if they supported a party that either didn't lose any seats or gained some seats but not enough to become the majority party. Finally, I classify respondents as nonpartisan if they did not support any party.

Figure 5.3 shows the predicted change in depression for respondents in each of these four groups following the election. Supporters of the winning party see a clear and statistically significant decline in depression following the election. In contrast, supporters of the losing party see an increase in depression following the election; however, this effect is not statistically distinguishable from zero, nor is it different from the estimated effects for nonpartisans or supporters of parties that neither won nor lost the election. These results are both provocative and tentative. They are provocative because they suggest electoral winning can decrease depression in parliamentary systems of government without electoral losing simultaneously increasing it. The implication is that there may be a way to design electoral systems so that electoral loss does not produce electoral blues. The results are tentative, however, because one case does not make a conclusion. Legislative elections in the Netherlands

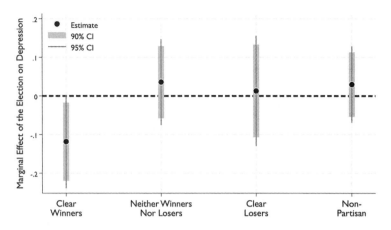

FIGURE 5.3. The Impact of Electoral Loss in the Netherlands
*Note*: The results are based on a regression of depression on the electoral status of respondents (clear winners, neither winners nor losers, clear losers, and nonpartisans), a binary variable for whether the respondent was interviewed after the election, and their interaction. The model includes survey weights and control variables for gender, age, education, marital status, employment status, and the number of days before or after the election that the interview occurred. More information about the analyses can be found in the appendix.

are arguably the most useful case to analyze in contrast to elections in the United States, but we need to first systematically replicate this pattern across many countries, years, and types of electoral systems before we can be fully confident in it.

## What's Next?

Using data from election polls, the Cooperative Election Study, Google Trends, the Behavioral Risk Factor Surveillance Survey, and the European Social Survey, I subjected the election-depression connection to the most rigorous testing to date. The evidence showed that elections can be a source of depression for losers and relief from depression for winners, but it also revealed some limits. In table 5.2, I consolidate what we learned about the scope of the election-depression connection in terms of the type of election, the timing of elections, the electoral system, the meaning of winning and losing, and the intensity of feelings.

These analyses doubled the amount of evidence we have on the election-depression connection but fall well short of exhausting what we

TABLE 5.2 **The Scope of the Election-Depression Connection**

| Scope Condition | Findings |
| --- | --- |
| Type of Election | Presidential elections consistently leave losers feeling depressed; midterm elections may also evoke feelings of depression, but the evidence is inconsistent and weaker. Legislative elections in the Netherland did not increase depression among losers but did decrease it among winners. |
| Timing of Elections | There is evidence that elections are depressing as far back as 2004, or 1992 if we include Levine's study of Perot supporters (1996). These years are less polarized than today, which indicates that the election-depression connection is not simply a product of today's polarized politics. |
| Electoral System | The election in the Netherlands made winners less depressed but not vice versa for losers. This suggests losing may not be depressing in all electoral and party systems even if winning can still have a "relief" effect. |
| Losers & Winners | People with stronger attachments to a candidate or party experience more intense emotions, both positive and negative. However, losing and winning is not limited to partisanship. Sharing a gender and/or racial identity with a *high-profile* candidate can make us more responsive to their electoral success or failure. |
| Intensity of Feelings | People consistently report feeling depressed by electoral loss, but it appears that electoral loss can also affect *generalized* feelings of depression as well as online search behavior. |

can learn. More work is needed before we can fully understand when and why electoral loss is depressing. So what comes next? For starters, studying elections in different times and places, including in nondemocracies, will go a long way to growing our knowledge. I focused here on the scope of the connection, but we also need to study how electoral outcomes are appraised. When is electoral loss seen as irrevocable, and who sees appraises it this way? We also need more work on how people cope with feelings of depression in the immediate aftermath of elections—do they become more disengaged, as my framework predicts?

How we answer these questions may have implications for the losers' consent and its role in making democracy work. As the political scientists Christopher Anderson, Andre Blais, Shaun Bowler, Todd Donovan, and Ola Listhaug point out in their book *The Loser's Consent*, "Losers determine whether the game will go on in the first place and whether it will continue to be played in the long run. . . . The consent of the losers is one of the central, if not *the* central, requirements of the democratic bargain" (2007, 2). They find that the transition of power is shaped by how losers react—for example, their perceptions of fairness, satisfaction with democracy, and protest potential. The importance of the loser's consent raises the possibility that depression may be a crucial element of making democracy work. Feelings of depression lead us to disengage from politics, and the disengagement of losers may be needed for winners to ascend to power.

Elites may play a critical role in producing the electoral blues that give rise to the loser's consent. Concession speeches communicate a sense of irrevocable loss and may therefore instill feelings of depression among supporters of the losing candidate. For instance, Republican John McCain told supporters in 2008, "It's natural, tonight, to feel some disappointment. But tomorrow, we must move beyond it and work together to get our country moving again ... we fought as hard as we could. And though we fell short, the failure is mine, not yours." In 1984, Democrat Walter Mondale told supporters, "My loss tonight does not in any way diminish the worth or the importance of our struggle ... Tonight, tonight especially, I think of the poor, the unemployed, the elderly, the handicapped, the helpless and the sad, and they need us more than ever tonight."

These speeches stand in stark contrast to the aftermath of the 2020 presidential election. Republican Donald Trump claimed the election was stolen and refused to give a concession speech, the first time in more than a century a losing presidential candidate had done so. Trump communicated to supporters that they had not lost, and by holding a rally on January 6, 2021, he communicated that the Electoral College certification of Democrat Joe Biden's victory was by no means irrevocable. Supporters of Trump subsequently stormed the Capitol in an anger-fueled attack that sought to undermine the peaceful transfer of power. Although anecdotal, this case suggest that elites are important to fomenting a sense of irrevocable loss and evoking the feelings of depression, rather than anger, that are necessary to securing the loser's consent.

If depression helps secure the loser's consent—even if only in high-profile elections—then it may not be possible to excise it without some consequence for democracy. In this case, the connection between electoral loss and depression becomes more complicated because it presents a trade-off between mental well-being and democratic functioning. However, if depression is ancillary to securing the loser's consent, we have to wonder if there is some way to do away with it. Can we design electoral institutions so that depression isn't a byproduct? And if we can't break the link between electoral loss and depression, what can be done to help citizens cope with these feelings in the aftermath of an election? Answering these questions will require digging deeper into the election-depression connection, but doing so is worthwhile given what is at stake for our mental well-being and democracy.

CHAPTER SIX

# The Polarization of Private Life

It's now standard operating procedure—not just for health and wellness blogs, but even for national news sites—to offer advice on dealing with political conflicts at Thanksgiving and Christmas. *Time* magazine ran a story with the headline, "Fighting with a Family Member of Over Politics? Try These 4 Steps." NPR put it this way, "If you find yourself fighting with a friend over politics, or frustrated and furious with your nearest and dearest over whom they're supporting for president, you're hardly alone" (Smith 2020). If a short advice column isn't enough, the podcast *I Think You're Wrong (But I'm Listening)* regularly discusses how to navigate difficult conversations about politics with partners, family, friends, neighbors, coworkers, and others.

This media trend points to one way politics infiltrates our personal relationships, often with harmful consequences. In October 2019, a *USA Today* survey asked Americans, "How have destructive partisan disagreements and divisiveness affected your life?" Respondent could select multiple answers, and about 40 percent of respondents reported experiencing "depression, anxiety or sadness" while 35 percent had "lost or had serious fights with friends or family." A study by political scientists Kevin Smith, Matthew Hibbing, and John Hibbing likewise found that "damaged friendships, ruined family reunions, and disrupted workplaces, not to mention feelings of guilt, regret, frustration, anguish, and remorse have all been attributed to political differences" (2019, 2).

Anecdotes abound about the polarized lives of Americans, from political elites to ordinary citizens. Claudia Conway, the daughter of former Trump advisor Kellyanne Conway, regularly discussed on social media how her mother's politics took a toll on her mental well-being. Stephanie Reagan, the daughter of a Republican primary candidate for the

Michigan state legislature, told her followers on X (the platform formerly known as Twitter) to vote against her father during the 2020 election season (Goldberg 2020). In an extraordinary case, Upworthy reported on a woman who was kicked out of her home after telling authorities that her parents attended the January 6 insurrection (Perry 2021).

So news stories, blog posts, survey results, and anecdotes show that mixing politics and personal relationships can be stressful, but is this stress depressing? I argue that the answer to this question is yes. When relationships become politically polarized, we can experience an irrevocable loss of social support that has depressing consequences. In this chapter, I explain how this happens by describing how politics is personalized, how it is polarized, and how this combination leads to a loss of social support in close relationships. I then present statistical and qualitative evidence from the United States and Great Britain that shows the political polarization of personal life is in fact depressing.

## What Is the Personalization of Politics?

A key feature of modern democracies is the political power it affords regular people. Nondemocracies concentrate political power in a single person or ruling class, but democracies diffuse power in the hope of determining a collective will. This power is codified in the right to vote. Democratic citizens decide who is put in office and who is thrown out and sometimes even vote directly on policies through ballot initiatives and referendums. Voting may be the official indicator of collective will in a democracy, but it isn't the only one. Politicians, journalists, and other officials often rely on polls, public demonstrations, social media, and other sources of information to determine what the public wants. By vesting power in regular people—whether formally or informally—democracy transforms them into political actors who shape the collective will through their rights to vote, protest, associate, and speak.

This diffusion of power blurs the distinction between public and private life. The activist Carol Hanisch captured this idea in a 1969 essay about the women's rights movement. She rejected the characterization of women's therapy groups as apolitical, arguing that the problems women discussed in these groups stemmed from a political system that perpetuated and enforced gender roles and norms in society. She wrote, "One of the first things we discover in these groups is that personal problems are political problems. There are no personal solutions at this time. There is only collective action for a collective solution" (1969). That is, what may appear as a personal problem—such as an *incident* of domestic violence—is often a collective problem—such as an *epidemic* of domestic violence. The title of Hanisch's essay—"The Personal Is Political"—became the protest slogan for second-wave feminists and has since been adopted and adapted by other activist groups. Twenty years later, legal scholar Kimberlé Crenshaw expounded on this idea: "This process of recognizing as social and systemic what was formerly perceived as isolated and individual has also characterized the identity politics of African Americans, other people of color, and gays and lesbians, among others" (1991, 1241–42).

The personal being political is not the only way public and private life blur. In 2009, the United Kingdom's Royal Society for the Arts Social Brain Project published an essay that argued, "Whether we like it or not, in late modernity citizens need to be able to reflexively chart their way through the choppy waters of a globalised economy. And whether we like it or not, they need to find ways of changing the way they live if they are to counteract problems like entrenched inequality and environmental degradation" (Grist 2009, 16). This idea inverts "the personal is political" into "the political is personal." For instance, according to this view, combating climate change isn't just a job for the government but is also the responsibility of regular people, whether that means taking public transportation or becoming a vegetarian. The blurring here is in believing that political problems have personal solutions. The political theorist David Chandler refers to this as "democracy unbound," in which "government is brought back 'to the people' and democracy is seen to circulate through the personal decisions made in everyday life" (2014, 42).

The blurring of the private and the public has ramifications for how we navigate our lives. We are no longer just regular people; we're political actors with the power to vote, contact elected officials, sign petitions, attend protests, volunteer, boycott and buycott, and form opinions. We begin to wonder about the political implications of our everyday problems (i.e., "the personal is political") and our everyday actions (i.e., "the political is personal"). Our relationships are also transformed as a result. We begin to see family members, friends, and colleagues as political actors whose preferences and actions are politically consequential. Everyone we encounter is now someone we might persuade or mobilize—or at least judge for their potential to be persuaded or mobilized. We ourselves become the target of persuasion, mobilization, and judgment.

It's not surprising, then, that how we think about and engage with the political process is profoundly shaped by our personal relationships. As the political scientist Katherine Cramer Walsh writes in her book *Talking about Politics*,

> Talking about politics is a common part of everyday life. Granted, informal political conversations may not be sustained, and they are not typically conducted for the purpose of reaching a decision. Instead, when the forum is friendly, we use politics like we use the weather, sports, and family—as a way to relate to one another. These conversations constitute a major part of the fabric of our civic life ... They are crucial public moments because they cause us to reflect on who we are, whom we consider to be people like us, and whom we want to lead us into the future. These conceptions, simply put, are social identities. They are tools of understanding that are integral to the way we interpret politics. (2003)

We see the political imprint of personal relationships most clearly with children. The family is where children first learn about politics, so parents are generally considered the most important "socializing agents" in their lives. Parents act as gatekeepers on what information and ideas children see, and there is considerable evidence that they "transmit" their political views to their children (Jennings et al. 2009). Indeed, all children are future political actors, so parents can only hope to impart their views on them. The political importance of personal relationships continues into adulthood, even if it becomes less visible. Partners, friends, and colleagues gradually replace parents in shaping our political identity, and we may even cultivate a community of "political" friends who fill this role.

Like our political identity, our engagement with politics often flows from our personal relationships. We typically think of political parties as the key mobilizers of the electorate, but parties pursue a strategy of *cascading mobilization* (Huckfedlt and Sprague 1992). They reach out to their most faithful supporters, knowing this outreach will *cascade* through those supporters' social networks. In effect, parties use personal relationships to their advantage. The importance of cascading mobilization endures even in the age of social media. In one famous study, about 61 million Facebook users were randomly selected to receive a political mobilization message during the 2010 Congressional election season. The researchers assessed how this message impacted users who received it, as well as users who did not receive it but were in the social network of someone who did. They found that "the effect of social transmission on real-world voting was greater than the direct effect of the messages themselves, and nearly all the transmission occurred between 'close friends' who were more likely to have a face-to-face relationship" (Bond et al. 2012, 495).

Democracy has always blurred public and private life because it turns regular citizens into political actors. Today, with the rise of the internet and the proliferation of smartphones, these boundaries seem blurrier than ever. People can more easily peer into the lives of others, which lowers the cost of assessing where the "personal is political" (Do they have the same problems as me?) and the "political is personal" (Do they pursue private solutions to political problems?). The personalization of politics can be good when it holds those in power accountable for their behavior, but it can be depressing, too. To understand why this is so, consider a second feature of modern democratic politics: political polarization.

## What Is the Polarization of Politics?

In the 1950s, the American Political Science Association published a report lamenting that the Democratic and Republican parties were disorganized and lacked cohesive platforms, writing that the "alternatives between the parties are defined so badly that it is often difficult to determine what the election has decided even in broadest terms" (1950, 30). Democracy, whether in the United Sates or elsewhere, is undermined when political parties fail to offer voters meaningful *choices*, which is why the report was titled "Toward a More Responsible Two-Party System." We've come a long way since that time. Today we are living through one of the more polarized periods in American history, in which the differences between Democrats and Republicans are deep and wide.

In any democracy, there is an ebb and flow to the polarization of political parties. Voter preferences change, coalitions shift, and party systems undergo dealignment and realignment. American history, for example, is characterized by periods of partisan polarization over certain issues, such as the schism between Federalists and Anti-Federalists over the ratification of the constitution in the 1780s, the split between Federalists and Jeffersonian-Republicans over federalism in the 1790s, and the divisions between Democrats and Republicans over slavery in the 1850s, currency in the 1890s, welfare spending in the 1930s, and civil rights in the 1960s. The unique aspect of the current moment in American politics, as political scientists Geoffrey Layman, Thomas Carsey, and Juliana Menasce Horowitz point out, is that partisan polarization is characterized by *multiple* divisive issues, whereas previous periods of partisan polarization typically revolved around a single issue (2006).

Democracy requires some polarization between parties if voters are to have a meaningful choice. However, too much polarization can also undermine democracy by making it impossible for parties to work together. Today in the United States, there is mounting evidence that elected officials in Congress and state legislatures no longer have an appetite to collaborate, compromise, or find consensus with officials across the aisle (Andris et al. 2015; Masket 2009). This Congressional dysfunction has reduced legislative output, created budgetary crises, and delayed confirmations of officials to the executive and judicial branches of government (McCarty 2015). Clearly "responsible" parties are not a panacea, or as the political scientist Nicol Rae put as the title of his review article on the subject, "Be Careful What You Wish For" (2007, 169).

It is against the backdrop of political polarization among elites that ordinary citizens find themselves highly polarized. Today Americans seem to be driven as much by *negative* partisanship—the rejection of a political party—as *positive* partisanship—the embrace of a political party. Indeed, partisan animosity is now widespread in the United States. Many Americans view members of the opposing party as closed minded, unpatriotic, immoral, and unintelligent (Pew 2019), leading the Pew Research Center to conclude that "partisan polarization remains the dominant, seemingly unalterable condition of American politics. Republicans and Democrats agree on very little—and when they do, it often is in the shared belief that they have little in common" (2022).

The escalation of polarization becomes especially harmful when it transforms out-party hostility into outright dehumanization. Dehumanization is subtle when another person is viewed as possessing the traits of animals (e.g., uncivilized) or automatons (e.g., emotionless). It is blatant when the entire essence of another person is seen as subhuman. American politics has been marred by both subtle and blatant dehumanization in recent years (Martherus et al. 2021). Perhaps most astonishing is how Democrats and Republicans evaluate one another on the "Ascent of Man" image, which famously depicts five silhouettes of a monkey morphing into a caveman morphing into a modern human. One study found that partisans in the United States rated members of the out-party as less human on this scale than members of their own party (Cassese 2021).

## What Happens When Personalization Meets Polarization?

The personalization and polarization of politics are not unrelated. For starters, growing polarization in the United States has intensified the politicization of our personal lives (Mason 2018). Where we live, whom we date, how we shop, and what we consume are all now influenced by whether we identify as Democrat or Republican. Partisan "sorting" in our personal lives, in turn, feeds back into affective polarization, creating a continuous loop. For example, one study looked at the preferences of liberals and conservatives on dating apps and found they almost exclusively sought dates with people who held similar views, thereby reducing their exposure to people who thought differently. The Pew Research Center found in 2020 that about 40 percent of registered voters did not have a single close friend who supported the opposing presidential candidate (Dunn 2020).

What are the consequences of the personalization of politics colliding with its polarization? Forming social ties with members of the same party—what social network scholars refer to as *partisan bonding*—can leave us in an "echo chamber" that cultivates extremist views and amplifies antipathy toward the other side. However, partisan bonding may also be a force for good in our lives, helping cultivate a sense of belonging and motivating political action. The opposite of partisan bonding is *partisan bridging*, which occurs when we form ties with someone from the opposite party. Bridging has negative and positive effects too. Political disagreements within opposite-party relationships may leave us with more negative views of the other side. However, compromise and consensus building are also potential outcomes of disagreement, and through these, bridging may mitigate our negative views of the other side.

To help us understand why the polarization of private life might be depressing, we can examine the stress-appraisal-coping framework. Politics is stressful because it is inherently conflictual, and the *personalization* of politics brings this conflict into our private life. How family, friends, and colleagues think about and engage with the political process matters. We feel stress when they act disagreeably, or when they hold views with which we disagree—even if disagreements are expressed respectfully. The *polarization* of politics amplifies the intensity of the stress we feel when family and friends hold differing political views. Polarization can make disagreements more conflictual and relationships more strained.

This stress becomes depressing when it leads to an irrevocable loss of *social support*. Social support is "the assistance and protection given to others, especially to individuals" (Langford et al. 1997, 95), and it has four defining attributes: *emotional* support, "the provision of caring, empathy, love, and trust" (96); *instrumental* support, "the provision of tangible goods and services, or tangible aid" (96); *information* support, "information provided to another during a time of support" (97); and *appraisal* support, "the communication of information which is relevant to self-evaluation, rather than problem-solving" (97). Social support thus shapes whether we experience stress and how we appraise and cope with it. Moreover, a lack of social support can itself be a source of stress. A meta-analysis of more than one hundred studies concluded, "The evidence is overall highly consistent and supports the notion that social support is an important protective factor against depression" (Garièpy et al. 2016, 289).

Social support becomes relevant to politics because of the collision of personalization and polarization. Partisan bonding can reduce stress and depression by allowing us to cultivate ties with people who can offer emotional, instrumental, information, and appraisal support when we need it. Partisan bridging, on the other hand, invites political conflict into our lives, or at least the potential for it. The potential for conflict in these relationships presents a subtle but serious problem: how much can we trust these people to offer social support, given that we may view them, consciously or not, with partisan antipathy and subtle dehumanization—and that we probably worry about their viewing us the same way? Whatever our answer might be, the need to consider this question at all indicates that there is at least some loss of social support in politically conflictual relationships compared to politically harmonious ones, and the degree to which social support is lost grows with the intensity of the political conflict. It is this loss that makes the political polarization of personal life so depressing.

## What Is the Evidence?

Personalization and polarization together make politics an unavoidable part of our relationships. I referred to this earlier in the chapter as the political polarization of personal life and argued that it can have depressing consequences because it leads to an irrevocable loss of social support. Is there empirical support for this argument? To answer this question, I analyze longitudinal data from Great Britain and the United States as well as interviews of mental health professionals. The longitudinal data provide systematic evidence that the polarization of personal relationships is depressing, while the interviews provide suggestive evidence that this effect stems from how political conflict impairs social support.

*The British Household Panel Survey*

The British Household Panel Survey (BHPS) is an annual, nationally representative survey of residents of Great Britain, Wales, Scotland, and Northern Ireland. This study began in 1991 with about 10,300 individuals residing in about 5,500 households in Great Britain. The Scottish and Welsh samples were added in 1991, and the Irish sample was added in 2001. This study is unique—and especially well-suited to studying the polarization of personal life—because members of the original households have been tracked and surveyed each year, even if they move out of their original home. The survey also targets whoever happens to live in the household of each original survey respondent as the survey continues through the years. This design generates rich longitudinal information about the household context of the survey respondents, a feature I exploit to assess whether political polarization within the household leads to higher levels of depression.

It will be helpful to describe the British party system before diving into measurement of polarization at the household level. In Great Britain, there are two dominant parties—Conservative and Labor—and two minor parties—Liberal and Scottish National. A handful of smaller parties typically don't seat representatives in the House of Commons but sometimes seat representatives in lower legislative bodies throughout the country. For instance, in the House of Commons in 2022, the Conservative Party had 358/650 seats, Labor had 199/650 seats, the Scottish National Party had 45/650 seats, and Liberals had 14/650 seats. The remaining 36 seats were distributed among seven smaller parties. In Scotland, Ireland, and Wales, many of these smaller parties are major parties, such as Sinn Féin in Northern Ireland or the Scottish National Party in Scotland. All of this is to say that there is a wider variety of political affiliations in Great Britain than in the United States.

The multiplicity of parties in Britain allows me to calculate the partisan fractionalization and the partisan strength of each household, which together indicate the level of polarization in the home. Fractionalization generally refers to how much a society is split into distinct socially relevant groups and is often used to understand political conflict in ethnically, linguistically, or religiously diverse societies (e.g., Alesina et al. 2003). Scholars have developed statistical techniques for measuring this kind of fractionalization, and I apply these techniques to capture how much a household is fractured each year in its support for political parties in Great Britain. This allows me to generate a "household partisan fractionalization" score for each household-year. This score ranges from 0 (all members of the household share the same partisan affiliation) to 1 (all members of the household hold different partisan affiliations).[1]

Partisan strength refers to how close a person feels to their preferred party. The closeness here is *psychological* rather than behavioral. Someone who feels a strong connection to a party may also be more active, such as volunteering, canvassing, phone banking, raising money, donating, or something else, but these activities are not a precondition for a strong psychological attachment. Likewise, someone who does all these activities may still only feel a weak psychological attachment—perhaps their engagement is driven more by the social benefits they receive than by their commitment to the cause. I classify respondents into five categories that capture the psychological strength of their partisan affiliation: (1) respondents who report no preferred party at all, (2) respondents who do not feel close to a party but nevertheless have a preferred party in a hypothetical election, (3) respondents who report feeling "not very close" to their preferred party, (4) respondents who report feeling "fairly close" to their preferred party, and (5) respondents who report feeling "very close" to their preferred party.[2] I calculate a "household partisan strength" score by averaging the partisan strengths of all members in a household-year. The final variable ranges from 1 (a household where all members report no preferred party) to 5 (a household where all members report feeling "very close" to their preferred party).

Polarization requires both fractionalization and strength. A household that is fractured but where no one feels strongly about a party is not polarized. A household where everyone cares strongly about a party but is unified in their affiliation is also not polarized. In contrast, a household is most polarized when it is comprised of strong and fully fractured partisans. This is where I expect to see the strongest impact on depression. Between these extremes are degrees of polarization—households that have at least some fractionalization and strength but vary in how much and in what combination. I therefore analyze how the partisan fractionalization and strength of a household *jointly* affect the depression of its residents.

Depression is measured using the General Health Questionnaire-12 (GHQ-12), which is popular in psychology, psychiatry, public health, and medicine. It asks respondents twelve questions, such as "Have you recently felt unhappy and depressed?" Each question has four "relative" response

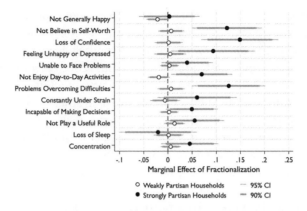

FIGURE 6.1. The Impact of Household Polarization on Components of Depression
*Note:* The results are marginal effects from ordinary least squares regressions of each depression item on household partisan fractionalization, household partisan strength, the square of these variables, and their interaction. I include the squared terms to allow for the possibility that the interactive effect is nonlinear. The model includes household random effects, wave fixed effects, and household clustered standard errors as well as control variables for gender, age, education, income, marital status, general health, employment status, household survey participation, household type, and household size. More information about the analyses can be found in the appendix.

options, such as not at all, no more than usual, rather more, and much more. I analyze the twelve items one at a time and altogether using the mean score across the items.

Figure 6.1 plots the impact of fractionalization on the GHQ-12 items for weakly and strongly partisan households. Partisan fractionalization has no substantive or statistical impact on any of the GHQ-12 items in households that are only weakly partisan. However, among households that are strongly partisan, fractionalization substantially and statistically significantly increases the probability of reporting lower self-worth, loss of confidence, feelings of unhappiness and depression, lack of enjoyment of day-to-day activities, problems overcoming difficulties, being incapable of making decisions, and not playing a useful role. This pattern supports the idea that polarization—defined as the combination of household partisan fractionalization and strength—can be depressing.

A similar pattern is seen in the left panel of figure 6.2, which plots the impact of household partisan fractionalization on the overall depression score across values of household partisan strength. Fractionalization has no effect in households full of weak partisans—people whose connection to a political party is limited to their vote—but matters increasingly as the partisan strength of the household grows. The predicted levels of depression are displayed in the right panel. When there is no fractionalization, depression levels are flat across the values of households' partisan strength. In fully fractionalized households, however, depression levels skyrocket as strength increases—the average level of depression in fully fractionalized goes from 1.87 (out of 4) in weak partisan households to 2.86 (out of 4) in strong partisan households. Altogether, these results provide strong evidence that political polarization in personal life is depressing.

## The National Longitudinal Surveys of Youth

Data available from the United States are considerably different—they are surveys of mother-child dyads rather than all members of a household—so I cannot conduct an exact replication. However, we can explore how *perceptions* of political differences shape feelings of depression. The National Longitudinal Survey of Youth 1979 (NLSY79) is a nationally

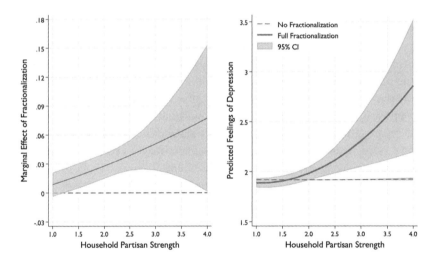

FIGURE 6.2. The Impact of Household Polarization on Overall Depression
*Note*: The results are based on an ordinary least squares regression of overall depression on household partisan fractionalization, household partisan strength, the square of these variables, and their interaction. I include the squared terms to allow for the possibility that the interactive effect is nonlinear. The model includes household random effects, wave fixed effects, and household clustered standard errors as well as control variables for gender, age, education, income, marital status, general health, employment status, household survey participation, household type, and household size. More information about the analyses can be found in the appendix.

representative sample of 12,686 Americans born between 1957 and 1964. The Bureau of Labor Statistics interviewed respondents annually from 1979 to 1994 and then biennially from 1996 to the present. I pair these data with the Children of the National Longitudinal Survey of Youth 1979 (CNLSY79), a sample of more than ten thousand children of women from the NLSY79. Starting in 1994, the CNLSY79 introduced a "Young Adult Survey" to children who were fifteen or older; this supplemented the data mothers provided on their children. Most importantly, the Bureau of Labor Statistics collaborated with the American National Election Study in 2006 to collect political information from mothers and their teenage and adult children.

Because the survey is limited to mother-child dyads who are mostly not living in the same home—in large part because these are *adult* children—I have incomplete data on the politics of each household. However, I do have rich data on the mother-child relationships. Both mothers and children are asked to report their party identification, so I know whether each identifies as a strong Republican, Republican, Republican leaner, Independent, Democratic leaner, Democrat, or strong Democrat. Children are also asked to report whether they think their mother and father are Republican, Independent, Democrat, or something else. This means I can analyze how *actual* and *perceived* partisan differences in the parent-child relationship affect feelings of depression. Depression is measured using seven items from the Center for Epidemiological Studies Depression Scale (Radloff 1977), which includes questions about feeling depressed, that everything was an effort, sad, not being able to get going, and more. I generate an overall depression score for each "child" in the data by averaging across answers to these items.

I begin by examining whether *actual* political differences between the mother and child are depressing to the child. I find that depression increases as the party identification of the mother diverges from the party identification of the child, but that these effects are not statistically significant. Overall, we can't be sure that actual political differences in mother-child relationships, at least with mostly adult children, are a source of depression. Even if actual political differences between mothers and children are not depressing, it is possible that what children *think* about their parents' partisan identities matters. This would be consistent with the idea that how we appraise stress matters. It would also be consistent with my own research on the intergenerational transmission of party identification, in which my coauthor and I find that children are more

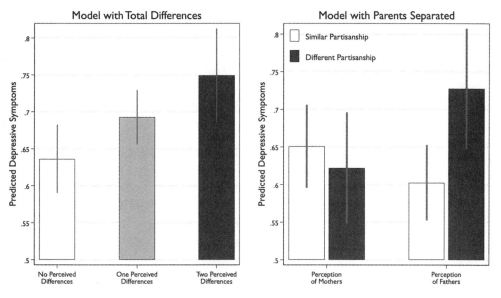

FIGURE 6.3. The Impact of Perceived Political Differences with Parents
*Note*: The results are based on three ordinary least squares regressions. I regress the child's depression on the mother's party identification in a model for Democratic children and a model for Republican children. Since political differences for Independent children could emerge in either direction—by mothers becoming more Democratic or more Republican—I used a "folded" measure of the mother's party identification. This folded measure is equivalent to "partisan strength" since it takes on values of Independent, leaner, partisan, and strong partisan. All models include survey weights and control variables for gender, race, age, education, and income. More information about the analyses can be found in the appendix.

likely to adopt the partisan views they thought parents had than parents' actual partisanship (Ojeda and Hatemi 2015). Perhaps something similar is going on here.

To test this possibility, I examine how perceptions of partisan difference with parents, both separately and jointly, affect depression. The results generally show that children become more depressed as they perceive more differences with parents. Figure 6.3 plots the predicted depressive symptoms for typical children who differ in their perceptions of their parents' partisanship. The left panel shows that perceiving one difference is more depressing than perceiving no difference and less depressing than perceiving two differences. Although the effects are not statistically significant when comparing no difference to one difference or one difference to two differences, the effect is statistically significant when comparing no difference to two differences. Children who perceive both parents to be outpartisans are more depressed than children who perceive both parents to be copartisans. When the results are split by parents, as is shown in the right panel of figure 6.3, it appears that perceived differences are only negatively and statistically significantly related to depression in the case of fathers. Altogether, these results suggest that perceived political differences with parents, especially fathers, can be depressing.

## Interviews of Mental Health Professionals

It's clear from the analyses of British households and American parent-child dyads that political polarization in our personal lives is depressing. I now turn to interviews of mental health professionals to highlight the role of social support. Over the past couple of years, I've conducted eighteen interviews with therapists, social workers, and psychiatrists throughout the United States. One of my motivations was to learn about political conversations in the therapy room. After a few warm-up questions about professional background and clientele, I would ask interviewees to recall a recent time that a client talked about politics—what issues were discussed, why, and with what impact? Interviewees often told me about multiple clients, and in almost all the interviews, the issue of politics as a source of interpersonal conflict would arise at least once during the conversation. I focus on five interviewees, who are given aliases to protect their identity, in order to showcase some of the ways political polarization in our personal lives leads to a loss of social support and ultimately to depression.

The first story comes from Tom, a psychiatrist in California, who worked in a medical and academic setting in the Midwest for years before moving to California and turning his small part-time private practice into a full-time job. He told me about two different clients who suffered from anxiety and depression and who both took medication for it. When I asked Tom to recall a conversation about politics, he was quick to answer, saying, "I have a client right now, a woman who's in her—probably about sixty years old—and she lives over by the ocean. And, um, her husband is a Trump supporter, and she just can't handle that." He elaborated that this issue had caused a "lot of tension in their relationship" and that his client brings it up at therapy because she is trying to figure out "how to deal" with her husband. The case of this client complements the first part of this chapter by illustrating in a personal way what the analyses showed using cold, hard statistics: disagreement over which candidate or party to support is an easy way for politics to infiltrate relationships.

The story of this woman, while interesting, doesn't shed light on the question of social support, and Tom didn't tell me much more about her case. However, he did quickly pivot to a second client, whose story inverts the first client's and speaks more directly to the issue of social support. As Tom told me, "I've got another guy . . . and he's like a closet Trump supporter. And he, like he thinks his girlfriend would dump him if she found out. So he, you know, wants to talk about that. How frustrated he feels he has to be in the closet." Whereas the first client was trying to cope with her husband openly supporting Trump, this client is privately struggling with the feeling that he can't open up about his support for Trump. Importantly, the stakes are high for this client as he sincerely believes that his relationship would end—what we might think of as the ultimate loss of social support—were this political preference to come out into the open.

Another mental health professional, Linda, also told me about a client who was dealing with "outpartisan" family members. Linda had worked as a counselor for various private and educational organizations for decades but had recently opened her own private practice at the time we spoke. In response to my question, she told me about a teenage girl who initially became her client after being sexually assaulted at school. Linda told me that "while she's not like of voting age, she's very much impacted by her parents' political viewpoints and not just her parents', because there are other people in her family that, um, have some pretty, um, hard-core right views, um, and you know, she kind of takes like the opposite." In fact, Linda told me that her client described her parents as "hardcore Trumpies."

Importantly, Linda didn't see a loss of social support as the *primary* reason that this political disagreement was a source of mental anguish. Instead, Linda told me, "I think because of the nature of the trauma that she went through she's very like anti-him [Trump] especially considering his history. Um, and a lot of the things that have come out there, but I think, um, a huge piece of it is just the underlying trauma and so, she focuses in very heavily on, like all of the sexual assault cases and things that have been brought up against him." To Linda, the parents' support of Trump was a problem for her client because it was a constant reminder of the sexual assault she had been through. Put another way, "retraumatization" seemed to be the most important factor in explaining why political disagreement lead to anxiety and depression for this client.

Even so, a loss of social support mattered in this case too. Linda told me at one point, "most of the time I just try to like let her kind of ventilate about what's been going on and just try to provide support." The implication here is that Linda's client felt she had to go to Linda, rather than someone in her family, to talk through the trauma of what happened to her and to vent about politics. That is, her client felt she lacked the requisite social support from her parents because of their support for Trump to be able to openly discuss these topics with them. This story highlights how political disagreement necessarily limits the social support we can receive from family and friends when coping with the stress of politics. Sometimes the social support we need is to talk about politics without being questioned, judged, or confronted, and mixed-partisan relationships make it more difficult to converse in this way.

The next story comes from Kim, who had recently graduated from a clinical mental health program and was actively pursuing her therapy license. When we spoke, she was working under supervision at a private practice where she had interned as a student. Her clientele were primarily adolescents, and she talked collectively about them when describing how political disagreements at home were challenging. To my question about politics, Kim told me, "It was really putting a strain on family relationships and friendships. And so I heard a lot of people say, you know, I don't really care that much. I really just want to be able to go home and watch football with my mom or my dad or have a conversation with my brother and my sister that's not about this. I just want to bury this and how that changed relationship dynamics."

I was curious whether any conversation about politics—conflictual or consensual—was stressful, or whether stress was limited to only the conversations that involved political disagreement. Kim elaborated, "It's not just the conversations about it. It's kind of the emotion behind the conversation. So misunderstanding, not feeling heard. It's bringing up maybe some old arguments, and it's becoming, with everything becoming so politicized . . . and having to deal with the stress that causes, of not feeling at peace in the family or connected." What Kim was hearing from her clients was that politics had turned the home into a place where they felt disconnected and misunderstood rather than welcomed and supported. In short, political conflict in the home had undercut the social support her adolescent clients felt from their parents and siblings.

The experiences of Kim's clients are how we might typically think about political disagreement in parent-child relationships—a parent holds one set of political views, a child holds another, and this difference creates conflict. Another interviewee, Sharon, who started her career working in trauma care before transitioning to couples' counseling, offered another perspective. When we spoke, she initially talked about the standard problems couples face when there is political disagreement. The core issue she found herself helping clients address was, "Can I still feel connected and close to you as my partner and know that we disagree around this issue?" Eventually our conversation turned to the issue of children, and Sharon pointed out that political disagreement among couples sometimes created conflict because of its implications for childrearing. One problem is how parents think about the political socialization of their child. As Sharon told me, "We're afraid that the child is going to take on, you know, my partner's political belief system. I'm worried they're going to grow up and be this as well." However, Susan saw this problem as minor because she found most parents could agree to expose the child to both views and then let them decide what views they wanted for themselves. The bigger problem was the child's exposure to political conflict between parents. As she told me, "The issue of the child comes up in the fact of the escalation of the conflict. We feel badly because we're arguing in front of the child.... How healthy is it for our child to be witnessing our escalation about this on a recurring basis?"

Although most interviewees highlighted ideological and partisan disagreements as a source of stress, some also pointed to differences in political engagement—cases where one person wanted to consume, discuss, and engage with politics a lot, and the other person did not. One such interviewee was Jared, a therapist who is one half of a husband-wife private practice that specializes in couples' therapy. Regarding a couple with differing backgrounds, ideological and partisan views, and political engagement, Jared told me, "Whereas one person from this region, who has more fiscally or socially conservative politics, politics is a regular component of their selfhood. And so they're talking about that frequently, and then this other person who may be, nascently Democratic from, you know, like a tradition, they grew up Episcopal in Pennsylvania and they're not talking about politics frequently." He saw these differences as leading to tension in the relationship, telling me that he would hear from his clients, "I don't like his or her political viewpoints, because I think that they are abhorrent or something. And I don't like how much they're engaging with politics."

Jared explained how political disagreement and differing engagement often work in tandem to start the "conflict cycle" among couples. He elaborated,

> And then that person might say, "Oh, I feel ignored, I feel unacceptable or I feel alone or I feel misunderstood," and then our conversation would pivot to,

"So then what do you do next when you feel those sorts of things" and it's like, "Oh well, then I get really defensive and I raise my voice and I start kind of loudly talking about my news sources" and then it's like "And then what does your partner do?" And it's like, "Oh, well, well, then she escalates, and she starts, you know, like loudly talking to me about how I'm an idiot and how could I ever, you know, like think these sorts of things, it doesn't, then what happens?" And then we blow up and we say things we regret, and we withdraw.

Here, his client felt ignored by their partner because they were highly engaged with the news and politics. When they confronted their partner, the conversation quickly morphed into a more intense conflict over their differing ideological and partisan views. The outcome of this "conflict cycle" is that both partners were left feeling misunderstood and alone and regretting what they said.

Although none of my interviewees mentioned differing levels of political engagement as a problem for clients in politically harmonious relationships, it seems feasible that a sense of loneliness can occur if one person in the relationship is so engaged in politics that they end up ignoring the other person. Interestingly, one interviewee, Adriana, discussed a mild version of this problem in terms of her own life. Adriana had become a therapist in middle adulthood after working in various other careers for decades. When we talked, she initially told me about clients who found the omnipresence of politics in their lives to be stressful at times, and then related her own struggles with this issue, telling me,

> I'm working from home lately, but I've been trying to really separate work from the rest of life. Because I feel like I'm talking about politics all the time with my clients and talking about people's hopelessness and empathizing with them, while feeling my own anxiety and fear and hopelessness and everything and I feel like I'm in it all workday. So I'm really trying to create, um, build some separation. So when I leave my work for the day, I'm not reading the news anymore, and I'm not talking about it. You know, I had some conflict [laughs] with my wife because she really wanted to watch the debates, the first debate, and I really opposed her. I was like, "I cannot, you know, just be with clients for eight hours talking about this, and then I walk out of this little office I'm using and walk into the, you know, the debate on the TV. I just need that to not, to not be happening." So reducing my own news consumption and trying to create a barrier between work and home life and trying to find some pleasant things to do in my off time. I've been baking a lot.

Although Adriana did not further elaborate on the conflict with her wife or give any indication that it led to serious mental anguish, her story nevertheless illustrates how differing levels of engagement even within politically harmonious relationships can be a source of stress.

These stories are in no way systematic or causal proof that the irrevocable loss of social support is why political disagreement is depressing.[3] Yet they offer unique insights that cannot be generated from mere number crunching. Analyzing just five interviews revealed a myriad of ways that people confront and navigate political disagreements in their relationships. Almost all the clients experienced political disagreement, a loss of social support, and feelings of depression, but how these components looked, combined, and interacted varied from story to story. This diversity of experience gets flattened and erased by statistical analyses. The interviews therefore act as both a proof of concept for the "irrevocable loss of social support" hypothesis and as an indication that understanding the political polarization of personal life—and its depressing consequences—is complex and requires more than this one promising hypothesis. More work is needed if we are to better understand the many ways political polarization manifests in our relationships, what types of social support are lost as a result, and how we are left feeling in the end.

## What's Next?

The widening gap between those on the left and those on the right is not limited to political elites. Affective polarization among ordinary people in the United States and other advanced Western democracies has given rise to unprecedented and concerning partisan animosity. With the personalization of politics, this partisan animosity is now directed both vertically—from citizens to out-party politicians—and horizontally—from citizens of one party to citizens of other parties. I argued that when political polarization seeps into our personal lives, it can lead to an irrevocable loss of social support in our closest relationships, which ultimately leaves us feeling depressed.

In analyses of Great Britain and the United States, I found that living in a polarized household and perceiving partisan differences in familial relationships is a source of stress and ultimately depression. Life outside the echo chamber—or what we might think of as the *noisy agora*, named for the public space where politics was debated in ancient Greece—can be especially depressing. The mental well-being of partisans, even fairly weak ones, is better off in a home of like-minded people than a home of diverse political views. Given these results, or perhaps because of them, it is not surprising that people today often seek relationships with those who share a similar political outlook.

However, this raises a troubling conundrum: How do we reconcile the dangers "echo chambers" pose to democracy with their benefits for mental well-being? One possibility is that "unblurring" the boundaries of political and personal life can be beneficial some of the time. Echo chambers may be bad for some sites where politics happens (such as social media), but not others (such as the home). Depolarizing the home and our most personal relationships may allow these "sites" to serve as a retreat from politics, and therefore an uncompromising source of social support. This may in turn better prepare citizens to enter the "noisy agora" and handle the stress of stepping into the public domain, be it online, a town hall meeting, or elsewhere.

Depolarization may seem daunting, but it isn't impossible. As I wrote this book, I heard many stories from family, friends, acquaintances, and even strangers about how politics has been depressing. One story came from a woman who told me, "I nearly destroyed my relationships with my two gay brothers over the church's involvement with Proposition 8 in California." As a bit of background, Proposition 8 was a ballot initiative that would have constitutionally banned same-sex marriage in California had it passed. The proposition ultimately failed, but the damage to her relationship was done. Her brothers and her didn't speak for the next four years. However, that wasn't the end of the story. She went on to tell me, "It took a lot of introspection for me to change my position . . . and a couple of attempts to apologize and rebuild, but sometimes those losses can be regained!"

It will take some time before we fully understand how the political polarization of personal life shapes depression. Do these results replicate in other places and at other times? Can this issue be studied experimentally so we can be more confident about the causal connection? Is the irrevocable loss of social support the mechanism connecting the polarization of personal life to depression, or is something else at work? And what is the role of mental health professionals in helping citizens cope with politically polarized relationships? These are just some of the important questions that lie ahead.

CHAPTER SEVEN

# The Pain of Public Policy

In July 2015, German chancellor Angela Merkel traveled to the northern city of Rostock to speak at a town hall meeting about the ongoing migrant crisis facing the country. Europe was grappling with an influx of migrants fleeing wars, political persecutions, and economic crises in Eastern Europe, the Middle East, and North Africa. As Pew Research reported, "A record 1.3 million migrants applied for asylum in the 28 member states of the European Union, Norway and Switzerland in 2015—nearly double the previous high water mark of roughly 700,000 that was set in 1992 after the fall of the Iron Curtain and the collapse of the Soviet Union" (2016). Aside from Italy and Greece, Germany saw the lion's share of migrants, processing nearly half the asylum claims filed in the European Union between 2015 and 2017 (Eurostat).

Merkel had unsuccessfully pushed for the European Union to impose immigration quotas across member states, and it was becoming clear that Europe's response to the migrant crisis would be a patchwork of policies across countries. In Germany, the Bundestag was considering legislation that would loosen residency laws and make it easier for migrant families to remain in Germany. As the *New York Times* reported, "An overhaul of residency laws would allow certain under-age asylum seekers who have attended German schools and have been assimilated the opportunity to stay in the country permanently, along with their parents" (Coburn 2015). However, this legislation, and the migrant crisis more generally, was dividing the German public and becoming a political flash point. The populist right-wing party Alternative für Deutschland, commonly known as AfD, had formed a couple years earlier on an anti–European Union platform but was now seizing on immigration to promote and popularize itself.

That summer, Merkel embarked on a "Living Well in Germany" campaign that sought to promote a greater acceptance of migrants while also making clear that her government would not support an open-door policy. This brings us to the town hall meeting in Rostock. The event was aimed at young people, and in the audience was a fourteen-year-old Palestinian girl, Reem Sahwil. Sahwil and her family had resided in Germany for the previous five years after migrating from a refugee camp in Lebanon. Because her parents were prohibited from working, the family had to survive on a government subsidy and live in an apartment owned by the government. Germany had denied her family's application for asylum — as had Sweden, years earlier — but the family had appealed to the German government for further consideration (Coburn 2015).

Sahwil was invited to the town hall meeting, which was hosted at a local school, and she attended without any plans to ask a question. However, she found herself compelled to share her family's story after hearing Merkel speak. Sahwil went on to the chancellor, "I don't know what my future looks like, as long as I don't know if I can stay" and later concluded by saying, "I also have goals, like other people. I'd like to go to college. That is really a wish, a goal I'd like to achieve. It's not so nice, watching how other people can make the most of their lives when one isn't able to make the most of one's own, along with them." Once Sahwil finished, Merkel responded, "I understand. It's sometimes hard, politics. You stand here in front of me. You are an incredibly appealing person." She elaborated, "You know that there are thousands and thousands of more refugees in the camps in Lebanon. We can't just say, 'You can all come. And all of you in Africa can come.' We can't manage that." Shortly after these words, Sahwil began to cry (Sorkin 2015).

The story of Reem Sahwil shows us how public policy, and the politics surrounding it, can be depressing. For Sahwil, Merkel's handling of the migrant crisis wasn't just about the fulfillment of political preferences. Whether the German government took a pro- or anti-immigration position mattered because the policies that ensued would drastically shape the lives of Sahwil and her family. Would they be granted asylum? Would they continue to live in Germany? Would her parents find meaningful work? Would Sahwil one day attend college? Would she ever fulfill her dream of becoming an interpreter for refugee communities in Germany? Or would they be deported? Sahwil had felt hopeful but worried when she arrived at the town hall — knowing the answer to these questions could be yes but uncertain that they would be. Her anxious optimism was quickly dashed by Merkel's response and replaced by a sense of despair as she lost hope in her dreams.

We know that stressors, such as being evicted, unemployed, or rejected from college, can be depressing, and we also know that public policy can systematically shape the distribution of these same stressors. In this chapter, I connect these two streams of knowledge by examining public policy as a source of depression. I argue that politics is often depressing *because* it produces policies that lead to an irrevocable loss of a personal object, such as health, wealth, family, home, possession, social status, or rights. We just saw this play out in the case of Reem Sahwil. Next, I present case studies relating to same-sex marriage, abortion, redistribution, and climate change that explore different ways public policy can leave us feeling depressed.

## Is LGBTQ Policy Depressing? The Case of *Obergefell v. Hodges*

Around the world, LGBTQ persons have some of the highest rates of depression, suicide attempts, and suicide. In the United States, the Census Bureau found that about 50 percent of LGBTQ persons between the ages of eighteen and twenty-nine exhibited symptoms of depression compared to 29 percent of non-LGBTQ persons of a similar age (2022). This gap diminishes with age but persists even among the oldest Americans. Among those over sixty-five, about 16 percent of LGBTQ persons had symptoms of depression compared to 11 percent of non-LGBTQ persons. In 2008, a meta-analysis of over twenty-five studies concluded that LGB adolescents and adults were twice as likely to report a suicide attempt in the past year compared to non-LGB persons (King et al. 2008). Other research replicates this pattern using more recent data (Moagi et al. 2021) and finds that rates of suicide are even higher among transgender persons (Berona et al. 2021).

Explanations for these statistics typically focus on the stigmatization, discrimination, bullying, and harassment that LGBTQ persons face in their homes, schools, workplaces, places of worship, and society more generally. In a review of the literature, a team of scholars concluded, "Over the past decade, consensus has grown among researchers that at least part of the explanation for the elevated rates of suicide attempts and mental disorders found in LGB people is the social stigma, prejudice and discrimination associated with minority sexual orientation" (Haas et al. 2010, 22). The depressing consequences of LGBTQ politics and policy have also received some attention. As the authors of the same review article noted in their conclusion, "Among the most salient findings to emerge from recent research are those linking public policies that discriminate against sexual minorities to elevated rates of mental disorders in LGB people" (Haas et al. 2010, 39).

One of the groundbreaking studies on LGBTQ policy and depression came from psychologist Glenda Russell. In her book *Voted Out: The Psychological Consequences of Anti-Gay Politics*, she dissected the impact of Colorado's Amendment 2, which passed in 1992 and more or less legalized discrimination against LBGTQ persons in the state (2000). The entirety of the amendment read, "Neither the State of Colorado, through any of its branches or departments, nor any of its agencies, political subdivisions, municipalities or school districts, shall enact, adopt or enforce any statute, regulation, ordinance or policy whereby homosexual, lesbian, or bisexual orientation, conduct, practices, or relationships shall constitute or otherwise be the basis of, or entitle any person or class of persons to have or claim any minority status, quota preferences, protected status or claim of discrimination. This section of the Constitution shall be in all respects self-executing" (Russell 2000, 2). Simply put, the amendment prohibited the Colorado government from adopting antidiscrimination policies for LGBTQ persons. Colorado was not alone in pursuing such an amendment; dozens of other states and localities were voting on ballot measures that limited LGBTQ rights at the time.

Through in-depth interviews and surveys, Russell found that LGBTQ persons in Colorado experienced a range of negative emotions, including fear and anger, but also feelings of depression. As one survey respondent wrote, "The biggest reaction I had was an overwhelming sense of dread and sadness. I just kept thinking, wherever I go, the majority of people hate me, even though they don't know me. The majority of people I run into today hate me, are scared of me. I almost couldn't leave my house, the feeling was so strong" (Russell 2000, 60). Perhaps more concerning, symptoms of major depressive disorder, generalized anxiety disorder, and posttraumatic stress disorder increased significantly in the wake of the bill's passage. By Russell's estimates, diagnosable cases of these disorders increased tenfold.

A decade later, psychologist Mark Hatzenbuehler and his colleagues published two studies highlighting the deleterious impact of anti-LGBTQ policies in the United States. One study from 2009 found that LGBTQ adults in states without protections against hate crime or employment discrimination had higher rates of mood disorders compared to their counterparts in protected states, a pattern that was not replicated among non-LGBTQ persons (Hatzenbuehler et al. 2009). A follow-up study of state constitutional bans on same-sex marriage found a similar pattern (Hatzenbuehler et al. 2010). A decade after Hatzenbuehler's studies, a different team of researchers found that mental well-being was better among LGBTQ persons living in states with more inclusive policies, such as hate crimes laws, gender-affirming transgender health coverage in Medicaid, or LGBTQ-inclusive adoption programs (White et al. 2023). Clearly, anti-LGBTQ policies contribute to the higher rates of depression, suicide attempts, and suicide among LGBTQ persons.

However, the political and policy landscape has changed dramatically over the past few decades. Although anti-LGBTQ policies are still pervasive around the world, many countries now recognize same-sex marriages, permit military service, and ban discrimination in employment, housing, public accommodations, and credit and lending. Do these policies reduce depression in the same way anti-LGBTQ policies increase it? I offer a preliminary answer to this question by examining the case of same-sex marriage in the United States. On June 26, 2015, the Supreme Court ruled in *Obergefell v. Hodges* that same-sex marriage was a constitutional right. The ruling invalidated the state-level bans that Hatzenbuehler and colleagues found to be depressing. This decision improved life satisfaction and happiness among LGBTQ persons (Flores et al. 2020), but did it also reduce depression?

I use the Behavioral Risk Factor Surveillance Survey (BRFSS) from the United States Center for Disease Control to answer this question. The BRFSS is an annual survey of hundreds of thousands of Americans and includes dozens of interviews every day throughout the year. One question asks respondents, "Now thinking about your mental health, which includes stress, depression, and problems with emotions, for how many days during the past 30 days was your mental health not good?" I classify respondents into two groups: those who report no depressed days and those who report at least one depressed day. I compare LGBTQ persons interviewed *before* the ruling in 2015 (January–June) to LGBTQ persons interviewed *after* the ruling in 2015 (July–December). Did the proportion of LGBTQ persons reporting at least one depressed day go down after the *Obergefell* ruling? I then split this comparison based on whether respondents lived in a state where same-sex marriage was already legal or a state where it was illegal until the *Obergefell* ruling. Did

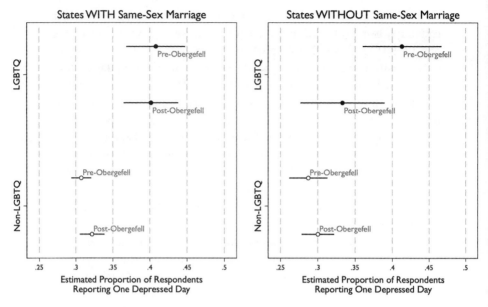

FIGURE 7.1. The Impact of the SCOTUS *Obergefell* Ruling
*Note:* The results are based on a logistic regression of depression on three binary variables—LGBTQ status, post–June 28 interview, change to state-level same-sex marriage policy—and their interactions. The model includes state-clustered standard errors and control variables for gender, race, age, education, and income. More information about the analyses can be found in the appendix.

the SCOTUS decision have a bigger impact on LGBTQ persons who were afforded new rights? Finally, I also include the same comparisons among non-LGBTQ persons to verify that the patterns were unique to LGBTQ persons.

Figure 7.1 shows the results of my analysis. In states where same-sex marriage was previously legal, the *Obergefell* ruling did not meaningfully change the proportion of LGBTQ persons reporting at least one depressed day in the prior month. However, in states where same-sex marriage was not previously legal, the *Obergefell* ruling lead to a substantial and statistically significant decrease. Before *Obergefell*, about 43 percent of LGBTQ persons in states without legal same-sex marriage reported at least one depressed day in the prior month on average, but this decreased to 33 percent in the six months following the ruling. Among non-LGBTQ persons, depressed days statistically significantly increased following the ruling regardless of the state's prior same-sex marriage policy, but the magnitude of this change is trivial, and additional analyses (included in the appendix) show that this effect is a yearly calendar pattern rather than a response to *Obergefell*.

There is growing evidence that anti-LGBTQ policies produce depression and pro-LGBTQ policies alleviate it, but a number of theoretical and empirical questions remain. The focus so far has been on rights, but these policies and the politics surrounding them often involve more than the loss or gain of rights. The context in which restrictive policies are passed is often filled with anti-LGBTQ rhetoric. For instance, in her study of Colorado's Amendment 2, Russell found that the proamendment campaign distributed materials that depicted LGBTQ persons as inherently immoral. She described this rhetoric as conceptually "liquidating" the existence of LGBTQ persons—what we might think of as a loss of dignity, humanity, and belonging. This rhetoric would have been harmful even if the amendment had failed and no rights had been lost. As one survey respondent testified, "I am so tired of all the negative stories, editorials, and television blurbs about gays and lesbians. It seems as if I am constantly bombarded everywhere I turn with 'how sick, immoral, and dangerous' gays and lesbians are. I'm worn down and tired. I've quit watching any television programs about gays and lesbians because I end up angry and depressed (same with newspaper and magazines)" (Russell 2000, 61).

Like rhetoric, public opinion is also important. The passage and persistence of policies, especially ballot initiatives, depends on public support. Everyone has some sense of the political views of their community and society, and these views can be psychologically damaging when they are—or are believed to be—antithetical to our identity. As with rhetoric, negative public opinion by itself doesn't cause the loss of rights but can bring about a loss of something less tangible. We might lose a sense of dignity, humanity, or belonging when society rejects our inclusion in public spaces or views us as less deserving of rights and liberties.

Although the past decade has seen substantial improvements in the rights and protections afforded LGBTQ persons, anti-LGBTQ politics and policies persist in many parts of the United States. Millions of LGBTQ persons still lack antidiscrimination protections at the state and local level, and LGBTQ issues have emerged as a key part of the culture wars in recent years with some states and localities attempting to restrict drag performances, ban LGBTQ literature in schools, prohibit transgender people using public restrooms that align with their gender, and more. Outside of the United States and western Europe, LGBTQ persons often face a much grimmer political context. To date, thirty-two countries have banned same-sex relations, and four of them have done so with the possibility of capital punishment for serial offenders. This diverse and shifting political landscape underscores the need for research to tease apart how policy, rhetoric, and public opinion independently and interactively depress LGBTQ persons.

## Is Abortion Policy Depressing? The Case of *Dobbs v. Jackson*

"The Supreme Court overturned Roe v. Wade and took away a woman's right to make decisions about her own body." This was one of several comments about abortion made by respondents in the autobiographical recall experiment I conducted. As you may recall, respondents were asked to remember and describe a time they felt X emotion (anger, anxiety, fear, or depression) in Y domain (personal life, politics), where the emotion and domain were randomly assigned. As I combed through the open-ended responses, I was struck by how often the issue of abortion came up in the depression/politics condition. It didn't take me long to realize that the survey was fielded shortly after the Supreme Court overturned the precedent set by *Roe v. Wade* in their *Dobbs v. Jackson* decision. The topic was clearly fresh on the minds of many Americans, even a few months later.

The timing of the survey with the Supreme Court decision was unintentional, but the coincidence prompted me to consider whether abortion policy could be depressing. Although I had an inclination that depression may be a relevant emotion, I knew this issue was typically associated with anger, anxiety, and fear. As political scientist Courtney Blackington concluded in her recent analysis of pro-choice activists in Poland,

> Anger and fear operate as important emotions for people who protest in support of abortion rights in Poland.... Anger at policies that individuals perceive to be unjust plays an essential role in helping to encourage people to begin protesting. These perceptions of injustice seem to provide a catalysing impulse. Moreover, as activists continue to feel anger, they keep going to the streets to vent their anger. Similarly, the fear that respondents feel can drive them to protest in support of abortion rights. A fear for their futures, for their lives, or for the lives and futures of close friends or family motivates some individuals to take to the streets and to continue protesting in the long-term (2024, 13–14).

Polling about the *Dobbs* decision confirms that Americans had diverse emotional responses to it, including anger, fear, and even depression. After the decision leaked, a poll by the Kaiser Family Foundation asked which emotions Americans might feel were *Roe* to eventually be overturned. About 53 percent said they would feel sad, 47 percent angry, 34 percent hopeful, 27 percent indifferent, and 22 percent enthusiastic. After the *Dobbs* decision was officially released, the *Boston Globe* asked residents of Massachusetts to give them a word or phrase about how they felt. About 16 percent said angry and mad, while another 16 percent said depressed, sad, unhappy, upset, or disappointed.

My autobiographical recall experiment reflected similar emotional diversity. Many respondents in the anger, anxiety, and fear conditions wrote about the *Dobbs* decision too. A respondent in the anger condition wrote, "Abortion rights being taken away. Roe v. Wade. It's unfair for the government to control women's bodies." This response highlights one of the quintessential elements of anger: a sense of unfairness. A respondent in the anxiety condition wrote, "I felt anxious about women's rights. I felt anxious because I wasn't sure how it would affect the future." Uncertainty about the future and whether something bad will happen, as this respondent seems to be expressing, is a hallmark of anxiety. In the fear condition, one respondent wrote, "Roe v. Wade being overturned because it was such a break from precedent and endangers the lives of so many people." Here the emphasis is on physical safety, which is a core component of fear.

These responses underscore the importance of *appraisal*. Respondents were thinking about the same political outcome—the Supreme Court decision that overturned *Roe*—but in very different ways. Viewing the decision through the prism of injustice led to anger. Viewing it through the prism of the future led to anxiety. Viewing it through the prism of physical danger led to fear. How we feel depends on how we think. The *Dobbs* decision is therefore a useful case for exploring the appraisal process and feelings of depression in the domain of abortion politics. Depression is a response to irrevocable loss, but what was irrevocably lost when the Supreme Court overturned *Roe*?

I use the dissenting opinion in *Dobbs* to analyze the concept of irrevocable loss among the pro-choice movement. Signed by Justices Stephen Breyer, Elena Kagan, and Sonia Sotomayor, the dissent concluded, "With sorrow—for this Court, but more, for many millions of American women who have today lost a fundamental constitutional protection— we dissent." Here, the justices signal that depression is their dominant emotion at seeing *Roe* overturned. The text of their dissent can therefore help us unearth the meaning of irrevocable loss and understand why so many Americans felt depressed in the wake of the *Dobbs* decision.

The court case turned on whether the Constitution of the United States includes a right to an abortion. Given this focus, it's not surprising that a loss of rights for women was explicitly highlighted in the concluding sentence of the dissent ("American women . . . lost a fundamental constitutional protection"). Elsewhere, the justices put it this way, "After today, young women will come of age with fewer rights than their mothers and grandmothers had." Women's rights were also mentioned by several respondents in the depression condition of my experiment. One wrote, "Roe v. Wade being overturned. A huge hit on women's rights. A women should always have a right to choose what to do with her own body." This loss of rights was tied up with other intangible losses for women. As the justices note, "When *Roe* and *Casey* disappear, the loss of power, control, and dignity will be immense." This idea was also reflected in the public discourse. For instance, the editorial board of the *New York Times* wrote, "For the first time in history, the Supreme Court has eliminated an established constitutional right involving the most fundamental of human concerns: the dignity and autonomy to decide what happens to your body."

The dissent does not make explicit why the loss of rights—as well as power, control, dignity, and autonomy—is irrevocable, but it hints at this idea. For instance, the phrase, "young women will come of age with fewer rights than their mothers and grandmothers" indicates that the justices anticipate the *Dobbs* decision will last decades. This belief is likely rooted in the justices' knowledge of the Supreme Court and how slowly the composition of the court changes. As the justices note about the fifty-year standing of *Roe*, "The Court reverses course today for one reason and one reason only: because the composition of this Court has changed." Similarly, the *New York Times* editorial board also appraised the decision as irrevocable, concluding their essay by writing, "We will be paying the price for decades to come." Even if the logic of irrevocability is not explicit, irrevocability itself is.

The loss of women's rights may have been the headline, but the dissenting justices also highlighted material loss. They wrote at one point, "A State can force her to bring a pregnancy to term, even at the steepest personal and familial costs." The idea here is that women may suffer losses related to personal preferences—to not have children, to maintain good health, or to save their time, energy, and money from extraordinary efforts (such as traveling to another state) to procure an abortion. In extreme cases, the justices argued that the material consequences of *Dobbs* may even be death for some women. As the justices noted, the history of abortion restriction is "a history of women dying." This concern was also mentioned by respondents in my experiment. One wrote, "When the abortion law was recently overturned. I'm sad because if abortion is completely banned and illegal, then I can foresee many females taking drastic measures to end a pregnancy. Ways that can be fatal to them."

Concerns about the future, such as the material losses women will face after *Dobbs*, are typically associated with emotions like anxiety and fear. However, in the dissenting opinion and in the comments from my respondents in the depression condition, the future is discussed with certainty, as if the losses are a foregone conclusion—women *will* suffer because of this decision. To better see this certainty, consider how a respondent in the anxiety condition talks about the future: "The Roe stuff is quite scary. I don't know how it'll play out. It's a very frightening time for women if you ask me." Here, the future is viewed with much greater uncertainty. Perhaps it will get bad, but perhaps it won't. The certainty with which the future is appraised by respondents in the depression condition makes the material losses seem irrevocable and thus depressing.

The meaning of irrevocable loss has focused so far on either a substantive preference (women's right to an abortion) or a personal preference (material well-being of women), but a third focus is on procedural preferences. In particular, the dissenting justices bemoaned the loss of judicial integrity. They wrote, "To hear the majority tell the tale, *Roe* and *Casey* are aberrations: They came from nowhere, went nowhere—and so are easy to excise from this Nation's constitutional law. That is not true." Later, they noted that by "overruling Roe and Casey, this Court betrays its guiding principles." The lost guiding principle: an adherence to precedent. This loss may have contributed to the sorrow of the dissenting justices, but it was not mentioned by respondents in my experiment and was typically only ever a secondary or tertiary framing of the case in the broader public discourse. For instance, the statement from editorial board of the *New York Times* only turned to this issue after focusing on the loss of women's rights.

For those in the pro-life movement, the *Dobbs* decision was a cause for celebration rather than despair. According to a CBS poll of Americans who approved of the decision, 79 percent felt hopeful and 70 percent felt happy. That said, it is unclear whether the *Roe* decision was depressing to the pro-life movement like the *Dobbs* decision was to the pro-choice movement. Only one respondent in the depression/politics condition of my experiment brought up abortion from a pro-life perspective, commenting that what they found depressing was "abortion rights and the right to kill an innocent baby that isn't born yet."

Depression is an emotion often discussed among the pro-life movement, but the discussion only partially focuses on the role of the Supreme Court. As the pro-life activist Clarissa Moll notes in an essay for *Christianity Today*, "For almost 50 years, pro-life evangelicals have grieved abortion statistics, procedures, and court documents. We've worked behind the scenes to support women choosing life for their unborn babies, and we're more than ready for this grief to end. And while the Supreme Court decision might present the illusion that our sad days are over, abortion will remain an ambiguous loss. Abortions past, present, and future will continue to provoke complex sorrow" (2022). In short, feelings of depression will continue to persist for some in the pro-life movement for as long as abortions occur, as they did legally under *Roe*, illegally under *Dobbs* in states that ban them, or legally under *Dobbs* in states that permit them. This view aligns with testimony from some pro-life activists, who attribute their activism to feelings of grief stemming from their personal decision to terminate a pregnancy (Maxwell 2002). The idea that having an abortion can induce depression, and emotional distress more generally, has become a popular argument against abortion in the pro-life movement (Whitesell 2023). However, there is no systematic evidence of "post abortion syndrome" (Dadlez and Andrew 2009), and even if there were, these feelings of depression do not seem to be dependent on whether *Roe* is or isn't the law of the land. So it remains an open question how much the *politics* of abortion, rather than just abortion itself, are depressing to those on the right.

Although the politics of abortion tend to be associated with emotions like anger and fear, it can evoke feelings of depression. Through a case study of the *Dobbs* decision, I explored what irrevocable loss looks like to supporters of abortion rights. My analysis reveals how the framing of a policy outcome can shape how we appraise and feel about it. Some frames invite appraisals of irrevocable loss, while others do not. Two frames in particular seemed to underpin depression: the long-term loss of rights brought about by the right-leaning composition of the Supreme Court and the certain hardships women will face in the future because of the decision. In contrast, the responses from my experiment suggested that frames about unfairness, uncertainty about the future, or physical insecurity were associated with anger, anxiety, and fear, rather than with depression.

## Is Redistributive Policy Depressing? The Case of the Welfare State

A few years ago, I came across a meme that asked in big bold letters at the top, "Feeling Sad and Depressed?" Beneath this headline was a doctor with a clipboard that read, "Are you anxious? Worried about the future? Feeling isolated and alone?" The punchline: "You might be suffering from CAPITALISM." In small print at the bottom was a list of potential symptoms, including "homelessness, unemployment, poverty, hunger, feelings of powerlessness, fear, apathy, boredom, cultural decay, loss of identity, extreme self-consciousness, loss of free speech, incarceration, suicidal or revolutionary thoughts, death." This meme is more anticapitalist propaganda than serious social science, but it highlights a well-documented phenomenon: the economic roots of depression.

The United States Center for Disease Control estimated that in 2014 about 15 percent of Americans living below the poverty line suffered from major depressive disorder compared to only 6 percent of Americans living at or above the poverty line. Similar "income-gradients" in depression have been observed in other countries and over time (Ridley et al. 2019). This has led scholars to conclude that poverty is one of the biggest risk factors for depression. Randomized control trials of antipoverty programs provide the strongest causal evidence for this conclusion. Meta-analyses show that antipoverty programs, such as cash transfers, training programs, savings incentives, access to healthcare, or other types of benefits, substantially reduce poverty and lower depression (Ridley et al. 2019).

Income inequality has also been linked to depression, especially among the poor. In one meta-analysis, a team of medical and public health scholars concluded that there is "greater risk of depression in populations with higher income inequality relative to populations with lower inequality" (Patel 2018, 76). Although the magnitude of this effect is small, the authors point out that its implications for population mental health are substantial. The fact that income inequality increases depression among the poor while antipoverty programs decrease it among recipients has led some scholars to call for a more robust welfare state, arguing for "a universal basic income, universal healthcare coverage, universal higher education access, progressive taxation, and mandated equity in compensation for women and ethnic minority groups" (Patel et al. 2018, 85).

The call for a robust welfare state to counter the depressing effects of poverty and income inequality makes sense at first glance. Income inequality and poverty are depressing, so redistributive polices that take from the rich and give to the poor could, in theory, knock out two birds with one stone. But I see a few issues with the underlying evidence; these need to be addressed before we can be confident in the claim that mitigating inequality would decrease depression. The first issue is that the role of government is rarely directly analyzed in studies of income inequality. Income inequality is typically measured as *market* income inequality (before taxes and transfers) rather than *disposable* income inequality (after taxes and transfers), so it's an open question whether government interventions like the ones proposed would work as intended. Redistributive policies may have hidden consequences that negate the benefits of reducing income inequality, reducing inequality through market mechanisms or civil society might be better. A similar problem arises in studies of antipoverty programs. A typical study analyzes *one* program at a time and focuses their assessment exclusively on *program recipients*. These studies cannot make reliable conclusions about who should administer these programs, whether rolling out several programs simultaneously and to a wider set of recipients would yield the same results, or how the general public might respond.

The second issue concerns the role of politics. In the process of studying how redistribution adds to the pocketbooks of program recipients, the *preferences* of citizens have been overlooked. Some people ideologically support these policies, while others oppose them. What happens when these preferences clash with material interests? What is redistribution's impact when someone gains financially but loses ideologically, or vice versa? To be clear, these questions should not be seen as implying equivalency between ideological loss and poverty. Poverty is arguably the single most important risk factor for depression, and it seems unlikely that ideological loss would matter as much or more. Rather, I think that ideological loss likely undercuts but does not erase the rewards of government benefits, while ideological gain soothes the financial pain of government taxes.

To summarize, an abundance of evidence shows that antipoverty programs reduce depression, and income inequality increases it, but questions remain about the role of government and the politics of redistribution. Does a strong welfare state reduce depression in general, and is the impact of redistribution affected by the substantive preferences of citizens? I offer some preliminary answers to these questions through an analysis of the European Social Survey. The European Social Survey (ESS) is a biennial study of tens of thousands of citizens across twenty-five-plus countries in Europe as well as Israel. Importantly, in 2006 and 2012, the ESS asked questions about depression: whether a respondent felt depressed, felt that everything was an effort, had restless sleep, felt happy, felt lonely, enjoyed life, and felt sad. With the responses to these questions, I can examine how levels of redistribution in a country affect depression, especially for people with different ideologies and incomes.[1]

Redistribution refers to "the difference between market income inequality and disposable income inequality, expressed as a percentage of market income" (OECD 2016, 3). Market means *before* taxes and transfers, while disposable means *after* taxes and transfers. The standardized difference between the two indicates how much a country taxes some citizens and transfers that money to others. The Standardized World Income Inequality Database contains measures of both market and disposable income inequality from 1960 onward (Solt 2020), so I merge this data with the ESS data for my analysis.

I begin by plotting in figure 7.2 the average level of depression in each country in 2012 across levels of income inequality (on the left) and redistribution (on the right). The lines of best fit indicate that income inequality is associated with more depression among the general public while redistribution is associated with less. An analysis at the individual level reproduces these patterns. The regression model predicts that depression will be 1.10, which is the equivalent to reporting "some of the time" to all the depression questions, when redistribution is at its lowest. Depression is cut in half when redistribution is at its highest—specifically, depression is estimated to be 0.55, which is equivalent to reporting "some of the time" to half of the depression question and "none or almost none of the time" to the other half. These analyses do not allow me to make strong causal claims, but they do show a strong association between income inequality and depression that endures even after accounting for potential confounding factors. By examining how overall redistribution in a country affects depression in the general public, these results build on studies that focus exclusively on recipients of antipoverty programs or income inequality before taxes and transfers.

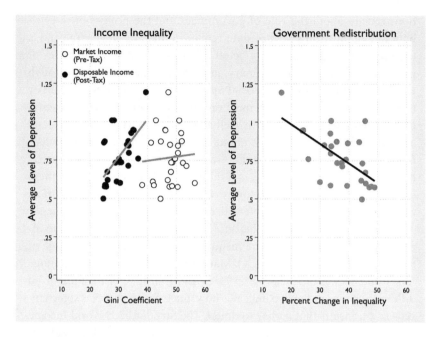

FIGURE 7.2. The Association between Inequality, Redistribution, and Depression in European Countries
*Note:* The results are based on an ordinary least squares regression of the average depression in a country on the country's level of market income inequality, disposable income inequality, or government redistribution. More information about the analyses can be found in the appendix.

Next, consider what happens when ideological preferences clash with material interests. In theory, the preferences and material interests of rich conservatives and poor liberals stand in direct opposition. Rich conservatives benefit both ideologically and financially from *less* redistribution, while poor liberals benefit ideologically and financially from *more*. Redistribution should therefore reduce depression least for rich conservatives and most for poor liberals. On the other hand, preferences and material interests do not align for poor conservatives and rich liberals. Poor conservatives ideologically prefer less redistribution but financially benefit from more of it, while the opposite is true for rich liberals. For these groups, redistribution should somewhat reduce depression—more than it does for rich conservatives, but less than it does for poor liberals.

The results of my analysis are reported in figure 7.3, which shows the effect of redistribution on depression at different combinations of ideology and income. On the whole, redistribution is consistently associated with *less* depression—its impact is negative across all values of ideology and income and statistically significant in all cases except for the poorest and most liberal respondents as well as the richest and most conservative respondents. Put another way, no group is made more depressed by redistribution. Turning to the dynamics of ideology and income, the results are somewhat expected. For people on the far right—as seen in the top right panel of figure 7.3—the negative effect of redistribution diminishes as income increases. This is consistent with my expectation. However, the opposite is true for the far left—as seen in the top left panel—which is

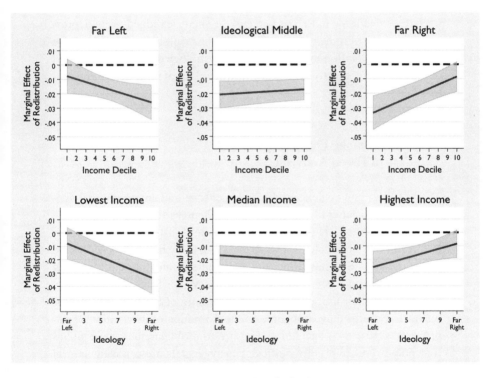

FIGURE 7.3. The Impact of Ideology, Income, and Redistribution
*Note*: The results are based on an ordinary least squares regression of depression on redistribution, ideology, income, and their interactions. The model includes survey weights, year fixed effects, country fixed effects, and country-clustered standard errors. It also includes individual-level controls for gender, age, education, marital status, unemployment status, and general health status. The country-level controls are population size, civil liberties, political freedom, GDP per capita, and long-term unemployment. More information about the analyses can be found in the appendix.

inconsistent with my expectation. I had thought that poor liberals who benefit both ideologically and financially from redistribution would see a greater decrease in depression than rich liberals, who benefit only ideologically, but in fact the opposite is true. These patterns are also reflected in the bottom panels, which show the marginal effect of redistribution across values of ideology for respondents at the lowest, median, and highest incomes.

All together these results show that redistribution can be a force for good when it comes to depression, but that its impact might vary by ideology and income in unexpected ways. I expected and found that rich conservatives benefit less than poor conservatives and rich liberals. However, I also found that the poorest and most liberal respondents, whom I expected to benefit the most, saw some of the smallest reductions in depression as a result of redistribution. This puzzling result indicates that a more granular investigation into the political psychology of redistribution and depression is needed to understand how ideological preferences and material interests interact.

## Is Climate Change Policy Depressing? The Case of Failed Activism

There is emerging evidence that climate change and environmental degradation more generally are depressing. Changes to the planet expose humans to continually more extreme natural disasters, weather irregularities, and other problems. The stress wrought by these changes can be traumatic and adversely affect our physical and mental health. As scientists Matilda van den Bosch and Andreas Meyer-Lindenberg recently concluded in their literature review, "A plethora of biophysical environmental exposures may contribute to the formation or prevention of depression" (2019, 252), including exposure to problems such as air pollution, polycarbonate plastics, pesticides, heavy metals, noise, pollen, natural disasters, and electromagnetic fields.

If exposure is one side of the coin, connection to nature is the other. In his book *Lost Connections*, journalist Johann Hari argues that interacting with nature is a crucial source of happiness. He writes, "Becoming depressed or anxious is a process of becoming a prisoner of your ego, where no air from the outside can get in. But a range of scientists have shown that a common reaction to being out in the natural world is the precise opposite of this sensation—a feeling of awe. Faced with a natural landscape, you have a sense that you and your concerns are very small, and the world is very big—and that sensation can shrink the ego down to a manageable size" (2018, 129). In other words, nature helps us manage the stress of everyday life, thereby improving our mental well-being. Scientific evidence bears out this idea. One team of scientists found that asking people to interact with nature in simple ways, such as taking a walk in the woods or through a park, substantially boosted their mood (Schertz et al. 2018). When humans are disconnected from nature, such as in heavily urbanized parts of the world with limited greenspace, depression is more pervasive.

While the problem may be clear—exposure to environmental degradation and disconnection from nature are depressing—any possible solutions are complex. Trade-offs and the challenges of collective action complicate the narrative. Some environmental changes that cause depression offer benefits that may simultaneously counteract other sources of depression. Pesticides, for example, may be bad for our physical and mental health but also improve agricultural yields and help combat poverty and famine. The environment is also vulnerable to overuse; if everyone started taking a walk in the woods to improve their mental well-being, crowds may decrease the needed sense of wonder, or in theory some wooded areas may fall victim to the tragedy of the commons, leaving everyone worse off in the long run. This is one way politics enters the story. How trade-offs are resolved and how commons are managed determine who is exposed to environmental degradation and who is disconnected from nature, with ramifications for depression.

Beyond exposure and disconnect, mere awareness of climate change and environmental degradation can be depressing. As the psychologists Susan Clayton and Bryan Karazsia note, "A growing number of media reports, however, as well as some scientific papers ... describe negative emotional consequences associated simply with perceptions of climate change: that is, people's awareness of the problem that is not linked to specific personal experiences" (2020, 1). The philosopher Glenn Albrecht coined the term "solastalgia" to describe this phenomenon—the psychological distress we feel in the face of a changing environment (Albrecht et al. 2007)—although a multitude of terms are employed in the literature, almost all of which involve some pairing of climate, environmental, or eco- with depression, grief, or melancholia (e.g., environmental melancholia).

The planet is losing biodiversity, green spaces, clean air, regular weather patterns, and more because of climate change, pollution, overfishing, deforestation, and other man-made problems. However, whether awareness of these problems leads to depression or some other emotion will depend on how we appraise them. To begin with, many people deny that climate change is real. A survey conducted by George Mason University in April 2022 found that only 72 percent of Americans reported believing that global warming was occurring. The other 28 percent were either uncertain or said it was not happening. However, even among those who are aware, not everyone views climate change as a problem. A survey conducted by Yale University in 2021 found that 34 percent of Americans were not worried about climate change. If the environment is not something of value, then its degradation will not register as a meaningful loss.

For those who are aware of and concerned about climate change, which negative emotions are evoked will depend on how they appraise the problem. We will feel anxiety if we appraise climate change as an ongoing problem that may get worse if action to combat it isn't taken. This anxiety can spur action by signaling to us that there is still an opportunity to secure the environment's future. Indeed, one study of citizens across thirty-two countries found that climate anxiety was "positively related to private-sphere pro-environmental behaviours, including actions like saving energy at home, using public transportation, and avoiding food waste" and "also positively predicted participation in climate protests" (Ogunbode et al. 2022).

In contrast, we will feel depressed if we appraise climate change as an irrevocable loss. Many changes to the environment are arguably irrevocable on the time scale of a human life. Forests can regrow, oceans can repopulate, and technologies may eventually cool the planet and revive extinct species, but these slow processes are unlikely to come to fruition any time soon, if at all. Given these prospects, it should not be surprising that many Americans feel depressed about changes to the environment. In a survey jointly conducted by George Mason University and Yale University in 2010, about 22 percent of Americans reported feeling moderately or very depressed about global warming, while about 45 percent said they felt moderately or very sad. Follow-up surveys in 2013 and 2020 revealed the consistency of these results, with about 24 percent of Americans being moderately or very depressed.

Climate anxiety and climate depression can be felt simultaneously if existing losses are appraised as irrevocable while new losses are anticipated if action is not taken. The term "climate distress" is often used to describe the mixture of feelings people have when thinking about the issue. Young people are especially prone to this distress, and their feelings are amplified by the view that governments around the world are not doing enough to combat the destruction of the planet. As one study in *Lancet Planet Health* recently concluded, "Distress appears to be greater when young people believe that government response is inadequate, which leads us to argue that the failure of governments to adequately reduce, prevent, or mitigate climate change is contributing to psychological distress, moral injury, and injustice" (Hickman et al. 2021, e870-e871). The distress felt by young people seems to be driven by their sense of powerlessness to get governments to act. The climate activist Greta Thunberg made this point in a speech at the World Economic Forum saying, "Adults keep saying: 'We owe it to the young people to give them hope.' But I don't want your hope. I don't want you to be hopeful. I want you to panic. I want you to feel the fear I feel every day. And then I want you to act. I want you to act as you would in a crisis. I want you to act as if the house is on fire. Because it is." The subtext of her statement is that leaders are the ones who have the power to act, but these positions are only ever occupied by adults, and rarely by young adults. The people whose futures are most affected are in the weakest position to act.

In recent years, there has been a growing interest in the behavioral consequences of depression, anxiety, and anger around climate change and environmental degradation. How do these feelings shape our behaviors around the environment, both individually (e.g., recycling) and collectively (e.g., contacting an elected official)? In other words, how do we *cope* with solastalgia? The pattern that seems to be emerging is consistent with what we might expect: depression seems to dampen environmental action, anger seems to spur it, and anxiety has a mixed impact (Stanley et al. 2021; Clayton and Karazsia 2020; Landry et al. 2018). This pattern points to a challenge for the environmental movement—how do you motivate green behavior when reminding people of these problems leaves them feeling depressed?

Exposure, awareness, and perceived government inaction represent how climate change can be depressing. Growing qualitative evidence suggests *failed activism* can be depressing, too. In 2021, National Public Radio reported on the suicide of climate activist Kevin Aaron. Aaron got involved in the environmental movement as a teenager after seeing the degradation caused by mass meat production in his home state of Kansas. Following college, he enrolled in graduate and law school in the Bay Area with the hopes of eventually working as a climate advocate. He was never able to live out this dream, however, because he died by suicide at the age of twenty-seven. According to Aaron's loved ones, his despair was driven at least in part by the sense that fighting climate change is a Sisyphean task. As NPR notes, "It was a feeling of doubt that his efforts—that all the combined environmental struggles—just wouldn't be enough. It added to the depression he was already struggling with" (2021). Following his death, Aaron's mom founded the organization The Resilient Activist to provide climate activists with the training and resources needed to effectively cope with the challenges her son faced.

Activism is a double-edged sword—some activism may mitigate feelings of depression, but too much activism may amplify them. One study of college students found that engaging in collective action helped mitigate feelings of depression by providing students with a sense of agency, hope, and belonging (Schwartz et al. 2022). Other activists have made this point as well. As the climate scientist Peter Kalmus wrote recently in the *Guardian*, "Therapy can help people struggling with climate anxiety and depression; but since climate emotions are driven by real, intensifying, physical processes on Earth, therapy only treats the symptom. Something that helps me is being part of a vibrant community of activists. I could not handle the weight of this knowledge if I had to do so alone." Thunberg echoed this view in a recent interview: "When I'm taking action, I don't feel like I am helpless and that things are hopeless, because then I feel like I'm doing everything I can" (Earth.org 2021).

At the same time, depression is a well-documented problem in the world of activism (Gorski 2019). The status quo bias of politics means that activists often face persistent political defeats in the pursuit of change. These defeats can leave activists feeling hopeless and as though they wasted immense amounts of time and energy. As the climate activist Yessenia Funes explained to *Atmos*, "Talk to anyone who works on climate change—whether they're an activist, a scientist, or a writer—and you'll hear the same thing. They're tired. They're tired of the inadequate climate policy, sure, but they're also tired of how they're treated.... You work crazy hours for a nonprofit that doesn't pay you enough to live comfortably. You pour your soul into an agency that, quite frankly, doesn't value you. Then, after all that, leaders in Congress fail to pass the sort of policy you've been breaking your back over" (2022). The website of The Resilient Activist puts it this way: "Those working to shift businesses and governments to sustainable processes can encounter naysayers who tell them that companies leading the sustainability frontier often end up losing. Often, projects are funded and defunded at the whim of whomever is in office or a position of responsibility. Many activists experience symptoms of deep grief in relation to these obstacles." One study of Norwegian climate activists provides more systematic evidence of this pattern (Marczak et al. 2023). Activists reported that a "loss of species, landscapes, ways of life, opportunities in the future" could lead to "sadness, grief, deep sorrow, emotional pain, sense of loss, despair, fear, shame" and that "being trapped in the political-economic system that is harmful for the natural environment" could lead to a range of feelings, including "frustration, guilt, anger, isolation, powerlessness" (5).

There is now growing attention to how activists can effectively cope with the disappointment of failure *before* it turns into full-blown depression and burnout. In interviews with environmental activists, sociologist Daniel Driscoll identified a range of coping strategies used to avert depression. For instance, he documents how "personalized mind-sets and orientations help activists persist. By focusing attention on their own small actions or behaviors, ignoring setbacks, and seeing the long-term trajectory of the environmental movement, they are able to stave off depression and burnout" (2020, 200). This appraisal-focused coping strategy works because it helps avoid thinking about loss as *irrevocable*, the hallmark of depression. As Driscoll goes on to note, "Activists are also, in a theoretical sense, strategically shifting their 'temporal horizons' . . . thinking short-term, to highlight small victories, but also long-term, to discount setbacks and frustrations" (2020, 200).

It is clear that climate change is depressing, but also that politics, especially "failed" activism, is an essential part of why this is so. Although the focus has been on climate change activism, burnout has been documented in areas such as social justice (Gorski 2019), human rights (Chen and Gorski 2015), and animal rights (Gorski et al. 2018). When efforts to enact change fail, as is often the case in politics, the sense of power that once motivated action now seems irrevocably lost. This can lead to depression and ultimately burnout, a pattern that is analogous to the learned helplessness felt by the trapped dogs in Martin Seligman's famous experiments. More investigation remains to be done, especially relating to understanding the challenges depression presents to collective action on the environment and the potential feedback loop it creates.

## What's Next?

This chapter has revealed how public policy, and the politics around it, can be a source of depression. The depressing consequences of politics aren't limited to elections and partisan conflict with family and friends but can also be felt through the policies produced by official political processes. We saw this with environmental activists responding to government inaction on climate change, pro-choice women responding to the Supreme Court decision in *Dobbs*, LGBTQ persons responding to same-sex marriage and antidiscrimination policies, and the general public responding to redistribution.

However, these cases do more than simply affirm that public policy can be depressing. They also illuminate different ways this process unfolds and how much more there is to learn. The Supreme Court rulings in *Obergefell* and *Dobbs* together provide evidence that the creation of rights can reduce depression, while the removal of rights can produce it. The case study on LGBTQ policy further highlighted the challenges in disentangling the impact of policy, rhetoric, and public opinion, while the case study on abortion policy demonstrated how irrevocable loss can take on meaning in the wake of political change. The case study of redistribution explored what happens when ideological preferences and material interests come into conflict. The case study of environmental politics spotlighted how repeated failures to enact change can be depressing.

By homing in on different aspects of the stress-appraisal-coping framework, these case studies generated new insights into the political production of loss, irrevocability, depression, and withdrawal. These studies are just the tip of the iceberg, however. Much more research is required before we can fully understand how politics and public policy are depressing and with what consequences. So what's next? This is the question I take up in the next and final chapter of this book.

CHAPTER EIGHT

# Democracy without Disruption

As a child, I strongly opposed capital punishment. I was disturbed by the idea that the death penalty deprived people of the opportunity to redeem themselves from whatever horrible crime they committed. Instead, I believed that capital punishment should be replaced with lifetime jail sentences. My passion for this issue led me to read books, watch movies, follow the news, and talk about it with whoever would listen. Most often this was my mother, given that my grade-school friends didn't seem to share my interest in the issue. Importantly, my passion also made me emotional. I recall crying whenever I read stories about people who had been executed by the state. In hindsight, I see now that I was grieving the irrevocable loss of life that came about because of the politics and policy of capital punishment. My views on the issue have evolved, and I no longer cry whenever I hear about it in the news, but looking back I'm struck by how little political scientists have to say about my experience and the depression I felt over this issue.

Emotions have long been a subject in the study of politics, dating back as far back as Aristotle's notion of *pathos*, but they've had a renaissance in political science over the past few decades. As the political scientists W. Russell Neuman, George Marcus, Ann Crigler, and Michael MacKuen write in the first sentences of *The Affect Effect*, "This book responds to a resurgent interest in the way emotion interacts with thinking about politics and, as a result, the way citizens engage in or withdraw from political activity. We have come to conclude that there is indeed an *affect effect*, actually, numerous, diverse, and significant effects" (2007, 1). Their volume was groundbreaking and to date remains the most comprehensive assessment of political emotions. Yet, while it gives considerable attention to anger, anxiety, fear, enthusiasm, and hope, it rarely mentions disappointment, sadness, and depression. In fact, disappointment and sadness do not appear in the index, and depression is listed only as a clinical disorder. I don't highlight these omissions to criticize the book—indeed, my work is only possible because of what these scholars have accomplished—but rather to reiterate just how invisible depression is in politics. Depression is such a private emotion that it has been overlooked by even the experts.

Just as depression has been overlooked in politics, politics has been overlooked in the study of depression. We've learned a considerable amount about the origins of depression over the past century, whether as an emotion or clinical disorder. The psychological sciences have illuminated the role of genes, neurobiology, cognition, and gender; sociology has focused on stress, discrimination, poverty, and broader cultural forces; and the health sciences have pointed to therapy, antidepressants, and other aspects of the healthcare system, to name just a few of the causes of depression. Politics lurks in the background of these explanations—clearly it matters to gender, discrimination, poverty, employment, and healthcare—but rarely is it in the foreground. It almost feels like we can glimpse the outline of politics in the distance if we squint, but never with the clarity needed to make out its features.

In fact, many people have been squinting in recent years. There seems to be a growing recognition that politics is a source of depression. Michelle Goldberg of the *New York Times* has been a proponent of this view, writing in one essay, "I've long thought that widespread psychological distress—wildly intensified by the pandemic—contributes to the derangement of American politics. But maybe the causality works the other way, too, and the ugliness of American politics is taking a toll on the psyche of the citizenry" (Goldberg 2022). In short, politics is so overwhelming, so stunted by gridlock, and so tainted by vitriol that it's doomed, or at least feels that way. Depression is the inevitable response. This idea has also popped up in conservative media outlets. For instance, two Stanford professors argued in the *National Review* that "election depression" could turn into a more general "political depression" if left untreated (Zaharna and Miller 2017).

In this book, I stopped squinting and pulled out the binoculars. After spending years writing about how depression shapes the political engagement of citizens (e.g., Ojeda 2015; Landwehr and Ojeda 2021), I decided it was time to consider how politics might be a source of depression. Using the stress-appraisal-coping framework, I explained that depression is a response to a loss (stress) that is perceived as irrevocable (appraisal) and which leads to withdrawal (coping). This idea comes from work in psychology, evolutionary science, and stress research, but I translated it into the language of political science. In doing so, I made it clear how politics can be a source of depression. Then using polls, survey experiments, longitudinal surveys, interviews, and case studies from the United States, Great Britain, the Netherlands, and Europe more broadly, I provided evidence to back up this idea. I can now confidently conclude: politics is depressing, and depression is demobilizing.

Despite my confidence in this conclusion, what I've done here is only a drop in the bucket. There is much more to learn about how politics and depression are connected and why this connection is important. In this chapter, I explore how we can move forward from here. I begin with a review of the stress-appraisal-coping framework, the loss-irrevocable-withdrawal argument, and the empirical evidence. As I make my way through the framework, the argument, and the evidence, I highlight some lingering questions and opportunities for further inquiry. I then turn my attention to the scope conditions of the book. Enumerating the scope conditions offers another way to identify avenues for future research. I then conclude with a few final thoughts.

## What Do We Know? What Is Next?

Stress begins when a change happens in the world, and depression begins when that change is a *loss*. The concept of loss is central to theories of depression, whether it's Freud pointing to the loss of a loved object, Seligman pointing to a loss of personal control, or evolutionary psychologists pointing to a loss of social status. I argued that loss occurs in politics, too. We lose in politics when our preferences cease to be fulfilled, when politics takes away an object of personal value, or when our attempt to enact change fails. These losses stem from the scarcity and competition that characterize politics. Scarcity means that not everyone can get what they want, and competition means that who gets what is constantly in flux. Loss is thus an unavoidable part of politics. I found that loss does in fact lead to feelings of depression. An analysis of hundreds of poll questions in the United States over the past half century reveals that feelings of depression are almost always asked about in connection to a real or hypothetical loss. A survey experiment showed that being exposed to trends in politics can be depressing when it conflicts with our preferences.

Having establishing that political losses are depressing, future research should consider whether some political losses are more depressing than others, whether some losses have associations only with specific members of the depression family, and whether some losses can evoke feelings of depression that are intense and prolonged enough to merit a clinical diagnosis. Another important issue is what happens when a loss for one preference is a gain for another. It is well established in behavioral economics that we are more sensitive to losses than gains—although I found limited support for this asymmetry in my "irrevocable loss" survey experiment—but this doesn't tell us how we reconcile losses and gains that are experienced simultaneously. Figuring this out is important because changes in politics are often cross-cutting. For instance, the Supreme Court's decision in *Dobbs* may have left pro-choice conservatives torn. For them, overturning the constitutional right to abortion may have been a loss while returning power to the states may have been a gain. More generally, anytime deal-making or logrolling occurs, the changes have the potential to pit preferences against one another. What is the impact on feelings of depression? I considered this issue with respect to how redistributive policies might bring ideological preference (i.e., ideology) into conflict with material interests (i.e., income). The results were perplexing and suggested that losses and gains may not simply offset one another.

Appraisal is how we think about the situation. Who or what caused the loss? Was the loss fair or unfair? How important was the lost object? How we answer these and other questions shapes our feelings about the situation and whether we feel depressed or some other emotion. I argued that we feel depressed when we perceive a loss to be *irrevocable*. I examined appraisals of control—which psychologists have identified as one way to capture irrevocability—and found that they did in fact condition the impact of political loss on feelings of depression. Yet there is much more we can learn. Beyond lacking control, psychologists have found that perceiving a lack of power or that the broader circumstances caused the loss also generate appraisals of irrevocability. Do these types of appraisals matter in politics? Do they matter more or less than appraisals about control?

More generally, we may need to revisit the concept of irrevocability and how it may apply in politics. As the political scientist Claudia Landwehr pointed out to me, a lack of control is probably less depressing, if at all, when we don't expect control in the first place. If this is the case—and I don't see why it wouldn't be—then any conception of irrevocability must include some notion of political agency. There is also a question about whether losses in politics can be irrevocable at all. As the literature scholar Sara Marcus points out in her book *Political Disappointment*, "Mourning and melancholia are commonly understood as responses to a loss that is final, or that at best could be remedied only in an entirely other reality, whether that be an eschatological afterlife or its secular equivalent. In cases of political loss, however, the finality of loss is itself a question, one that disappointment aims to address" (2023, 19). In other words, the nature of politics means that change is always possible, and so losses rarely, if ever, seem final. This implies that disappointment may be more common than, say, sadness or depression—a pattern that we saw in the political polls—but it also raises questions about what it means for something to be irrevocable in politics. Losses in politics are not final in the same way that the death of a loved one is final. Yet many people reported feeling depressed about politics, which suggests that at least some people perceive political loss as irrevocable. What does this concept mean to them? Does irrevocability somehow look different in politics than in other domains?

Coping is what we do about how we feel. I argued that feelings of depression make us less likely to pursue a problem-focused strategy, especially in politics where problem-solving almost always requires collective action. In short, depression makes us *withdraw* from politics. There may be more to the story, however. Withdrawal is one response to depression—perhaps even the most prominent and immediate—but it is not the only response. As Marcus argues, "Disappointment in representational politics occurs not periodically but perennially, and as long as this disappointment does not turn into disillusionment, there is always an outlet for it in the political realm. A desire to build a legislative majority for one's party can always be acted on politically—find a new candidate, strategize, and regroup, start a lobbying firm—so although such a desire can also shape culture and aesthetics, it does so in tandem with concurrent political action" (2023, 20). This story may seem at odds with the one I told about withdrawal, but in fact they are just different chapters of the same book. When we feel depressed, withdrawal is often the most immediate response. Depression tells us we've lost something that cannot be (easily) gotten back. Most of the time, however, withdrawal is temporary because its purpose is not to permanently sideline us but rather to provide an opportunity to reappraise the situation and determine the best course of action. As I noted before, it is this reappraisal function that has led some scholars to call sadness the "architect of cognitive change" (Karnaze and Levine 2018, 46).

Studying this reappraisal process will help us better understand how feelings of depression shape the way citizens think about and engage with politics. Marcus highlighted how disappointment can prompt political actors to restrategize, because it signals that the current tactics are not working. More intense feelings of depression may lead to more dramatic reappraisals. The case of grieving White Southerners following Lincoln's elections and the secession of the Confederacy is a good example. The historian Michael Woods points out that many of the Southerners who felt sorrow at the dissolution of the Union would go on to become some of the strongest supporters of the Confederacy: "By placing this grief into a cultural context, it is easier to understand how mourning for the Union promoted secessionism and hastened the transfer of loyalties from the United States to the Confederacy. Because feelings of resignation and hope veined their grief, reluctant secessionists acquiesced more readily to the new reality of disunion and shifted their affections and patriotism onto the new proslavery republic" (2014, 231). The grief felt by these White Southerners, while most immediately leading to some degree of withdrawal, also made them susceptible to pro-Confederacy messages of hope. Eventually many of them reappraised their political views and became active supporters of the Confederacy. I did not find that depression in politics led to any more reliance on appraisal-focused strategies when compared to anger, anxiety, and fear, which may appear to be evidence against the idea of depression as a source of reappraisal. However, it may be that *how* the reappraisal process unfolds and what *types* of reappraisals are made differs between these emotions.

In the middle of the stress-appraisal-coping framework is a response, which in this book is depression. The term depression has many vernacular uses, ranging from an adjective to describe something pathetic to a clinical term to describe a mental health disorder. I used it to refer to a family of feelings characterized by a sinking feeling. The idea of families is rooted in psychological scholarship, which argues that there are six basic emotion families: anger, contempt, disgust, enjoyment, fear, *sadness*, and surprise (Ekman 1992). The depression family, or what Ekman calls the sadness family, is comprised of feelings such as disappointment (least intense), discouragement, resignation, helplessness, hopelessness, misery, despair, grief, sorrow, and anguish (most intense). When feelings in the depression family are especially intense, persist for longer periods of time, and disrupt day-to-day life, they are no longer just feelings but a clinical disorder. Given this conceptualization, my analyses focused on either feeling disappointed, sad, and depressed about something in politics *or* on general symptoms of depressive mood disorders (e.g., feeling sad, lonely, fatigued, etc.). Both approaches capture the underlying concept ("a sinking feeling") and together allow me to establish that the connection between politics and depression is not simply an artifact of how it is measured.

For all that members of the depression family have in common, they are also distinct in ways that go beyond mere intensity. These differences may be important to the way each family member gets produced by politics and with what consequences. We already saw that disappointment was more common than sadness and depression, which is to be expected given that it is the least intense member of the depression family. However, we also saw that it was tied to different politics topics in the eyes of pollsters. Whereas depression and sadness were mostly connect to elections, political violence, scandals, or politics in general, disappointment was often asked about with respect to evaluations of elected officials, policymaking by legislatures, the performance of political parties, decision making by courts, and cabinet appointments.

One potential difference between disappointment and other members of the depression family is that disappointment is a response to dashed expectations. Dashed expectations are a type of irrevocable loss but one that is less "final" than other types of irrevocable losses (Marcus 2023). For instance, if a leader makes a misstep, the opportunity to act has been irrevocably lost, but the possibility for future action remains. This possibility takes us back to the case of disappointed Democrats and the Biden administration. When irrevocable loss is more strongly characterized by finality, such as a loss following an election, it may leapfrog over disappointment and to more intense feelings of depression. This is largely speculative, and more theorizing and analyses are needed before we know if and how members of the depression family differ as political emotions.

## What Are the Scope Conditions?

My overarching argument was that politics is depressing, and I used the stress-appraisal-coping framework to explain when and why. In reality, however, I only end up arguing and showing that some aspects of politics are depressing in some places, at some times, and for some people. These qualifiers are what social scientists refer to as scope conditions, or the "circumstances in which a theory is applicable" (Harris 1997, 123).

Defining the scope of my argument and analyses is another way to identify how we can continue to refine our understanding of the connection between politics and depression.

It's clear that many aspects of politics in *Western democracies* can be depressing, as we saw in analyses of the United States, Great Britain, the Netherlands, and Europe more broadly. It's unclear, however, to what extent politics is depressing in democracies outside the West, such as Brazil, India, Japan, or South Africa, or when it comes to nondemocratic politics, such as the process of democratization, democratic backsliding, authoritarian states, conflict zones, and international relations. The question here seems to be less whether politics can be depressing—there isn't any obvious reason the logic of irrevocable loss wouldn't apply—and more about *how* politics might be depressing in these cases *or* why it is overshadowed by other political emotions if it is not especially prevalent.

Temporally, my emphasis has been *the late twentieth and early twenty-first centuries*. Is the connection between politics and depression a new phenomenon, or would politics be depressing in earlier times as well? There has been some discussion in the media recently about how the current political climate in the United States seems to be creating an epidemic of depression. Young adults, especially young liberal women, are reporting unusually high levels of depression (Gimbrone et al. 2022). This pattern raises the possibility that there is something unique about the current moment—social media? polarization? globalization?—that makes politics especially depressing. Investigating how the politics-depression connection varies over time is an important next step.

Throughout the book, my focus was on *ordinary citizens*, so I generally ignored political elites. Can politics be depressing for elected officials, bureaucrats, judges, journalists, activists, and consultants? One possibility is that politics is *especially* depressing to the political class, because they are closer to the action. Losing an election as a candidate is surely more depressing than losing as a voter. A bill failing in Congress seems like it would be more depressing to its sponsor than to a citizen who supports it. At the same time, there are reasons to think that the political class may be somewhat immune to depression. The authority of political elites means they have greater control over politics than ordinary citizens, and so they may be less likely to appraise losses as irrevocable. Their self-selection into these political roles suggests they may view politics as generally more controllable compared to ordinary citizens.

Political parties are a staple of modern democracies, and *partisanship* has become one of the primary prisms through which ordinary people make sense of politics. Party labels are often how we know who wins and loses. Although partisan politics was not my exclusive focus, I did not thoroughly investigate settings where partisanship may not be predominant, such as citizen interactions with bureaucrats, interest groups, or the judiciary, or nonpartisan aspects of citizens, such as gender, race, class, education, or issue position. Social identity may be especially important. Not only does it have the power to shape whether citizens see themselves as winners or losers, but it may also impact appraisals of irrevocability. Members of less powerful groups in society, such as women and the poor, may be especially likely to perceive a lack of control when confronting a loss.

## Is It the End?

As Americans confronted the resignation of Richard Nixon and the end of the Vietnam War, professor and political activist Michael Harrington described these events as "the most wrenching and disillusioning experiences in the nation's history: our first truly unpopular war and our greatest political scandal" (1974, 111). For Harrington, they created a "collective sadness" that overtook the country. The emotional consequences were much darker for Vietnam veterans who suffered major depressive disorder and posttraumatic stress disorder in the years to come. Indeed, a recent study found that veterans who were deployed to the Vietnam theater are today twice as likely to be diagnosed with depression than nontheater veterans and three times as likely as nonveterans (Cypel et al. 2022).

Today we seem to be in the throes of another national malaise, one created by rising income inequality, high inflation, widening political polarization, the seeming inevitability of climate change, a spate of international conflicts, and the erosion of democratic institutions. What's more, these problems are merely the backdrop to the political theater that dominates the daily news—contentious Supreme Court nominations, the messy withdrawal from Afghanistan, the January 6 attacks and subsequent investigation, the war in Ukraine, battles over unionization, the overturning of *Roe v. Wade*, and whatever issue tomorrow brings. In fact, these issues may be irrelevant—or at least faded memories—by the time you read this book, replaced by a slew of new and more salient stories.

In polarized times like these, it's hard to imagine a world in which politics isn't depressing. And, in fact, it's possible that depression cannot be entirely eradicated from politics. Politics will always be contentious. Some people will get less than they want, others will get more, and this balance will shift as competition ensues. The political production of loss is never-ending, and the steep costs of collective action in the face of these losses often leave us feeling powerless. From this, it is easy to conclude that constructing a democracy without depression is a hopeless project, one that is doomed from the start. However, if we step back and reappraise the situation, we can realize that the goal is not the absolute eradication of depression from politics. Sometimes feeling disappointed, sad, or depressed can be helpful. It can prompt us to step back and reconsider our situation. It is when these feelings are intense enough to disrupt our lives in undesirable ways that we should be concerned. Simply put, the goal is not a politics free of depression but a politics free of disruption. As we move forward, let's work to bring an end to the disruption.

# Acknowledgments

This book benefited from the generosity of so many people. I am especially thankful to Claudia Landwehr, Julie Pacheco, Eric Plutzer, and Gary Segura. Their friendship and mentorship over the years has been invaluable to me. Thanks also to Scott Carlson, Aditya Dasgupta, Elaine Denny, Justin Friel, Lee Hannah, Marlon Johnson, Nolan Kavanagh, Nate Kelly, Anil Menon, Courtneay Monroe, Jana Morgan, Anthony Nownes, Richard Pacelle, Justin Phillips, Tesalia Rizzo Reyes, Mark Shadden, Anne Whitesell, and Matthew Wilson for their feedback and advice.

I was a fellow at Harvard University's Ash Center for Democratic Governance and Innovation in 2021–2022. A special thanks to Archon Fung for inviting me to the Ash Center to work on this book. Thank you also to the wonderful community of fellows who provided invaluable feedback, including Selene Campion, Jonathan E. Collins, Dimitri Courant, João Fabiano, Janice Gallagher, Selina Gallo-Cruz, Marshall Ganz, George Greenidge, Nikolas Kirby, Anna Krämling, Huck-ju Kwon, Tina Law, Quinton Mayne, Ashley Nickels, Pedro Arcain Riccetto, Celina Su, and Tova Wang.

Through the generous support of the Center for Analytical Political Engagement at the University of California, Merced, I hosted a book workshop in 2022. I am especially grateful to Bethany Albertson, Andrea Louise Campbell, Ann Crigler, Christopher Den Hartog, Benjamin Highton, Herschel Nachlis, Michael Sances, Jessica Trounstine, and Charley Wilison. Their insights, comments, advice, and support transformed the book in ways I couldn't have imagined. Thank you also to Nathan Monroe and Austyn Smith for helping support and organize the workshop.

I had the good fortune of presenting portions of the book at Pennsylvania State University's McCourtney Institute for Democracy, the

Johannes Gutenberg University of Mainz, the University of California, Merced, and the annual meetings of the American Political Science Association and Midwest Political Science Association. I am especially grateful to Allison Anoll, Christopher Beem, Michael Berkman, Claudia Landwehr, and Amy Linch for giving me these opportunities. Thank you also to everyone who attended these talks and offered feedback and support, especially Lee Ann Banaszak, Roberto Carlos, Melody Crowder-Meyer, Andrew Engelhardt, Sarah Gollust, Leonard Häfner, Jake Haselswerdt, MacKenzie Israel-Trummel, Dan Meyers, Kevin Munger, Michael Nelson, Tanika Raychaudhuri, Armin Schäfer, Jenna Spinelle, Lea Stallbaum, Daniel Tavana, and Nicholas Valentino.

Many research assistants contributed their hard work and talents to various aspects of this book over the years. Thank you to Selene Bahena, Katelin Cortez, Leilani Garcia, Jacqueline Giacoman, Eshaan Kajani, Jessica Lopez, Elena Ramirez, Ricardo Robles, Jorge Rodriguez-Mota, Justin Rose, and April Westmark. Thank you also to Ana Shaw for her truly excellent copyediting skills.

Thank you to Sara Doskow, Rosemary Frehe, and the whole team at the University of Chicago Press. Sara invited me to write this book when it was still just an idea, and I'm not sure it would have happened without her encouragement and support. Thank you also to the anonymous reviewers who offered detailed and insightful comments.

Finally, I am thankful to my family for their love and support over the years. Thank you to Richard Eyer, Michelle Cummings, Kevin Cummings, Panchito Ojeda, Kristylea Ojeda, Mia Showker, Victora D'Amore, and Wolfgang Burgo-Ojeda. I'm especially grateful to my mother, Joanna Eyer, who has always been my most ardent supporter and a source of inspiration. A very special thanks goes to my partner, William Burgo, who not only supported me throughout this process but read and commented on several versions of the manuscript. I truly could not have done this without his love, care, and understanding.

# Appendix

The appendix provides details about the analyses reported in the main text. I organize the appendix by dataset rather than chapter. This structure allows me to avoid repetition in describing datasets that are used across multiple chapters. The datasets are presented in sections based on the order in which they appear in the main text and then by chapter within each section when appropriate:

- Interviews of Therapists (chapters 2, 6)
- Cooperative Election Study (chapters 2, 3, 5)
- Political Polls (chapters 3, 5)
- Irrevocable Loss Experiment (chapter 3)
- Coping Experiment (chapter 4, 7)
- Psychology Websites (chapter 4)
- Google Trends (chapter 5)
- Behavioral Risk Factor Surveillance Survey (chapter 5, 7)
- European Social Survey (chapter 5, 7)
- British Household Panel Study (chapter 6)
- National Longitudinal Survey of Youth (chapter 6)

Importantly, I limit the appendix to the details I deem essential to understanding the analyses. More detailed information, including descriptive statistics, full results, robustness checks, replication materials, and more, can be found on my website.

## Interviews of Therapists

I conducted eighteen semistructured interviews of mental health professionals across the United States, especially in California and Tennessee, between 2020–2022. The sample was drawn from the *Psychology Today* directory and included social workers, therapist, psychologists, psychiatrists, and couples' counselors. Interviews were conducted over videochat and lasted approximately forty-five to sixty minutes.

The interview protocol covered the professional background of the interviewee, instances when clients talked about politics with the interviewee, how the interviewee responded to the client when politics came up, how the interviewee saw politics impacting the mental well-being of their client, and how training and professional guidelines prepared the interviewee to handle political conversations. The protocol also included two questions about partisan and ideological differences in how clients talk about politics as well as other pathways by which politics might enter the therapy room, although there was rarely enough time in the interview to cover these questions. The interview protocol concluded with a short series of questions on the interviewee's demographic background and political attitudes.

A total of eighteen interviews were completed (out of 109 interview requests, a response rate of 16.5 percent). The age of the sample ranged from twenty-six to sixty-eight with an average of forty-three. The racial composition of the sample was seventeen White and one Asian. Two interviewees identified as Latino and another two identified as Jewish. The partisan composition of the sample was eleven Democrat, two Independent, and five who were either unsure, not interested in labels, or refused to say.

The audio of the interviews was recorded and then later transcribed (by me and research assistants). Each audio recording was deleted following its transcription. A research assistant then read through the transcripts and summarized the key stories, topics, and themes that emerged in each interview, which later served as a guide as I sifted through the interview data. I selected quotes and stories from the interview for inclusion in the main text based on my assessment of how well they illustrate different types of political loss (chapter 3) and the role of social support (chapter 6). Importantly, this sampling procedure and analytic strategy do not allow me to draw causal inferences about whether or how politics is depressing, so the "results" reported in the main text should not be interpreted as evidence for or against my arguments. Rather, the primary purpose of these interviews is to help build narrative and to provide illustrative examples of the phenomena under study.

## Cooperative Election Study

The Cooperative Election Study (CES) is an annual survey of over fifty thousand adults in the United States. The survey is conducted by YouGov. Election-year data collection consists of two waves—a ten-minute survey before the election and a five-minute survey after the election. All respondents fill out a "Common Content" questionnaire, while researchers can design special modules for a random selection of one thousand respondents from the full sample. I administered special modules in 2020 and 2022.

*Chapter 2: When Politics Produces Loss*

I use quotes from respondents in the 2020 and 2022 CES to illustrate the three types of political loss. My analysis is based on three questions from the postelection surveys. First, respondents were asked, "Have you ever met regularly with a therapist, counseling center, psychiatrists, or support group?" Response options included yes (currently), yes (in the past), and no. Next, respondents who indicated going to therapy, either currently or in the past, were asked, "When you attend therapy/counseling, whether currently or in the past, how often do you talk about what is going on in politics?" Response options included rarely or none of the time, some or a little of the time, a moderate amount of time, or most or all of the time. Finally, respondents who indicated talking about politics at least some or a little of the time were asked, "What aspects of politics did you talk about more frequently during therapy/counseling sessions, and why?" Respondents were provided a large text box to type out their answer. These open-ended responses provide the data for my analysis.

*Chapter 3: When Loss Becomes Depressing*

I included a special module on the 2022 CES to assess the role of irrevocability. Respondents on the preelection survey were asked, "Please try to recall an unpleasant political experience from the past year when you thought [Democrats / Republicans / circumstances beyond anyone's control] were responsible for what happened. Remember this experience as vividly as you can." They were then instructed, "Can you briefly describe this unpleasant political experience and why you felt [Democrats / Republicans / circumstances beyond anyone's control] were responsible for it?" Respondents were randomly assigned to see Democrats, Republicans, or circumstances beyond anyone's control. The purpose of this randomization was to ensure that responses cover a wide range of problems from a variety of sources.

Following the recall task, respondents were asked to appraise the experience and say how it made them feel. Appraisals were measured by asking respondents, "To what extent would you say this unpleasant political situation was . . . important, unpleasant, unfair, solvable, within your control." For each appraisal dimension, the order of which was randomized, respondents selected from an eleven-point scale with labels of not at all (0), a moderate amount (5), and a great deal (10). Feelings were measured by asking respondents, "Now recall the emotions you felt during this unpleasant politics experience. How much did you feel each emotion? Depressed, hopeful, angry, anxious, happy, fearful, disappointed." The order of the emotions was randomized, and the response options were the same as for the appraisal questions. Feelings about the experience are the key dependent variables. Appraisals of solvability and control are the key independent variables in one set of these analyses.

The other key independent variables are the respondent's position within the political system. Political position was measured based on gender, race, ethnicity, education, age, and income. *Gender* is a binary variable where 1 indicates that the respondent self-reported as a woman, and 0 indicates otherwise. *Age* is a continuous variable based on the survey year minus the respondent's birth year; it ranges from 18 to 93. *Education* is an ordinal variable with six categories that capture the highest level of schooling a respondent has completed; the categories are no high school, high school graduate, some college, two-year college degree, four-year college degree, and at least some postgraduate schooling. *Race* is a categorical variable with three groups: White, Black, and other; the latter group serves as the baseline category in the model. *Ethnicity* is measured using a preset variable that is 1 if a respondent self-reports being Hispanic, and 0 otherwise. *Income* is a sixteen-point ordinal variable based on income brackets in increments of $10,000 USD from 0 to $100,000 and then in increasingly larger brackets with the highest being $500,000 or more.

I also include control variables for party identification and political

TABLE A.1 **The Impact of Irrevocability as Solvability and Control**

| Model | Key Estimates | | | |
|---|---|---|---|---|
| | Solvable | Within Control | N | $R^2$ |
| Depressed | −0.109** | 0.025 | 679 | 0.30 |
| | (.038) | (.042) | | |
| Disappointed | −0.0001 | −0.094** | 679 | 0.50 |
| | (.032) | (.036) | | |
| Happy | 0.025 | 0.376** | 677 | 0.38 |
| | (.031) | (.034) | | |
| Hopeful | 0.071** | 0.364** | 679 | 0.34 |
| | (.033) | (.037) | | |
| Angry | −0.029 | −0.050 | 678 | 0.49 |
| | (.033) | (.037) | | |
| Anxious | −0.028 | 0.057 | 679 | 0.37 |
| | (.036) | (.040) | | |
| Afraid | −0.055 | 0.005 | 678 | 0.33 |
| | (.037) | (.041) | | |

\* $p < 0.05$; \*\* $p < 0.10$
*Note*: Data come from a special module of the 2022 Cooperative Election Study. Estimates are coefficients (and standard errors) from ordinary least squares regressions of each emotion on appraisals of solvability and control. All models control for appraisals of importance, unpleasantness, and unfairness, as well as gender, race, ethnicity, education, age, income, political interest, party identification, and treatment condition.

interest in the analyses below. Party identification is a preset variable measured on a seven-point scale: strong Republican, Republican, lean Republican, Independent, lean Democrat, Democrat, strong Democrat. Political interest was measured by asking respondents, "Some people seem to follow what's going on in government and public affairs most of the time, whether there's an election going on or not. Others aren't that interested. Would you say you follow what's going on in government and public affairs . . ." Response options included hardly at all, only now and then, some of the time, and most of the time.

I estimate two sets of regression models. The first set are ordinary least squares regressions of feelings on appraisals of solvability and control. These models include controls for appraisals of importance, unpleasantness, and unfairness, as well as gender, race, ethnicity, age, education, income, party identification, political interest, and whether respondents were randomized to see Democrats, Republicans, or circumstances when recalling the unpleasant experience. I exclude respondents who gave "straightline" responses to all the questions about feelings and appraisals. Table A.1 presents the results for the key variables from these models.

TABLE A.2 **The Impact of Irrevocability as Political Power**

|  | Depression | Disappointment |
|---|---|---|
| Female | 0.675** | 0.452* |
|  | (.271) | (.267) |
| Black | −0.1475** | −0.712* |
|  | (.400) | (.392) |
| Other Race | −0.520 | 0.404 |
|  | (.431) | (.426) |
| Hispanic | 0.120 | 0.304 |
|  | (.543) | (.536) |
| Education | 0.086 | 0.012 |
|  | (.098) | (.097) |
| Age | −0.015* | −0.009 |
|  | (.008) | (.008) |
| Income | −0.083* | 0.094** |
|  | (.043) | (.042) |

\* $p < 0.05$; \*\* $p < 0.10$
*Note*: Data come from a special module of the 2022 Cooperative Election Study. Estimates are coefficients (and standard errors) from ordinary least squares regressions of depression and disappointment on position in political system (operationalized as gender, race, ethnicity, education, age, and income). All models control for political interest, party identification, and treatment condition.

The second set of models are ordinary least squares regressions of feelings on the indicators of political position, including gender, race, ethnicity, education, age, and income. These models control for party identification, political interest, and randomization status. I exclude respondents who gave "straightline" responses to all the questions about feelings. Table A.2 presents the results for the key variables from these models.

*Chapter 5: Election Blues*

I included a special module on the 2020 CES to assess whether *partisan* electoral loss is depressing. Specifically, I add a battery of questions about generalized depression to both the pre- and postsurvey, which allows me to analyze whether changes in depression are a function of electoral winning and losing.

Depression is measured using an abridged version of the Center for Epidemiologic Studies Depression (CES-D) scale, which has been validated and used extensively in the field of psychology (Radloff 1977). Respondents were asked, "Below is a list of the ways you might have felt or behaved. Please tell me how often you have felt this way during the past week." It then presents respondents with a list of symptoms, including (1) I felt depressed, (2) I felt like everything was an effort, (3) I felt lonely or remote from other people, (4) I felt hopeful about the future, (5) I could not shake off the blues even with help from my family and friends, and (6) My sleep was restless. Respondents were given the option of selecting rarely or none of the time, some or a little of the time, a moderate amount of time, and most or all of the time.

Overall pre- and postelection depression scores are calculated as the mean of the six items (after reverse coding responses to "I felt hopeful about the future"). Higher values thus indicate more depression. The Cronbach's alpha for the items on the preelection survey is 0.84 and on the postelection survey is 0.85, indicating high reliability. The correlation between the pre- and postelection depression scores is 0.78. A *change* in depressive symptoms is calculated by taking the difference between the overall pre- and postelection scores; positive values on the change variable indicate that symptoms increased, while negative values indicate that symptoms decreased. About 44 percent of respondents saw a decrease in symptoms, 20 percent saw no change, and 36 percent saw an increase in symptoms.

Party identification is measured on the postelection Common Content portion of the survey and is based on the standard wording from the American National Election Study. Respondents were asked, "Generally speaking, do you think of yourself as a . . . ?" with response options of Republican, Democrat, Independent, and other. Respondents who answered Republican or Democrat were then asked, "Would you call yourself a strong [Republican/Democrat] or not so strong [Republican/Democrat]?" with response options of strong [Republican/Democrat] and not so strong [Republican/Democrat]. Respondents who selected Independent or other were asked, "Do you think of yourself as closer to the Democratic or the Republican party?" with response options of the Democratic Party, the Republican Party, or neither. These questions allow for the construction of a seven-point party identification measure: strong Democrat (25.9 percent of respondents), Democrat (12.0 percent), lean Democrat (10.7 percent), Independent (13.8 percent), lean Republican (8.8 percent), Republican (8.2 percent), strong Republican (17.4 percent). About 3.2 percent of respondents reported that they were "not sure" of their party identification.

I also use candidate preference as an alternative measure for determining who is a partisan loser and winner. Since party identification is measured on the postelection survey, using it as a key predictor creates the potential of introducing posttreatment bias. Since candidate preference was measured on the preelection survey, it circumvents the problem. Respondents were asked, "Do you intend to vote in the 2020 general election on November 3rd?" Those who voted early were asked, "For which candidate for President of the United States did you vote?" They were given the options of Trump, Biden, someone else, not sure, or won't vote. Respondents who had not yet voted (on the first question) or said they were not sure or wouldn't vote (on the second question) were then asked, "Which candidate for President of the United States do you prefer?" The response options were the same. I create a three-category measure of candidate preference: (1) Trump (38 percent), (2) Biden (46 percent), and (3) someone else/not sure/won't vote (16 percent).

I include several control variables in the regression models. *Gender* is a binary variable where 1 indicates that the respondent self-reported as a woman. *Age* is a continuous variable based on the survey year minus the respondent's birth year; it ranges from 18 to 93. *Education* is an ordinal variable with six categories that capture the highest level of schooling a respondent has completed; the categories are no high school, high school graduate, some college, two-year college degree, four-year college degree, and at least some postgraduate schooling. *Marital status* is a binary variable where 1 indicates that the respondent self-reported as married or in a civil partnership. *Race* is a categorical variable with groups for White, Black, and neither White nor Black; the latter group serves as the baseline category in the model. *Income* is a sixteen-point ordinal variable based on income brackets in increments of $10,000 USD from 0 to $100,000 and then in increasingly larger brackets with the highest being $500,000 or more.

I estimate ordinary least squares regressions of changes in depression on either party identification or candidate preference. In the candidate preference models, the omitted category is Biden supporters. I use team module weights calculated by YouGov and control for gender, race, age, education, marital status, and income. Table A.3 presents the results for the key variables from these models.

## Political Polls

The poll questions come from Cornell University's Roper Center. The Roper Center hosts a digital archive for polling firms and pollsters to

## APPENDIX

TABLE A.3 **The Impact of Electoral Loss in the United States**

|  | Party Identification | | Candidate Preference | |
|---|---|---|---|---|
|  | 1 | 2 | 3 | 4 |
| Party Identification | 0.027** | 0.027** | | |
|  | (.009) | (.010) | | |
| Trump Supporter | | | 0.152** | 0.155** |
|  | | | (.042) | (.048) |
| Other Preference | | | 0.123* | 0.162** |
|  | | | (.072) | (.056) |
| Observations | 851 | 777 | 871 | 793 |
| Survey Weights | ✓ | ✓ | ✓ | ✓ |
| Control Variables | | ✓ | | ✓ |

\*\* $p < 0.05$; \* $p < 0.10$
*Note:* Data come from a special module of the 2020 Cooperative Election Study. Estimates are coefficients (and standard errors) from ordinary least squares regressions of pre-/postelection changes in depression on party identification or candidate preference. In the candidate preference models, the omitted category is Biden supporters; the "Other Preference" category are respondents who indicated they were going to vote for a third-party candidate, were not sure who they supported, or were not going to vote in the election. All models control for gender, race, age, education, marital status, and income.

voluntarily deposit polling data, questionnaires, toplines, metadata, and other relevant information. Below, I provide more detailed information on the data collection process and analytic strategy used to generate the results reported in chapter 3 (all polls) and chapter 5 (election polls only).

### Data Collection

Data collection proceeded in two steps. The first step was a search of the archives. I instructed an undergraduate research assistant to search the *longstanding methods collection* of the archives for *questions* in which the outcome was feelings of depression, sadness, and disappointment. These instructions mean that questions which appear only in the *recently developed methods collection* of the archives might be excluded from the search results. It also means that the unit of analysis is the poll question rather than the poll itself, and so the final dataset can include multiple questions from the same poll. The research assistant searched the archives using stems of the key emotions (e.g., depress*) but iterated through with variants of the terms to ensure that nothing was missed (e.g., depressed, depression).

The second step was extracting relevant information from the search results. Relevant questions were those that allowed a respondent to report feeling depressed, sad, or disappointed. Irrelevant questions were ones that asked about how someone else feels (e.g., whether the respondent's child was depressed), included the feelings in the question wording without ultimately being about them, or referred to an alternative meaning of the feeling (e.g., the Great Depression). These search parameters resulted in an initial dataset of 725 relevant questions. For these questions, the research assistant logged the study title, archive number, study date, sample parameters and size, question wording, response options, and topline summary. They then categorized each question as emotional, political, or other. The "emotional" questions were ones that asked about generalized feelings (e.g., "How depressed have you felt over the past two weeks?") rather than about feelings in connection to a specific object. The "other" questions were ones that asked about feelings of depression in connection to a nonpolitical object (e.g., watching television, the dissolution of a relationship, etc.).

The "political" questions were ones that tied the feelings to a political object, such as an institution (e.g., legislatures, courts, etc.), group or actor (e.g., Democrats, Lyndon Johnson, etc.), aspect of the policymaking process (e.g., pending legislation), or event or outcome (e.g., 9/11, political scandal). The assistant, who was an undergraduate honors student majoring in political science at the time, was instructed to err on the side of including questions rather than excluding them. The logic here was that I could later get rid of irrelevant questions that were included, but I could not later add relevant questions that were excluded. The research assistant labeled 438 questions as political, 209 as other, and 78 as emotional.

*Analytic Strategy*

The analysis has three parts, all of which focus only on the "political" questions. The first part is a description of which aspects of politics are covered by these questions and whether certain political topics and feelings go together. The second part is a content analysis of the questions in terms of their potential to be appraised as an irrevocable loss. The third part is a statistical analysis of the percentage of respondents who report feeling depressed, sad, or disappointed. I describe the analytic strategy for each part below.

*Part I: Descriptive Analysis.* I narrowed the 438 questions classified by the research assistant as "political" to 414 questions. I eliminated questions that were fielded in countries outside the United States, such as Japan, Great Britain, and France, and questions that were ultimately deemed to be nonpolitical. This includes questions about mass shootings, global warming, or other subjects that, while often highly politicized, are not explicitly political (i.e., about political institutions, actors, processes, events, or outcomes). I then divided the final set of political questions into categories based on the object that is the focus of the depressed feelings: campaigns and elections; political violence; evaluations of elected officials; policymaking by legislatures; general impressions of politics; the scandals, impeachments, resignations, and deaths of political actors; the performance of political parties; decision making by courts; cabinet appointments; and miscellaneous. These categories were not theoretically motivated, nor are they comprehensive of every aspect of politics; rather they were selected because they generally align with subfields of the political science discipline and do a nice job of showcasing the breadth of political questions focused on feelings of depression.

*Part II: Content Analysis.* Each question was assessed for its potential to be appraised as an irrevocable loss. I first examined the temporal dimension of each question—coding questions as being about the past, present, or hypothetical past (e.g., if X happens in the future, how would you feel) or about an uncertain outcome in the future (e.g., what do you think about the possibility of X happening?). Questions about the future are unlikely to elicit appraisals of irrevocable loss. Next, I coded questions about the past, present, or hypothetical past based on whether they asked about change or the status quo. Since loss requires change, questions about the status quo are less likely to evoke feelings of depression.

*Part III: Statistical Analysis.* I used the question's topline information provided by the archives to determine the percentage of respondents who reported feelings of depression, sadness, and disappointment. As part of this process, I coded the format of the question: open-ended or, if close-ended, ordinal, binary, or categorical. For the open-ended, categorical, and binary questions, the overall percentage was based on the sum of percentages to each response option that indicated these feelings. For ordinal questions, the overall percentage was calculated as the percentage of respondents selecting the most emotionally intense category. Of the 414 questions, 27 could not be classified and 2 were missing the topline information. An overwhelming majority of the unclassified questions included response options that mixed depressed and nondepressed feelings in their response options (e.g., sad or angry, depressed or anxious).

## Irrevocable Loss Survey Experiment

The "irrevocable loss" survey experiment was inspired by the article "How do politicians respond to opinion polls? An experiment with Swedish politicians" by Gijs Schumacher and Patrik Öhberg (published in the *Research & Politics*, 2020). Schumacher and Öhberg presented Swedish elected officials with information from public opinion polls that showed the favorability of the official's political party either improving or worsening. From this, I adapted the idea of strategically selecting time-series data to construct political trends showing losses, gains, or no change. Chapter 3 drew on this experiment as a test of my argument about the role of irrevocable loss. Below, I provide more information on the protocol, data, measures, analytic strategy, and results of this study.

### *Protocol*

*Consent and Pretreatment Questionnaire.* Respondents were first shown an informed consent page of the online survey, which explained the purpose, procedures, risks, benefits, confidentiality, cost, right to refuse or withdraw, and contact information of the principal investigator. Consent was obtained when respondents continued with the survey.

*Treatment.* Respondents were presented with a page of text that read, "We now want to ask you about some recent trends in the United States. On the following screen, we will present a trend that is based on real data. Please look over it carefully and then answer the following questions." Respondents were then randomly presented with a loss, gain, or no change trend from one of nine topics that addressed either a process issue (corruption, democracy, or trust in government) or substantive issue (abortion, guns, taxes, same-sex marriage, healthcare, or immigration). Respondents who saw a loss or gain trend were randomly assigned to see either no additional information, a statement that the trend was revocable (i.e., "Analysts think this change is temporary."), or a statement that the trend was irrevocable (i.e., "Analysts think this change is permanent."). After the presentation of the trend, respondents answered questions about how they felt and thought about the trend. I describe these questions below. Respondents then repeated this task two more times, so each respondent saw and evaluated a total of three trends.

The trends are based on real time-series data. All trends take the most recent year of the time series (either 2022 or 2023 in all case) as the base year and then construct loss, gain, or no change trends through the cherry-picking of a past reference year. The first priority was to generate losses and gains of comparable sizes, and the second priority was to minimize the difference in years across trend types. When the trend was based on public opinion polls, some aspects of the question wording was randomized to ensure that the overall results were an artifact of the framing. For instance, trends about public opinion on abortion were either phrased in terms of more or less support for either the pro-life *or* the pro-choice position, even as the statistics remain unchanged. In order to save space, I do not present the text of all trends here. The text for the corruption trends can be found in the main chapter, while the text for the remaining topics can be found on my website.

For the process issues, trends are considered a loss if they show an increase in corruption, a decrease in democracy, or a decrease in trust, and vice versa for gains. However, the substantive issues cannot be as easily classified as losses or gains. Whether a directional trend—such as an increase or a decrease in support for gun control—is a loss or gain depends on the preference of the respondent. I considered the trend to be a loss when it conflicts with the preferences of the respondents and a gain when it aligns with their preferences. Trends showing no change do not depend on the preferences of the respondent. I classify the substantive trends as showing a leftward or rightward shift and then compare this shift to the self-reported party identification of the respondent to determine if they are a loss or gain. Party identification is measured on a six-point scale—strong Republican, Republican, lean Republican, lean Democrat, Democrat, and strong Democrat. Note that respondents who identified as Independent or something else were required to give a response to the leaner question. Leftward shifts are losses for all Republican-affiliated respondents and gains for all Democrat-affiliated respondents. The opposite holds for rightward shifts.

*Emotions and Appraisals.* Following each trend, respondents were asked, "To what extent does this trend make you feel . . . ?" They are presented with the following emotions: depressed, sad, happy, disappointed, angry, anxious, afraid, and hopeful. For each emotion, they could select not at all, a little, somewhat, moderately, or very. Next, respondents were asked "To what extent would you characterize this trend as . . . ?" They were presented with the following dimensions: permanent, bad for me personally, bad for the country, and within my control. Respondents could select very much, somewhat, neither, somewhat, or very much.

*Posttreatment Questionnaire.* The survey concluded with a handful of questions: feelings about politics today, feelings about life overall, political interest, demographics, and voting history.

*Data, Analysis, and Results*

I fielded the survey experiment using the online survey platform Cloud Research Connect to 1,800 respondents in the United States on April 11–13, 2024. The survey was targeted to panelists in such a way to ensure that it would be nationally representative.

I estimate two sets of models using the data in a "long" format where the unit of analysis is the respondent-task. The first set of models are ordinary least squares regressions of each trend-specific emotion on the loss/gain ("stressor") treatment (with "no change" as the control variable). The second set of models build on the first regressions by adding the permanent/temporary ("appraisal") treatment (with "no information" as the control group) as well as an interaction between the stressor and appraisal variables. These models included fixed effects for task number and topic and clustered standard errors by respondent. Tables A.4 and A.5 present the results for the key variables from these models.

TABLE A.4 **The Impact of Losses and Gains**

| DV | Key Coefficients | | N | $R^2$ |
| --- | --- | --- | --- | --- |
|  | Loss | Gain |  |  |
| Depressed | 0.342** | −0.232** | 5,468 | 0.07 |
|  | (.045) | (.041) |  |  |
| Sad | 0.521** | −0.372** | 5,468 | 0.12 |
|  | (.052) | (.049) |  |  |
| Disappointed | 0.594** | −0.549** | 5,468 | 0.15 |
|  | (.059) | (.057) |  |  |
| Angry | 0.488** | −0.279** | 5,468 | 0.11 |
|  | (.050) | (.046) |  |  |
| Anxious | 0.447** | −0.182** | 5,468 | 0.08 |
|  | (.047) | (.044) |  |  |
| Afraid | 0.416** | −0.179** | 5,468 | 0.08 |
|  | (.047) | (.043) |  |  |
| Happy | −0.342** | 0.702** | 5,468 | 0.17 |
|  | (.044) | (.049) |  |  |
| Hopeful | −0.469 | 0.635* | 5,468 | 0.16 |
|  | (.049) | (.054) |  |  |

\* $p < 0.05$; \*\* $p < 0.10$

*Note*: Data come from an original "irrevocable loss" survey experiment. Estimates are coefficients (and standard errors) from an ordinary least squares regression of each emotion on the loss/gain treatment (with "no change" serving as the control group). All models include fixed-effects for task number and topic and cluster standard errors by respondent.

TABLE A.5  **The Impact of Irrevocable Losses and Gains**

| DV | Stressor | | Appraisal | | Interaction | | N | $R^2$ |
|---|---|---|---|---|---|---|---|---|
| | Gain | Loss | Temporary | Permanent | Gain × Temp | Gain × Perm | | |
| Depressed | -0.073 | 0.449** | -0.002 | 0.080 | -0.019 | -0.140* | 4,790 | 0.08 |
| | (.112) | (.116) | (.063) | (.060) | (.076) | (.073) | | |
| Sad | -0.249* | 0.618** | -0.143** | 0.073 | 0.107 | -0.171** | 4,790 | 0.13 |
| | (.134) | (.137) | (.071) | (.067) | (.087) | (.085) | | |
| Disappointed | -0.422** | 0.653** | -0.062 | 0.137* | 0.060 | -0.251** | 4,790 | 0.17 |
| | (.147) | (.148) | (.076) | (.072) | (.097) | (.093) | | |
| Angry | -0.195 | 0.563** | -0.080 | 0.083 | 0.122 | -0.134 | 4,790 | 0.12 |
| | (.141) | (.145) | (.069) | (.066) | (.084) | (.083) | | |
| Anxious | -0.032 | 0.574** | -0.073 | 0.058 | 0.069 | -0.128 | 4,790 | 0.09 |
| | (.121) | (.125) | (.065) | (.063) | (.082) | (.078) | | |
| Afraid | -0.133 | 0.418** | -0.027 | 0.059 | 0.021 | -0.153** | 4,790 | 0.08 |
| | (.127) | (.131) | (.063) | (.061) | (.079) | (.076) | | |
| Happy | 0.581** | -0.309** | -0.048 | -0.097** | 0.152* | 0.327** | 4,790 | 0.19 |
| | (.110) | (.103) | (.052) | (.048) | (.087) | (.085) | | |
| Hopeful | 0.496** | -0.479** | -0.044 | -0.099** | 0.123* | 0.275** | 4,790 | 0.18 |
| | (.124) | (.116) | (.058) | (.052) | (.089) | (.087) | | |

\* p < 0.05; \*\* p < 0.10

*Note:* Data come from an original "irrevocable loss" survey experiment. Estimates are coefficients (and standard errors) from ordinary least squares regressions of each emotion on the loss/gain treatment (with "no change" serving as the control group), the permanent/temporary treatment (with "no information" serving as the control group), and their interactions. All models include fixed-effects for task number and topic and cluster standard errors by respondent.

TABLE A.6  **The Impact of Repeated Loss**

| DV | Repeated Loss | N | $R^2$ |
|---|---|---|---|
| Depressed | 0.072 | 1,823 | 0.02 |
|  | (.057) |  |  |
| Sad | 0.128** | 1,821 | 0.01 |
|  | (.053) |  |  |
| Disappointed | 0.178** | 1,823 | 0.02 |
|  | (.055) |  |  |
| Angry | 0.098* | 1,820 | 0.02 |
|  | (.055) |  |  |
| Anxious | −0.019 | 1,821 | 0.01 |
|  | (.055) |  |  |
| Afraid | −0.002 | 1,819 | 0.01 |
|  | (.055) |  |  |
| Happy | −0.096** | 1,821 | 0.03 |
|  | (.032) |  |  |
| Hopeful | −0.069 | 1,821 | 0.01 |
|  | (.044) |  |  |

* $p < 0.05$; ** $p < 0.10$

*Note*: Data come from an original "irrevocable loss" survey experiment. Estimates are coefficients (and standard errors) from ordinary least squares regressions of each emotion on repeated losses, which is defined here as the sum of the "stressor" treatments (gain, no change, loss) across the three tasks. All models include topic fixed-effects from each task.

I also estimate a set of models using the data in a "wide" format where the unit of analysis is the respondent. The key independent variable is the mean of the "stressor" treatment, where -1 indicates the respondent saw three "gain" trends, 0 indicates three "no change" trends, and 1 indicates three "loss" trends. Notably, this variable can take on a range of values between -1 and 1 depending on the combination of trends. I call this the "repeated loss" treatment. The dependent variables are feelings about politics in general today. These models are ordinary least squares regressions of general feelings about politics on repeated loss. These models include topic fixed effects across the three tasks. Tables A.6 presents the results for the key variables from these models.

## Coping Experiment

This experiment was adapted from the paper "Investigating the Appraisal Patterns of Regret and Disappointment" by Wico W. van Dijk and Marcel Zeelenberg (published in *Motivation and Emotion*, 2002). The key changes from the original van Dijk and Zeelenberg experiment are which emotions are used as treatments and the randomization of domain when recalling experiences. Chapter 4 drew on this experiment as a test of my argument about the impact of depression on coping strategies. Below, I provide more information on the protocol, data, measures, analytic strategy, and results of this study.

*Protocol*

*Consent.* Respondents were first shown an informed consent page of the online survey, which explained the purpose, procedures, risks, benefits, confidentiality, cost, right to refuse or withdraw, and contact information of the PI. Consent was obtained when respondents continued with the survey.

*Treatment.* Respondents were presented with the following question: "Please recall a time when you felt [emotion] because of something that happened in [domain]. This may be something recently, a few months ago, or even a few years ago. If nothing comes to mind immediately, please give yourself a few moments to think carefully. Can you think of a time you felt [emotion] about something in [domain]?" Respondents were randomly assigned to one of four emotion treatments—anger, anxiety, sadness/depression, fear—and one of two domain treatments—politics, life. Respondents who said "yes" were asked to write a brief description of what happened and why they felt the way they did. This emotion- and domain-specific memory is the "treatment." Respondents who answered "no" were then asked the same question but where the emotional treatment was reworded to be about "negative feelings" while the domain treatment remained the same. Respondents who answered "yes" undertook the same descriptive exercise, while those who said "no" to this second question were directed to recall and describe something "bad" happening in the same domain (i.e., language around emotions and feelings was stripped out).

This three-question procedure was developed after an initial pilot study found that respondents occasionally said they did not feel the emotion in question. This led to nonsense answers to the open-ended question, effectively making the data unusable. Rather than screening out these kinds of respondents, however, I reformulated the treatment so respondents who said "no" would go through this cascade of questions, which ultimately allows me to retain the respondents in the data. Overall,

TABLE A.7 **The Categorization of Coping Strategies**

| Focus | Strategy |
|---|---|
| Emotion | I got upset and let my emotions out |
| | I discussed my feelings with someone |
| | I used alcohol or drugs to make myself feel better |
| Attention | I turned to work or other substitute activities to take my mind off things |
| | I kept myself from getting distracted by other thoughts or activities |
| Appraisal | I tried to grow as a person as a result of the experience |
| | I said to myself "this isn't real" |
| | I put my trust in God |
| | I laughed about the situation |
| | I got used to the idea that it happened |
| Problem | I tried to get advice from someone about what to do |
| | I concentrated my efforts on doing something about it |
| | I talked to someone to find out more about the situation |
| | I made a plan of action |
| Unclear | I admitted to myself that I can't deal with it, and quit trying |
| | I restrained myself from doing anything too quickly |

about 84 percent of respondents took the "emotion" treatment, 8 percent the "negative feelings" treatment, and the final 8 percent took the "something bad" treatment.

*Coping Strategies.* Respondents were then asked about how they coped with the situation, "There are lots of ways people respond to unpleasant situations. Thinking about the situation you just described, please tell us how you responded at the time." Respondents were presented with sixteen items, which are listed and categorized in table A.7, and could select from one of four response options for each item: (0) I didn't do this at all, (1) I did this a little, (2) I did this a medium amount of time, and (3) I did this a lot. The order of the items was randomized across respondents.

*Political Action.* Next, respondents were asked about how they might respond politically to the situation were it to happen today: "Thinking about the situation you described, what actions do you think you would take if a similar situation occurred today? (select all that apply)." Respondents were presented with the following political actions:

1. Attend a political meeting
2. Give money to a political organization
3. Attend a protest march, rally, or demonstration
4. Post a message or comment online

APPENDIX                                                                 171

5. Try to persuade others to vote one way or another
6. Wear a campaign button, put a sticker on your car, or display a sign at your home
7. Give money to a candidate, political party, or any other group involved in elections
8. Engage in political discussion with family or friends
9. Other [text box]

*Other Questions.* Finally, respondents were prompted, "We now want to ask some questions unrelated to the situation you described. Forget about that situation and instead just answer the questions as you normally would when taking a survey." They were subsequently asked standard questions about political trust, political efficacy, ideology, partisanship, political participation, year of birth, race, ethnicity, gender, education, income, county of residence, and voter registration status.

## Data, Analysis, and Results

The study was fielded using the online survey platform Cloud Research to 1,200 respondents on September 12–13, 2022. Initial analyses of the data, which are reported on my website, show that the randomization worked well and that the sample is nationally representative along key demographics.

The two key outcomes are the coping strategies and political action. I create a separate variable for the four coping strategy categories. Respondents might have different interpretations of the response options, and so I calculate the percentage of a respondent's overall coping strategy that is comprised of each category rather than average across strategies. For each respondent, I summed up their responses across all the items (excluding the two unclear items). The lowest possible score in theory is 0 (a score of 0 on each item), while the highest possible score is 42 (a score of 3 on each item). I then sum up their responses within each of the four categories. For instance, the attention-focused strategy can range from 0 (a score of 0 on the two items) to 6 (a score of 3 on the two items). I then divide each category score by the total score to determine the proportion of a respondent's overall strategy that is characterized by each type of strategy.

A few notes about the creation of these categories. First, I reverse coded the item "I kept myself from getting distracted by other thoughts or activities" so that higher values correspond to a more attention-focused

TABLE A.8  **The Impact of Depression on Coping with Politics and Personal Life**

| | Coping Strategy Models | | | | |
|---|---|---|---|---|---|
| | Emotion-Focused | Attention-Focused | Appraisal-Focused | Problem-Focused | Political Action |
| Depression | 0.089* | -0.01 | 0.036 | -0.115** | -0.116 |
| | (.048) | (.054) | (.046) | (.052) | (.114) |
| Politics | 0.105** | 0.083* | 0.044 | -0.262** | 0.561** |
| | (.035) | (.043) | (.034) | (.041) | (.068) |
| Depression × Politics | -0.229** | 0.193** | -0.003 | 0.009 | -0.060 |
| | (.071) | (.090) | (.070) | (.084) | (.143) |
| Marginal Effect of Depression | | | | | |
| *Politics Condition* | -0.027** | 0.036** | 0.006 | -0.017 | -0.217** |
| *Personal Condition* | 0.017* | -0.003 | 0.007 | -0.021** | -0.084 |
| Marginal Effect of Politics | | | | | |
| *Depression Condition* | -0.024** | 0.057** | 0.008 | -0.041** | 0.444** |
| *Anger, Anxiety, & Fear Conditions* | 0.020** | 0.016* | 0.008 | -0.045** | 0.577** |
| N | 1,195 | 1,195 | 1,195 | 1,195 | 1,195 |

\* $p < 0.05$; \*\* $p < 0.10$

*Note*: Data come from an original "coping" survey experiment. Estimates are coefficients (and standard errors) in the upper panel and marginal effects in the lower panel from fractional logistic regressions of coping strategy and a Poisson regression of political action on the depression treatment (with anger, anxiety, and fear as the control group), politics treatment (with personal life as the control group), and their interaction.

strategy—that is, *not* paying attention to the problem situation. Second, I did not include the two items in the "unclear" category. There is some uncertainty about how these items should be counted. The question about quitting implies that the person was pursuing a problem-focused strategy but then stopped. This makes it unclear how it should be included. The same is true of the restraint question; this implies that a person was being thoughtful about their actions, but it remains unclear what strategy they ultimately pursued after this initial pause from acting too quickly.

For political action, I create a variable that is a count of the selected acts, excluding the "other" option. The "other" option required respondents to enter text describing what they did. A scan of the responses reveals that most respondents who selected this option were in the "personal life" condition and used the text box to indicate that the political action questions were irrelevant to their situation. In fact, roughly 50 percent of respondents in the personal life condition selected the "other" category compared to only about 10 percent from the politics condition. The final count variable ranges from 0 to 8; the most common responses were 0 (20 percent), 1 (41 percent), 2 (14 percent), and 3 activities (12 percent).

I estimate four fractional logistic regressions of each coping strategy variable and a Poisson regression of political action on a binary indicator for whether a respondent was in the politics condition (vs. personal condition), a binary indicator for whether a respondent was in the depression condition (vs. anger, anxiety, or fear condition), and their interaction. Table A.8 presents the results for the key variables from these models.

## Psychology Websites

I analyzed text from psychology websites in chapter 4 to assess what recommendations mental health professionals make about coping with the stress of politics. My analysis is based on the most visited psychology websites, which are listed in table A.9. To identify relevant pages, I searched each website using terms such as "politic*," "stress," and "coping" in permutations that always included the political term. Most of the time, this process yielded a single relevant page to include in the analysis.

Three aspects of the data collection process require elaboration. First, *Psychology Today* has an extensive set of professional bloggers, and many of them had their own take on how to cope with politics. Rather than including all of these pages, I only included the page that was labeled

TABLE A.9  **List of Psychology Websites and Pages**

| Website | Monthly Traffic | Page Analyzed |
|---|---|---|
| Psychology Today | 24 million | Politics |
| Verywell Mind | 19 million | No Matter What Party Is in Power, Politics Can Harm Mental Health |
| Scientific American Mind | 11 million | 5 Self-Care Tips for Today's Political Climate |
| Better Help | 10.4 million | What Is Post-Election Stress Disorder, and What Can You Do About It? |
| American Psychological Association | 7.7 million | Managing Stress Related to Political Change |
| Psych Central | 2.8 million | 1) How to Avoid Losing Friends Over Politics, and 2) Depressed by the News? Here Are 7 Strategies for Self-Care |
| HeadSpace | 2.7 million | 4 Ways to Cope When Politics Are Stressing You Out |
| Good Therapy | 2.0 million | Political Anxiety |
| Happier Human | 537,000 | 9 Tips to Avoid the News to Reduce Your Life Stress |
| PsychReg | 272,000 | How to Manage Our Mental Health During Tense Political Times |

*Note*: Data on monthly traffic for each website comes from SimilarWeb.com.

"Reviewed by Psychology Today Staff." Second, *Psych Central* produced two relevant pages—one about political news and one about talking about politics with family and friends—so I included both. Third, several popular psychology websites did not have a page about coping with politics, including Simply Psychology (monthly traffic: 2.7 million), Calm (2.1 million), Positive Psychology (2.0 million), PsychNews Daily (1.6 million), Psychiatric Times (1.0 million), BPS Research Digest (840,000), PsyPost (795,000), PsyBlog (175,000), MentalHealth.gov (150,000), and Mind Hacks (81,000).

Next, I downloaded each page and eliminated all text that was not a recommendation about how to cope. I then divided the remaining text into discrete recommendations. The articles often presented recommendations in a list format, which means there were already broken up. However, sometimes a single "recommendation" in the list would implicate other coping strategies, so I counted these separately. I then organized these recommendations into the nine categories presented in the main text.

I present two cross-sections of the data here: the categorization of responses from Verywell Mind and the responses in the "manage exposure" category. The Verywell Mind page was one of two that recommended six of the nine strategies, which makes it one of two to recommend the most

APPENDIX 175

strategies. Likewise the "manage exposure" category was the most recommended across websites. These cross-sections therefore offer the most in-depth peek into the data. Tables A.10 and A.11 show snippets of these recommendations. Importantly, as I note above, some text may implicate another strategy, in which case it would be counted as recommending both.

TABLE A.10 **Recommended Coping Strategies from Verywell Mind**

| Strategy | Website Text |
| --- | --- |
| Manage Exposure | Restructuring the time you spend consuming news media and limiting time spent on social media ... online discussions heighten stress levels and contribute to political polarization. |
| Self-Care | I recommend first prioritizing self-care and meeting their basic needs of healthy sleeping, eating and exercising. |
| Become Engaged | It can also be incredibly beneficial, both to you and your community, to get involved locally ... |
| Seek Social Support | Finding support instead from friends and family |
| Change Discussions | – |
| Go to Therapy | Seeking out a therapist is also always a healthy means of support |
| Self-Reflect | – |
| Learn about Politics | If you consistently feel overwhelmed by politics, educate yourself about the systems in place ... |
| Take Medication | – |

TABLE A.11 **Recommendations on How to Manage Exposure to Politics**

| Website | Website Text |
| --- | --- |
| Headspace | Sometimes a little bit of ignorance is bliss. If scrolling through your newsfeeds makes your blood pressure rise, it may be wise to take a step back. Those who check social media frequently are more likely to report that political discussions on social media cause them stress, and more than half of Americans (56 percent) say that while they want to stay informed about the news, doing so causes them stress ... |
| Verywell Mind | Restructuring the time you spend consuming news media and limiting time spent on social media. Indeed, research has shown that social media and online discussions heighten stress levels and contribute to political polarization. |
| APA | Stay informed, but know your limits. Consider how much news you take in and how that information is affecting you. If you are preoccupied by national events and it is interfering with your daily life, this may be a sign to cut back on your news intake and limit social media discussions ... |
| Psych Central (1) | People with depression often use television as a coping mechanism. This is counterproductive for obvious reasons if you're watching the news: News programs are rarely uplifting (there's an old expression among news people: "If it bleeds, it leads") ... Read positive news, too ... |
| GoodTherapy | Limiting social media involvement can also be helpful for some individuals. While social media can be a good way to stay informed, it can also be stressful, as it often involves heated debates and nasty comments. |

(*continues*)

TABLE A.11 (*continued*)

| Website | Website Text |
|---|---|
| Happier Human | Cancel Subscriptions. Do you still read the newspaper every day? Most of us don't, but if you do, go ahead and unsubscribe. You can get your news online when you want it. Unsubscribing isn't just for the daily newspaper that most of us don't get anymore. When we suggest canceling.... |
| PsychReg | Switching off your social media for a while may prove to be a great boon to your mental health. If you must be on social media, you can unfollow some of the people who are constantly sharing their vitriol. In extreme cases, you can block them too. Excuse yourself from the media for a while, perhaps a day or two. This includes TV, social media, and radio. Instead, watch a favourite film, or listen to music. |

*Note*: *Psychology Today*, *Psych Central* (2), and *Scientific American* are not included here because they did not recommend managing exposure as a strategy for coping with politics.

## Behavioral Risk Factor Surveillance Survey

The Behavioral Risk Factor Surveillance Survey (BFSS), which is administered by the United States Center for Disease Control, is "the nation's premier system of health-related telephone surveys that collect state data about U.S. residents regarding their health-related risk behaviors, chronic health conditions, and use of preventive services. Established in 1984 with 15 states, BRFSS now collects data in all 50 states as well as the District of Columbia and three U.S. territories. BRFSS completes more than 400,000 adult interviews each year, making it the largest continuously conducted health survey system in the world" (CDC). The BRFSS allows me to test my arguments because of the unique way in which the survey is carried out. Interviewing regularly occurs over the course of the year, meaning that tens of thousands of adults are surveyed each month. I therefore have a random sample of Americans reporting feelings of depression before and after political events of interest.

### *Chapter 5: Election Blues*

I use the BRFSS data from 2008 (Obama's win, Palin's loss), 2012 (Obama's win), 2016 (Clinton's loss), and 2020 (Harris's win) to test whether high-profile electoral wins or losses affect feelings of depression among citizens who share a gender or racial identity with these candidates.

The key outcomes are distressed days, depressed days, and anxious days, which are measured by asking respondents the following questions:

- **Distressed days**: "Now thinking about your mental health, which includes stress, depression, and problems with emotions, for how many days during the past 30 days was your mental health not good?"
- **Depressed days**: "During the past 30 days, for about how may days have you felt sad, blue, or depressed?"
- **Anxious days**: "During the past 30 days, for about how many days have you felt worried, tense, or anxious?"

In all cases, respondents could select between zero and thirty days. The measure of distressed days appears in most years as part of the core questionnaire, so it is asked of all respondents when it appears. The measures of depressed and anxious days are not administered in every year and only in a few states when they appear, because they are added by state-level officials in the portion of the survey that can be customized by state. I use these measures where possible because depressed days better capture depression than distressed days, while the anxiety days measure serves as a "placebo test."

I report the results of five analyses in the chapter. As I note there, "The results are based on negative binomial regression models of mental health days, depressed days, and anxious days for respondents who were interviewed in October, November, or December of the election year. The key independent variables are whether the survey interview occurred before or after the election as well as a "running" variable. The running variable is the number of days before or after the election the interview occurred, where zero is election day. I include survey weights; state fixed-effects; control variables for gender, race, age, education, income, marital status, and employment status; and self-rated health."

I make a few adjustments to this basic model in a few of the analyses. For Harris's win in 2020, I extend the sample through January 2021 and add a binary variable to the model for whether the survey interview occurred after the inauguration. For Palin's loss in 2008 and Clinton's loss in 2016, I add an interaction between gender and the electoral outcome for the state where the respondent resides, measured either as a binary variable indicating whether the state voted for Palin/Clinton or as a continuous variable based on the vote share for Palin/Clinton.

Below, I report the results for the key variables from the regressions models. I report the regression coefficients, standard errors, and average marginal effects for the first analysis (Obama in 2008) but only report the

TABLE A.12  **The Impact of Obama's Election in 2008**

|  | Distressed Days | | Depressed Days | | Anxious Days | |
|---|---|---|---|---|---|---|
|  | 1 | 2 | 3 | 4 | 5 | 6 |
| Postelection | 0.003 | 0.010 | −0.133 | −0.387** | −0.152** | −0.240** |
|  | (.033) | (.042) | (.241) | (.051) | (.037) | (.086) |
| Black | 0.374** | 0.185** | 0.382* | 0.033 | 0.039 | −0.150 |
|  | (.067) | (.080) | (.199) | (.123) | (.087) | (.218) |
| Female | 0.294** | 0.344** | 0.353** | 0.141 | 0.224** | 0.214** |
|  | (.027) | (.033) | (.008) | (.139) | (.055) | (.103) |
| Post × Black | −0.257** | −0.311** | −0.875** | −0.564** | −0.281 | 0.096 |
|  | (.078) | (.108) | (.179) | (.039) | (.177) | (.397) |
| Post × Female | 0.038 | 0.056 | −0.001 | 0.176 | 0.079* | 0.172 |
|  | (.034) | (.048) | (.159) | (.118) | (.035) | (.117) |
| Black × Female | −0.196** | −0.429** | −0.194 | −0.275** | −0.190** | −0.223 |
|  | (.074) | (.098) | (.217) | (.055) | (.076) | (.235) |
| Post × Black × Female | 0.258** | 0.390** | 1.014** | 0.792** | 0.303 | −0.183 |
|  | (.098) | (.119) | (.270) | (.086) | (.204) | (.392) |
| Running Variable | −0.001** | −0.001* | 0.003 | 0.004** | 0.002 | 0.002** |
|  | (.001) | (.001) | (.004) | (.0004) | (.003) | (.0003) |
| Observations | 102,606 | 88,883 | 3,349 | 2,912 | 3,336 | 2,909 |
| State Fixed-Effects | ✓ | ✓ | ✓ | ✓ | ✓ | ✓ |
| State Clustered SEs | ✓ | ✓ | ✓ | ✓ | ✓ | ✓ |
| Respondent Controls |  | ✓ |  | ✓ |  | ✓ |
|  | Average Marginal Effect of the "Election Treatment" | | | | | |
| Black Men | −0.899** | −0.875** | −2.314** | −2.087** | −1.743** | −0.592 |
| Black Women | 0.195 | 0.485* | 0.023 | 0.049 | −0.254 | −0.630** |
| Non-Black Men | 0.010 | 0.028 | −0.309 | −1.056** | −0.671** | −1.092** |
| Non-Black Women | 0.158 | 0.271* | −0.443 | −0.721** | −0.416 | −0.421** |

** p < 0.05; * p < 0.10
*Note*: Data come from the Behavioral Risk Factor Surveillance Survey. Estimates are coefficients (and standard errors) in the upper panel and marginal effects in the lower panel from negative binomial regressions of distressed days, depressed days, and anxious days. Control variables are gender, race, age, education, income, marital status, employment status, and self-rated health.

average marginal effect thereafter since it is ultimately the quantity of interest. However, the full regression results for not only the key independent variables but also the control variables can be obtained through the replication files posted on my website. The following results are presented in chronological order: Table A.12 for Obama's win in 2008, table A.13 for Obama's win in 2012, table A.14 for Harris's win in 2020, table A.15 for Palin's loss in 2008 and Clinton's loss in 2016.

## Chapter 7: The Pain of Public Policy

I use the BRFSS data from 2015 to test whether the SCOTUS decision in *Obergefell v. Hodges*, which ruled that there was a constitutional right to same-sex marriage, reduced depression among LGBTQ persons, especially in states where same-sex marriage was not previously legalized.

The dependent variable is based on the question, "Now thinking about your mental health, which includes stress, depression, and problems with emotions, for how many days during the past 30 days was your mental health not good?" Respondents could select between zero and thirty days. I convert this measure to a binary variable where 1 indicates that a respondent reported at least one distressed day, and 0 otherwise. About 30.6 percent of respondents report at least one distressed day over the past month. The measures of depressed days and anxious days were either not asked or did not have enough coverage in this year to be useful for the analysis.

The key independent variables are self-reported LGBTQ status of respondents and the same-sex policy of the state where the respondent resides. LGBTQ status is measured by asking respondents, "Do you consider yourself to be: (We ask this question in order to better understand the health and health care needs of people with different sexual orientations.)" Respondents could select straight, lesbian or gay, bisexual, other, or not sure. Respondents who do not give an answer are coded in the data as "refused." I generate a binary variable where 1 indicates respondents who are

TABLE A.13 **The Impact of Obama's Election in 2012**

|  | Distressed Days | | Depressed Days | | Anxious Days | |
| --- | --- | --- | --- | --- | --- | --- |
|  | 1 | 2 | 3 | 4 | 5 | 6 |
| Black Men | 0.666* | 0.501 | −1.426 | −3.319 | 2.552 | 0.751 |
| Black Women | 0.013 | −0.051 | 0.296 | 0.643 | 2.001 | 1.952 |
| Non-Black Men | −0.045 | −0.022 | 0.134 | 0.468 | −0.480 | 0.295 |
| Non-Black Women | 0.161 | 0.090 | 0.961 | 1.070 | 1.197 | 0.653 |
| Observations | 110,559 | 93,836 | 2,864 | 2,449 | 2,867 | 2,459 |
| State Fixed-Effects | ✓ | ✓ | ✓ | ✓ | ✓ | ✓ |
| State Clustered SEs | ✓ | ✓ | ✓ | ✓ | ✓ | ✓ |
| Respondent Controls |  | ✓ |  | ✓ |  | ✓ |

\*\* $p < 0.05$; \* $p < 0.10$
Note: Data come from the Behavioral Risk Factor Surveillance Survey. Estimates are marginal effects from negative binomial regressions of distressed days, depressed days, and anxious days. Control variables are gender, race, age, education, income, marital status, employment status, and self-rated health.

TABLE A.14 **The Impact of Harris's Election in 2020**

|  | Election Only | | Inauguration Only | | Election and Inauguration | |
|---|---|---|---|---|---|---|
|  | 1 | 2 | 3 | 4 | 5 | 6 |
|  | Average Marginal Effect of the Election | | | | | |
| Women of Color | 0.319* | 0.255 | | | 0.385* | 0.275 |
| Men of Color | -0.104 | -0.203 | | | -0.072 | -0.191 |
| White Women | 0.135 | 0.256 | | | 0.238* | 0.328** |
| White Men | 0.074 | 0.084 | | | 0.124 | 0.134 |
|  | Average Marginal Effect of the Inauguration | | | | | |
| Women of Color | | | -0.766** | -0.801** | -0.757** | -0.725** |
| Men of Color | | | -0.269 | -0.290 | -0.104 | -0.065 |
| White Women | | | -0.556 | -0.118 | -0.038 | -0.508 |
| White Men | | | -0.772** | -0.403** | -0.727** | -0.347** |
| Observations | 131,172 | 104,134 | 143,093 | 2,449 | 143,093 | 113,466 |
| State Fixed-Effects | ✓ | ✓ | ✓ | ✓ | ✓ | ✓ |
| State Clustered SEs | ✓ | ✓ | ✓ | ✓ | ✓ | ✓ |
| Respondent Controls | | ✓ | | ✓ | | ✓ |

** p < 0.05; * p < 0.10
*Note:* Data come from the Behavioral Risk Factor Surveillance Survey. Estimates are marginal effects from negative binomial regressions of distressed days. Control variables are gender, race, age, education, income, marital status, employment status, and self-rated health.

TABLE A.15  **The Impact of Palin's Loss in 2008 and Clinton's Loss in 2016**

|  | 2008 Election | | 2016 Election | |
|---|---|---|---|---|
|  | Winning State | Losing State | Winning State | Losing State |
| Women | 0.335* | 0.148 | 0.208 | 0.463** |
| Men | −0.001 | −0.180 | −0.095 | 0.221* |
| Observations | 88,883 | | 99,224 | |
| White Women | 0.335 | 0.112 | 0.184 | 0.708** |
| White Men | 0.195 | −0.126 | −0.091 | 0.233 |
| Non-White Women | 0.375 | 0.293 | 0.328 | −0.159 |
| Non-White Men | −0.740** | −0.422 | −0.112 | 0.188 |
| Observations | 88,883 | | 99,224 | |

\*\* $p < 0.05$; \* $p < 0.10$
Note: Data come from the Behavioral Risk Factor Surveillance Survey. Estimates are marginal effects from negative binomial regressions of distressed days. The results in the upper panel include an interaction between the election treatment and gender; the results in the lower panel include a triple interaction between election treatment, gender, and race. All models control for age, education, income, marital status, employment status, and self-rated health.

gay or lesbian, and 0 indicates otherwise. Not sure and refused are coded as missing. About 1.4 percent of respondents identify as gay or lesbian.

For prior state policy, I create a binary variable where 1 indicates that the state of residence had not recognized same-sex marriage prior to the SCOTUS ruling, and 0 otherwise. This variable captures whether a state saw a change to its same-sex marriage policy because of the ruling. States that had not recognized same-sex marriage at the time of the *Obergefell* ruling are Arkansas, Georgia, Kentucky, Louisiana, Michigan, Mississippi, Missouri, Nebraska, North Dakota, Ohio, South Dakota, Tennessee, and Texas.

I estimate logistic regression models of depression on three binary variables—LGBTQ status, post–June 28 interview, change to state-level same-sex marriage policy—and their interactions. I also cluster the standard errors by state and control for gender, race, age, education, and income. Table A.16 presents the results of the key variables from these models.

## European Social Survey

The European Social Survey (ESS) is a biennial nationally representative survey of citizens in over twenty-five European countries and Israel. The 2006 and 2012 waves, which include more than ninety thousand respondents, asked about depression, so I use these waves in my analyses.

TABLE A.16  **The Impact of the SCOTUS *Obergefell* Ruling**

|  | I | II |
|---|---|---|
| Postruling | 0.050** | 0.073** |
|  | (.015) | (.017) |
| Gay/Lesbian Status | 0.618** | 0.472** |
|  | (.064) | (.074) |
| State Change | −0.080 | −0.103 |
|  | (.055) | (.076) |
| Postruling × Status | −0.125 | −0.101 |
|  | (.113) | (.118) |
| Postruling × State Change | 0.011 | −0.006 |
|  | (.030) | (.038) |
| Status × State Change | 0.107 | 0.126 |
|  | (.089) | (.112) |
| Postruling × Status × State Change | −0.413* | −0.334* |
|  | (.152) | (.203) |
| Observations | 157,528 | 133,966 |
| State Clustered SEs | ✓ | ✓ |
| Control Variables |  | ✓ |

** $p < 0.05$; * $p < 0.10$

*Note*: Data come from the Behavioral Risk Factor Surveillance Survey. Estimates are coefficients (and standard errors) from logistic regressions of a binary variable indicating the experience of at least one distressed day in the past month. Control variables are gender, race, age, education, and income.

Specifically, I use the 2006 wave in chapter 5 to test whether electoral loss is depressing outside the United States, and I use 2006 and 2012 waves in chapter 7 to assess the impact of redistribution.

Depression is measured identically in the 2006 and 2012 waves with an abridged version of the Center for Epidemiologic Studies Depression Scale (Radloff 1977). Respondents were asked, "I will now read out a list of the ways you might have felt or behaved during the past week. Using this card, please tell me how much of the time during the past week" and then shown the following items: (1) you felt depressed, (2) you felt that everything you did was an effort, (3) your sleep was restless, (4) you were happy, (5) you felt lonely, (6) you enjoyed life, (7) you felt sad, (8) you could not get going, (9) you had a lot of energy, and (10) you felt peaceful. Response options were none or almost none of the time, some of the time, most of the time, and all or almost all of the time. Depression was calculated as the mean of the ten items (after reverse-coding "you were happy," "you enjoyed life," "you had a lot of energy," and "you felt peaceful"). Higher values indicate more depression. The Cronbach's alpha for the items is 0.86, indicating high reliability.

## Chapter 5: Election Blues

I use the 2006 wave to test my argument about electoral blues because it the only wave that includes a measure of depression and where one of the participating countries in the ESS—in this case the Netherlands—held an election midway through the data collection. The Dutch election therefore offers a quasi-natural experiment, because random samples of Dutch citizens were surveyed before and after the election. I can therefore assess whether changes in depression are tied to the *partisan* electoral winning and losing.

Respondents are classified as electoral winners or losers on the basis of (1) which party they support and (2) how each party performed. I assess each respondent's connection to a party using a question that asked, "Is there a particular political party you feel closer to than all the other parties?" Respondents who said yes to this question were then asked, "Which one?" and presented with a list of fifteen political parties from which to select. Whether supporters of each party are winners or losers depends on how the party in question performed. Table A.17 provides details on these performances. Notably, the survey also included questions about party membership and vote choice in the previous election. However, these measures are not adequate for my purposes. Only 95 (or 5 percent of) respondents reported any partisan membership, while vote choice for the prior election will be a noisier indicator of whom a respondent supports in the current election than the question about closeness.

From these two pieces of information—respondent's partisan support and the party's performance—I create two measures of losing:

TABLE A.17  **The Categorization of Party Success in the 2006 Dutch Elections**

| Category | Political Parties |
|---|---|
| Clear winners | Christian Democratic Appeal (major party in ruling coalition) |
| Partial winners | Socialist Party (gained 16 seats, not part of ruling coalition) |
|  | Party for Freedom (won 9 seats as new party) |
|  | Christian Union (gained 3 seats, part of ruling coalition) |
|  | Party for the Animals (won 2 seats as new party) |
| Neutral | Reformed Political Party (neither lost nor gained seats) |
| Clear Losers | GroenLinks (lost 1 seat) |
|  | Democrats 66 (lost 3 seats) |
|  | People's Party for Freedom and Democracy (lost 6 seats) |
|  | Pim Fortuyn List (lost 8 seats) |
|  | Labour Party (lost 9 seats) |

1. Losing as *not being part of the ruling coalition*. Respondents who support the Christian Democratic Appeal are electoral winners, while anyone who supports a different party is a loser. Since the final coalition was not formalized until months after the election, only supporters of the Christian Democratic Appeal—the party tapped to form the coalition—are considered winners. The inclusion of the Christian Union in the ruling coalition was not a forgone conclusion following the election.
2. Losing as *losing seats in Parliament*. Respondents who support the Labour Party (lost nine seats) People's Party for Freedom and Democracy (lost six seats) Democrats 66 (lost three seats) Pim Fortuyn List (lost eight seats), and GroenLinks (lost one seat) are losers, while supporters of any other party are winners (or at least not losers).

These two measures of losing allow me to classify respondents who support a party as winners or losers. I also create a third category for respondents who did not report being close to any party, and this category serves as a "control" group when assessing the electoral impact of winning and losing.

I estimate an ordinary least squares regression of depression on an indicator for whether the respondent took the survey before or after the election, whether the respondent is a winner or loser, and their interaction. Nonpartisan respondents are the omitted category. I also include a "running" variable that is the number of days before or after the election when the respondent took the survey; this variable is coded so that 0 indicates election day. I use survey weights and control for gender, age, education, income, marital status, and unemployment status. Table A.18 presents the results for the key variables from these models.

*Chapter 7: The Pain of Public Policy*

I use both the 2006 and 2012 waves to study the politics of redistribution. I assess how redistribution at the country level affects depression at the individual level and how this impact varies across the ideology and income of respondents.

The key independent variables are income, ideology, and redistribution. *Income* is measured by asking respondents, "Using this card, if you add up the income from all sources, which letter describes your household's total net income? If you don't know the exact figure, please give an estimate. Use the part of the card that you know best: weekly, monthly

TABLE A.18  **The Impact of Electoral Loss in the Netherlands**

|  | Losing Is Not Winning | | Losing Is Losing Seats | |
|---|---|---|---|---|
|  | 1 | 2 | 3 | 4 |
| Postelection | 0.018 | 0.031 | 0.019 | 0.037 |
|  | (.052) | (.055) | (.052) | (.054) |
| Electoral Losers | −0.015 | 0.008 | −0.029 | 0.015 |
|  | (.029) | (.030) | (.031) | (.032) |
| Losers × Postelection | 0.007 | 0.013 | 0.016 | 0.008 |
|  | (.049) | (.050) | (.055) | (.056) |
| Electoral Winners | 0.027 | 0.017 | 0.044 | 0.044 |
|  | (.040) | (.039) | (034) | (.034) |
| Winners × Postelection | −0.168** | −0.126** | −0.099* | −0.074 |
|  | (.062) | (.063) | (.054) | (.055) |
| Interview Day | 0.0002 | 0.0001 | 0.0001 | 0.0001 |
|  | (.0004) | (.0005) | (.0004) | (.0005) |
| Observations | 1,888 | 1,638 | 1,888 | 1,638 |
| Survey Weights | ✓ | ✓ | ✓ | ✓ |
| Individual Controls |  | ✓ |  | ✓ |

** $p < 0.05$; * $p < 0.10$
*Note*: Data come from the European Social Survey. Estimates are coefficients (and standard errors) from ordinary least squares regressions of depression. Control variables are gender, age, education, income, marital status, and unemployment status.

or annual income." The ESS makes responses commensurable across countries by creating categories that are "deciles of the actual household income range in the given country." The final income variable ranges from 1 (bottom income decile) to 10 (top income decile). *Ideology* is measured by asking respondents, "In politics people sometimes talk of 'left' and 'right.' Using this card, where would you place yourself on this scale, where 0 means the left and 10 means the right?" Respondents could choose a number between 0 (left) and 10 (right).

The measure of *redistribution* comes from the Standardized World Income Inequality Database (SWIID), which provides estimates of income inequality for 198 countries from 1960 onward (Solt 2020). I calculate redistribution by first taking the difference between market and disposable income (which is considered absolute redistribution) and then dividing this difference by market income inequality (which is considered relative redistribution). I use the measure of relative redistribution in the analysis.

I include several individual-level control variables in the model, which come from the ESS. *Gender* is a binary variable where 1 indicates that the respondents self-reported as a woman. *Age* is a continuous variable based on respondent self-report; it ranges from 14 to 103. *Education* is an ordinal variable with seven categories that capture how much schooling a respondent has completed. These categories are based on the International Standard Classification of Education set by the United Nations Educational, Scientific and Cultural Organization (UNESCO). The seven categories correspond to less than lower secondary (ES-ISCED I), lower secondary (II), lower-tier upper secondary (IIIb), upper-tier upper secondary (IIIa), advanced vocational or subdegree (IV), lower tertiary education/BA level (V1), and higher tertiary level/MA level or higher (V2). *Marital status* is a binary variable based on respondent self-report where 1 indicates married or in a civil partnership and 0 otherwise, such as separated, divorced, widowed, never married, or something else. *Self-reported health status* is a self-reported ordinal variable based on the question, "How is your health in general? Would you say it is . . .?" Response options include very bad, bad, fair, good, and very good. Higher values indicate better health. *Employment status* is a categorical variable based on the question that prompts respondents, "Using this card, which of these descriptions applies to what you have been doing for the last 7 days?" and then presents them with different activities, such as paid work, education, and more. From these questions, the ESS constructs a preset variable that captures a respondent's "main activity." I code respondents as unemployed if their main activity is either "unemployed, looking for work" or "unemployed, not looking for work." All other respondents are coded as 0, including those whose main activity is paid work, education, retirement, permanently sick or disabled, caretaking, or other.

I estimate two models. The first is an ordinary least squares regression of depression on redistribution, income, and ideology. The second model builds on the first by including interactions between redistribution, income, and ideology. Both models cluster standard errors by country and include survey weights, time-fixed effects, country-fixed effects, and control variables. The individual-level controls are gender, age, education, marital status, unemployment status, general health status, income, and ideology. The country-level controls are population size, civil liberties, political freedom, GDP per capita, and long-term unemployment. Table A.19 presents the results for the key variables from these models.

## British Household Panel Study

I use the British Household Panel Study (BHPS) in chapter 6 to test my argument that political polarization in our personal life is depressing. The

TABLE A.19 **The Impact of Ideology, Income, and Redistribution**

|  | 1 | 2 |
|---|---|---|
| Redistribution | −0.018** | −0.006 |
|  | (.004) | (.007) |
| Income | −0.017** | 0.064 |
|  | (.001) | (.044) |
| Ideology | −0.006** | 0.116** |
|  | (.001) | (.037) |
| Redistribution × Income |  | −0.002* |
|  |  | (.001) |
| Redistribution × Ideology |  | −0.003** |
|  |  | (.001) |
| Income × Ideology |  | −0.019** |
|  |  | (.007) |
| Redistribution × Income × Ideology |  | 0.001** |
|  |  | (.0002) |
| Observations | 46,391 | 46,391 |
| Countries | 21 | 21 |
| Survey Weights | ✓ | ✓ |
| Control Variables | ✓ | ✓ |
| Year Dummy | ✓ | ✓ |
| Country Fixed-Effects | ✓ | ✓ |
| Country-Clustered SEs | ✓ | ✓ |

\*\* $p < 0.05$; \* $p < 0.10$

*Note*: Data come from the European Social Survey and Standardized World Income Inequality Database. Estimates are coefficients (and standard errors) from ordinary least squares regressions of depression. All models control for gender, age, education, marital status, unemployment status, general health status, income, and ideology at the individual level, and for population size, civil liberties, political freedom, GDP per capita, and long-term unemployment at the country level.

BHPS is an annual and nationally representative survey of residents of Great Britain, Wales, Scotland, and Northern Ireland. It began in 1991 with over 10,300 individuals residing in about 5,500 households in Great Britain; the Scottish and Welsh samples were added in 1991, and the Irish sample was added in 2001. I use data from 1991 to 2018 in my analyses. The survey is household based, which means it follows all members of the original households and surveys them and their housemates as they move and/or the composition of their household changes.

The key dependent variable is depression. The BHPS includes a battery of questions known as the General Health Questionnaire-12 (GHQ-12). The GHQ-12 is a validated measure that is often used in psychology, psychiatry, and medicine. The twelve items are described in table A.20. The items have a Cronbach alpha of 0.89, indicating high reliability. I reverse code the positively worded items (3, 4, 7, 8, 12) and then average across items to generate an overall depression score, ranging from 1 to 4. The

TABLE A.20 **Items in the General Health Questionnaire-12**

|   | Category | Question ("Have you recently...") | Response Options |
|---|---|---|---|
| 1 | Concentrate | Been able to concentrate on whatever you're doing? | better than usual, same as usual, less than usual, much less than usual |
| 2 | Lost Sleep | Lost much sleep over worry? | not at all, no more than usual, rather more, much more |
| 3 | Felt Useful | Felt that you were playing a useful part in things? | more than usual, same as usual, less so, much less |
| 4 | Make Decisions | Felt capable of making decisions about things? | more than usual, same as usual, less so, much less |
| 5 | Constant Strain | Felt constantly under strain? | not at all, no more than usual, rather more, much more |
| 6 | Overcome Difficulties | Felt you couldn't overcome your difficulties? | not at all, no more than usual, rather more, much more |
| 7 | Enjoy Activities | Been able to enjoy your normal day-to-day activities? | more than usual, same as usual, less so, much less |
| 8 | Face Problems | Been able to face up to problems? | more than usual, same as usual, less so, much less |
| 9 | Felt Depressed | Been feeling unhappy or depressed? | not at all, no more than usual, rather more, much more |
| 10 | Lost Confidence | Been losing confidence in yourself? | not at all, no more than usual, rather more, much more |
| 11 | Felt Worthless | Been thinking of yourself as a worthless person? | not at all, no more than usual, rather more, much more |
| 12 | Felt Happy | Been feeling reasonably happy, all things considered? | more than usual, same as usual, less so, much less |

overall depression score variable has a mean of 1.93 and a standard deviation of 0.45.

The key independent variables are household partisan fractionalization and household partisan strength, which are described in detail in the main text.

I include several control variables in the model. *Gender* is a binary variable where 1 indicates that the respondent self-reported as a woman. *Age* is a continuous variable based on respondent self-report; it ranges from 15 to 101. *Education* is a ordinal variable with thirteen categories that capture the respondent's highest educational qualification: still at school, no qualification, other qualification, apprenticeship, CSE grade 2–5, commercial qualification, GCE O levels or equivalent, GCE A levels, nursing qualification, other higher qualification, teaching qualification, first degree, and higher degree; it is coded so higher values indicate higher educational qualifications and is added to the models as a continuous variable. *Marital status* is binary variable based on respondent self-report where 1 indicates married and 0 otherwise, such as separated, divorced, widowed, and never married. *Self-reported health status* is an ordinal variable based on the question, "Please think back over the last 12 months about how your health has been. Compared to people of your own age, would you say that your health has on the whole been ... ?" Response options include very poor, poor, fair, good, and excellent. Higher values indicate better health. *Employment status* is a preset variable from BHPS indicating whether a respondent is employed, not employed, or under the age of sixteen. No respondents under the age of sixteen are included in the analyses, so the variable is coded as 1 if employed, 0 otherwise. *Household size* is a continuous variable that captures the number of respondents residing in the household. *Household survey participation* is the proportion of household members that took the BHPS survey. *Household type* is a categorical variable indicating whether a household is (1) single nonelderly, (2) single elderly, (3) couple with no children, (4) couple with dependent children, (5) couple with nondependent children, (6) lone parent with dependent children, (7) lone parent with nondependent children, (8) 2 or more unrelated adults, or (9) other household.

I estimate an ordinary least squares regression of depression on household partisan fractionalization, household partisan strength, the square of these variables, and their interactions. The model uses household random effects, wave fixed effects, and household clustered standard errors and includes the control variables listed above. I exclude single-person households or households where only one member took the survey. Table A.21 presents the results for the key variables from this model.

TABLE A.21 **The Impact of Household Polarization on Overall Depression**

|  | 1 | 2 |
|---|---|---|
| Fractionalization | −0.111 | −0.114 |
|  | (.100) | (.100) |
| Frac × Frac | 0.233 | 0.211 |
|  | (.188) | (.188) |
| Strength | −0.025** | −0.007 |
|  | (.005) | (.004) |
| Frac × Strength | 0.273* | 0.277* |
|  | (.146) | (.151) |
| Frac × Frac × Strength | −0.561** | −0.519* |
|  | (.277) | (.287) |
| Strength × Strength | 0.008** | 0.002 |
|  | (.001) | (.001) |
| Frac × Strength × Strength | −0.104** | −0.112** |
|  | (.049) | (.052) |

(*continues*)

TABLE A.21 (*continued*)

|  | 1 | 2 |
|---|---|---|
| Frac × Frac × Strength × Strength | 0.221** | 0.225** |
|  | (.094) | (.100) |
| Observations | 172,722 | 144,595 |
| Households | 77,575 | 68,290 |
| Household Random Effects | ✓ | ✓ |
| Wave Fixed Effects | ✓ | ✓ |
| Household Clustered Standard Errors | ✓ | ✓ |
| Control Variables |  | ✓ |

\*\* $p < 0.05$; \* $p < 0.10$
*Note*: Data come from the British Household Panel Study. Estimates are coefficients (and standard errors) from ordinary least squares regressions of depression. Households with only one resident or households where only one resident participated in the survey are excluded. Control variables are gender, age, education, marital status, self-reported health status, employment status, household size, household survey participation, and household type.

## National Longitudinal Survey of Youth

I use the National Longitudinal Survey of Youth 1979 (NLSY79) and the Children of the National Longitudinal Survey of Youth 1979 (CNLSY79) in chapter 6 to test my argument that political polarization in our personal life is depressing. The NLSY79 is a nationally representative sample of 12,686 Americans born between 1957 and 1964. Conducted by the Bureau of Labor Statistics, respondents were interviewed annually from 1979 to 1994 and then biennially from 1996 to present. The CNLSY79 is a sample of over 10,000 children of women from the NLSY79. The CNLSY79 introduced a "Young Adult Survey" to children who were fifteen or older starting in 1994, which supplemented the mother-reported data. It is important to keep in mind that these "children" are mostly adults; less than a quarter of the sample are minors. The NLSY paired with the American National Election Study in 2006 to collect political information about the mothers and their teenage and adult children.

The key dependent variable is the child's feelings of depression, which are measured using a seven-item battery. Respondents are asked, "Please tell me how often you felt this way during the past week . . ." and then presented with the following symptoms: (1) I did not feel like eating; my appetite was poor, (2) I had trouble keeping my mind on what I was doing, (3) I felt depressed, (4) I felt that everything was an effort, (5) my sleep was restless, (6) I felt sad, and (7) I could not get "going." For each symptom, respondents could indicate that it occurred rarely or none of the time (less than 1 day), some or a little of the time (1–2 days), occasionally or a moderate amount of time (3–4 days), or most or all of the time (5–7 days). Responses are coded to range from 0 to 3, where higher values indicate more depression. An overall measure of depression is generated by taking the mean response across the seven items. The items have a Cronbach's alpha of 0.72. The mean is 0.67 (out of 3) with a standard deviation of 0.55.

The key independent variables are actual and perceived partisan difference between the child and the parent determined from the child's PID, mother's PID, child perception of mother's PID, and child perception of father's PID, which are described below.

- **Child party identification**: Standard three questions about party affiliation, strength, and leaning; coded on a seven-point scale for calculating *actual* difference between child and mother and on a three-point scale for calculating *perceived* difference between child and parents; leaners counted as partisans
- **Mother party identification**: Standard three questions about party affiliation, strength, and leaning; yields a seven-point scale from strong Republican to strong Democrat
- **Child perception of mother**: "When you were growing up, did your mother think of herself mostly as [a Democrat, a Republican (or reversed)], an Independent, or what?" [Response options: Democrat, Independent Republican]
- **Child perception of father**: "When you were growing up, did your father think of himself mostly as [a Democrat, a Republican (or reversed)], an Independent, or what?" [Response options: Democrat, Independent Republican]

I create measures of perceived partisan differences for mothers and fathers. Each measure is coded 1 if the child perceives any partisan difference between themselves and the respective parent, and 0 if they perceive a shared party identification. Since the perception measures are on a three-point scale, I convert the child's party identification to a three-point scale for the purposes of generating the perceived differences measures. I also create a "count" of perceived differences, which takes on values of 0 (no perceived difference with parents), 1 (perceived difference with only one parent), and 2 (perceived differences with both parents).

I include several control variables in the models. *Gender* is a binary variable where 1 indicates that the respondent self-reported as a woman. *Race* is a categorical variable with groups for White, Black, and neither

TABLE A.22  **The Impact of Actual Political Differences with Parents**

|  | Democratic Children | | Independent Children | | Republican Children | |
|---|---|---|---|---|---|---|
|  | 1 | 2 | 3 | 4 | 5 | 6 |
| Mother's Party Identification | −0.004 | 0.001 |  |  | −0.016 | −0.003 |
|  | (.013) | (.014) |  |  | (.012) | (.013) |
| Mother's "Folded" PID |  |  | 0.010 | 0.021 |  |  |
|  |  |  | (.024) | (.022) |  |  |
| Observations | 1,099 | 995 | 752 | 693 | 464 | 434 |
| Survey Weights | ✓ | ✓ | ✓ | ✓ | ✓ | ✓ |
| Respondent Controls |  | ✓ |  | ✓ |  | ✓ |

** $p < 0.05$; * $p < 0.10$
*Note*: Data come from the National Longitudinal Survey of Youth. Estimates are coefficients (and standard errors) from ordinary least squares regressions of depression. Control variables are gender, race, age, education, and income.

TABLE A.23  **The Impact of Perceived Political Differences with Parents**

|  | Parents Combined | | |
|---|---|---|---|
|  | 1 | 2 | 3 |
| Perceived Partisan Differences | 0.028 | 0.057** | 0.050** |
|  | (.018) | (.021) | (.021) |
| Observations | 3,942 | 3,483 | 3,380 |
| Survey Weights | ✓ | ✓ | ✓ |
| Respondent Controls |  | ✓ | ✓ |
| Lagged DV Control |  |  | ✓ |

|  | Parents Separated | | |
|---|---|---|---|
|  | 1 | 2 | 3 |
| Perceived Difference with Mother | −0.058 | −0.029 | −0.031 |
|  | (.046) | (.052) | (.050) |
| Perceived Difference with Father | 0.100** | 0.125** | 0.108** |
|  | (.047) | (.051) | (.047) |
| Observations | 3,492 | 3,135 | 3,060 |
| Survey Weights | ✓ | ✓ | ✓ |
| Respondent Controls |  | ✓ | ✓ |
| Lagged DV Control |  |  | ✓ |

** $p < 0.05$; * $p < 0.10$
*Note*: Data come from the National Longitudinal Survey of Youth. Estimates are coefficients (and standard errors) from ordinary least squares regressions of depression. Control variables are gender, race, age, education, and income.

White nor Black; the latter group serves as the baseline category in the model. *Age of child* is a continuous variable based on respondent self-report; it ranges from fourteen to thirty-five. *Education of child* is an ordinal self-reported variable that captures the highest grade completed; it ranges from zero to twenty. *Economic status of child* is measured as the poverty level of the child's household and is calculated by taking the self-reported income measure and indexing by Census Bureau poverty thresholds based on household size and composition.

I estimate two sets of models. The first set are ordinary least squares regressions of the child's depression on the mother's self-reported party identification (for Democratic and Republican children) or the mother's "folded" party identification (for Independent children). These models use survey weights and control for gender, race, age, education, and income. Table A.22 presents the results for the key variables from these models.

The second set of models are ordinary least squares regressions of the child's depression on perceived partisan differences with their parents. The setup of these models is identical to the first set of models except they also include actual partisan differences and lagged depression as control variables. Table A.23 presents the results for the key variables from these models.

# Notes

**Chapter One**

1. Persistent depressive disorder can also be diagnosed as the result of chronic major depressive disorder. Other mood disorders include bipolar I (a mix of manic and depressive states), bipolar II (a mix of hypomanic and depressive states), cyclothymic disorder (a long history of less intense hypomanic and depressive states), disruptive mood dysregulation disorder (an irritable temperament among children), and premenstrual dysphoric disorder (disruptions to mood in the week prior to and during menstruation).

2. Emotion families were first popularized by the psychologist Paul Ekman. In "An Argument for Basic Emotions," Ekman writes, "Each member of an emotion family shares certain characteristics, for example, commonalities in expression, in physiological activity, in nature of the antecedent events which call them forth, and perhaps also in the appraisal processes" (1992, 172). He goes on to argue that there are seven emotion families that are universally felt by humans—anger, happiness, sadness, contempt, surprise, fear, and disgust—which he refers to as the "basic" emotions (1992). What I call the depression family is what Ekman calls the sadness family. Other scholars disagree with the idea that any emotion is truly universal. For a useful review, see Lisa Feldman Barrett's *How Emotions Are Made* (2017).

3. As the psychologist James Gross writes, "One thing that makes the emotion literature challenging is that many different terms are used to refer to emotion-related processes, including affect, emotion, stress, and mood (Davidson 1994). Unfortunately, these terms are used in different ways by different researchers, leading at times to some degree of 'conceptual and definitional chaos' (Buck 1990, 330). To organize this chaotic landscape, I find it useful to view affect as the umbrella term . . . these affect states include (1) emotions such as anger and sadness, (2) stress responses to circumstances that exceed an individual's ability to cope, and (3) moods such as depression and euphoria" (2015, 5–6).

4. For a primer on the cultural meaning of different emotions, including members of the depression family, see *The Book of Human Emotions* by Tiffany Watt Smith (2015).

5. Moving forward, the term depression will primarily refer to the feeling family. Sometimes, however, depression will refer to itself as a family member. For instance, respondents in some surveys rate how depressed they feel about political events. Here depression refers to a specific feeling rather than the collective family. References to other members of the feeling family (e.g., disappointment) are generally meant to be specific to them as family members. Although the term "feeling" encompasses more than just emotions, I use these terms interchangeably to describe members of the depression family. This seems reasonable given that all moods and mood disorders begin as emotions.

6. Stress is a tricky concept to define. The World Health Organization describes it as "any change that causes physical, emotional or psychological strain" (2022). Others define stress differently. The sociologist Peggy Thoits describes it as "any environmental, social, or internal demand which requires the individual to readjust his/her usual behavior pattern" (1995, 54). According to these definitions, stress is neither what happens in the world nor our negative responses, but the combination of the two. I try to split the difference between the title of the framework—which was proposed by Lazarus and Folkman and which continues to be used today in psychology—and the technical meaning of the term "stress" by using the word "stressor" to refer to the first part of the framework.

**Chapter Two**

1. Bowlby (1961) and Parkes (1972) each identified four stages of grief-shock-numbness, yearning-searching, disorganization-despair, and reorganization. Elizabeth Kübler-Ross (1969) later hypothesized five stages: denial, anger, bargaining, depression, and acceptance. Each model thus recognizes depression/disorganization/despair as a grief response. Despite using the term stages, Kübler-Ross and other scholars (e.g., Corr et al. 2007) recognize that these responses may be experienced in different orders by different people. Indeed, there is strong evidence of the various reactions but mixed support for the idea that they proceed in stages (Maciejewski et al. 2007). For instance, one study found that many individuals expressed acceptance immediately following the loss of a loved one, while others went through some stages of the process but not always starting with disbelief or proceeding in the hypothesized order; feelings of depression were found to peak about six months following the loss of a loved one and then recede to their minimal value about two years after the loss (Maciejewski et al. 2007). The consensus thus seems to be that these hypothesized reactions have some legitimacy, but that the idea of stages does not.

2. It is not clear that the social risk theory integrates diverse evolutionary theories as much as it replicates the social competition theory. As the evolutionary psychologist Edward Hagen writes in his review essay, "The evidence Allen and Badcock present is also consistent with other theories that explain sadness and low mood as functional responses to social adversity. Their own comparison of the social risk hypothesis to the social competition hypothesis notes few differences" (2011, 719). Put another way, it is not clear that the concept of social investment potential differs meaningfully from the concept of social status.

3. Early means stress tends to be more depressing when experienced at a young age. Chronic means ongoing stress is more depressing than discrete or one-time stress. Continuing means current stress tends to be more depressing than past stress. Cumulative means more stress tends to be more depressing than less stress. Proximal means stress is more depressing when it more directly impact our lives.

4. Preferences are comparative subjective evaluations of two or more objects. We might rate our personal taste for jazz music and rock music—the subjective evaluation—and then conclude that we prefer jazz to rock—the comparison. Someone else might conclude the opposite based on their own evaluation, while another person might be indifferent between the two. Preferences reflect what we value in politics, and so it is the fulfillment of these preferences that might be lost, gained, maintained, or lacked.

5. Importantly, the absence of absolute scarcity doesn't necessarily mean everyone gets what they want. The sociologist Adel Daoud offers a useful example of how distributional problems can arise for even something that may seem absolutely abundant. He writes, "There could be more than enough land in order to meet all the food needs of a population (arable land is absolutely abundant in terms of food needs), but land may be needed for the production of housing or industry (relatively scarce in terms of alternative use). Conversely, land may be enough for agriculture, housing, and industry (relative abundance), but still misallocated in terms of agriculture (absolute scarcity); that is, more land is used for housing and industry which generates absolute abundance or over production in these sectors and absolute scarcity in agriculture" (2010, 1216–17). This example underscores how problems with distributing and accessing goods don't disappear simply because their supply is greater than their demand.

6. Importantly, this type of loss must be perceived by the loser for it to resonate emotionally, and this perception is only possible when people consume information about politics. If a person is unaware that a change has occurred, they cannot perceive themselves to be a loser or winner. It's also possible for people to mistakenly perceive themselves as losers or winners when in fact they are not. The gap between what people believe about politics and political reality can lead to either type of misperception.

## Chapter Three

1. Respondents who indicated that they identified as Independent or something else were forced to indicate whether they leaned toward the Republican or Democratic party.

2. To validate that the trends are appropriately classified as losses and gains, I asked respondents to evaluate how bad each trend was for themselves and for the country as a whole. On average, respondents evaluated the loss trends as worse and the gain trends as better on both dimensions when compared to the "no change" trends, which indicates the treatments are working as designed.

3. For the validity test, respondents were asked whether they thought the trend was permanent. On average, respondents who received the irrevocability treatment said trends were more permanent compared to respondents who received no information. In contrast, respondents who received the revocability treatment reported that the trends were less permanent, but their responses are not statistically distinguishable from those of respondents in the "no information" condition.

## Chapter Four

1. It is worth noting that emotion regulation and coping are distinct but overlapping concepts that both involve the regulation of affect. Coping emphasizes strategies for reducing negative emotions, a tendency that is reflected in the definition offered here. In contrast, the process model of emotion regulation explicitly recognizes that we can and do upregulate and downregulate both positive and negative emotions. Emotion regulation and coping also differ in their affective focus. Emotion regulation is narrowly focused on emotions, while coping is focused on any kind of affect, including emotions, moods, personality traits, and mental health disorders. Some coping strategies therefore require a longer timeline than emotion regulation strategies in order to accommodate longer-lasting types of affect.

2. Political participation is sometimes undertaken for solidarity or material reasons rather than political ones (Van Deth 2014). In these cases, participation may be pursued as a problem-focused coping strategy for a personal problem that is social (e.g., lack of friends) or economic (e.g., lack of money). The social aspect of participation also means it may be used as part of a coping strategy focused on appraisal, attention, or emotions. For instance, participation might be the way we seek social support when confronted with a problem. For these reasons, we might occasionally see participation used as a coping strategy for nonpolitical problems or as a way to cope when politics is depressing.

3. These results are expected values based on a Poisson regression of the count of political actions. The key predictors are a binary indicator for the depression

NOTES TO CHAPTER FIVE                                                    199

treatment, a binary indicator for the politics treatment, and their interaction. The full output of the regression models is reported in the appendix.

**Chapter Five**

1. The study of Clinton's loss by Yan and colleagues also analyzed another question, "Has a doctor, nurse, or other health professional ever told you that you had any of the following? Tell me yes, no, or not sure." The enumerator than read out a list of health conditions, which includes "(Ever told) you that you have a depressive disorder, including depression, major depression, dysthymia, or minor depression?" I do not consider this measure, because it does not as cleanly capture feelings of depression and most likely is biased against people of color and lower socioeconomic status who often face steeper barriers to seeking mental health care.

2. The CDC allows state government health agencies to control a portion of the survey, so these questions occasionally appear when a state opts to include them. As a result, there are many fewer respondents to analyze using these questions than the psychological distress question, which appears on the core questionnaire.

3. The results reported here are based on negative binomial regression models of mental health days, depressed days, and anxious days for respondents who were interviewed in October, November, or December of the election year. The key independent variables are whether the survey interview occurs before or after the election as well as a "running" variable. The running variable is the number of days before or after the election the interview occurs, where 0 is election day. I include survey weights, state fixed effects, and control variables for gender, race, age, education, income, marital status, employment status, and self-rated health. I use this basic setup for all the BRFSS analyses, except when idiosyncrasies of an election required adjustments. The appendix reports more details on the data, measures, and results.

4. Notably, the characteristic break at the discontinuity is missing for distressed days but present for depressed days and anxious days. Since respondents are asked to reflect on the past thirty days, it makes sense that we would not see an immediate drop but that one would emerge over time. I suspect the difference is that depression and anxiety call forth a more immediate feeling than stress, so they are subject to recency bias. Excited about the election results, respondents may give responses rosier than the reality of their past thirty days. The initial reduction in depressed days persists for the duration of the year, while anxiety returns to its preelection level. I explore this possibility by estimating a series of models that shifted the "treatment" (election) by one day over the course of November to better assess what is occurring with measures of depression and anxiety. For depressed days, there is a statistically significant effect in the first four days

after the election—respondents report two fewer depressed days on average—but this goes away five days after the election when the initial excitement has worn off. The effect of the election returns after twenty-one days, which is roughly what we would expect if respondents are giving answers that truly reflect the past month. For anxiety, there is a similar pattern to depression, but the effects are not statistically significant. For Black women and White Americans, either men or women, there is no evidence that Obama's election reduced the number of stressed, depressed, or anxious days. The full results of this analysis are reported in the appendix.

5. The European Social Survey collects information about depression in Wave 3 (2006) and Wave 6 (2012). I looked up whether each participating country in these two years had an election at the time. There were elections in fourteen countries in 2006 and in eight countries in 2012. I then determined whether the election date overlapped with the dates of the survey, which vary somewhat from country to country. Only the Netherlands in 2006 and Slovenia in 2012 had overlap, and the overlap in Slovenia was so minimal that there were not enough respondents in the preelection group to conduct meaningful analyses. This left me with only the Netherlands, which incidentally is one of the better cases to use because it is "most different" vis-á-vis the United States. The election for the Tweede Kamer took place on November 22, 2006, while Wave 3 of the European Social Survey was administered to Dutch respondents between August 30, 2006, and March 30, 2007. As a result, 2,493 respondents (about 37 percent of the Dutch sample) were interviewed on or before election day, while 4,298 (about 63 percent of the Dutch sample) were interviewed after election day.

**Chapter Six**

1. The calculation of household partisan fractionalization is based on the party affiliation of survey respondents. This is assessed using three questions. First, respondents are asked, "Do you think of yourself as a little closer to one political party than to the others?" Respondents who say "yes" are asked, "Which one? (Party do you regard yourself as being closer to than the others)," while respondents who say "no" are asked, "If there were to be a General Election tomorrow, which political party do you think you would be most likely to support?" For these latter two questions, respondents can choose from thirteen political parties, or they can report no partisan affiliation. Respondents who do not answer the question or who report they are too young to vote (if asked the third question) are coded as missing, which means they do not factor into the fractionalization measure. I then calculate the proportion of each household-year that belongs to each party. For instance, if all members of a household in a given year report a preference for the Conservative party, then the Conservative proportion of that

household would be 1 and the proportion for all other parties/nonpartisan would be 0. For each household-year, I then square each of these proportions, sum across these values, and then subtract the sum from 1. This gives me my final measure of fractionalization. I then merge this household-year data back into the individual-year data for the analyses.

2. These categories are based on a combination of questions, including the ones mentioned above in the calculation of fractionalization as well as another question posed to respondents who reported feeling close to a political party. This new question asked, "Would you call yourself a very strong supporter of [PARTY], fairly strong, or not very strong?" Respondents could choose from the three options in the question. Those who did not answer the question or said "don't know" were coded as missing.

3. A few obvious problems: neither political disagreement nor the loss of social support is randomly assigned to clients; the stories represent the experiences of only a small portion of the small portion of Americans who go to therapy; the clients under study are selected on the dependent variable; and the analysis entails a triple interpretation of the data—my interpretation of the mental health professional's interpretation of the client's interpretation of their own experience.

**Chapter Seven**

1. Since countries use different currencies with different purchasing powers, the survey presents respondents with 10 income categories that correspond to the income decile within their country. It is these income deciles that are used in the analysis. For ideology, respondents were asked to locate their left-right ideology on a card that ranges from 0 (left) to 10 (right).

# References

Albertson, Bethany, and Shana Kushner Gadarian. 2015. *Anxious Politics: Democratic Citizenship in a Threatening World*. New York: Cambridge University Press.
Albrecht, Glenn, Gina-Maree Sartore, Linda Connor, Nick Higginbotham, Sonia Freeman, Brian Kelly, Helen Stain, Anne Tonna, and Georgia Pollard. 2007. "Solastalgia: The Distress Caused by Environmental Change." *Australasian Psychiatry* 15, no. S1: S95–S98.
Allen, Nicholas B., and Paul B. T. Badcock. 2003. "The Social Risk Hypothesis of Depressed Mood: Evolutionary, Psychosocial, and Neurobiological Perspectives." *Psychological Bulletin* 129, no. 6: 887–913.
American Political Science Association. 1950. "Part I. The Need for Greater Party Responsibility." In "Towards a More Responsible Two-Party System," special issue, *American Political Science Review* 44, no. 3, part 2: 15–36.
American Psychiatric Association. 2022. *Diagnostic and Statistics Manual of Mental Disorders*, 5th ed. Arlington, VA: American Psychiatric Association.
Anderson, Christopher J., André Blais, Shaun Bowler, Todd Donovan, and Ola Listhaug, eds. 2007. *Losers' Consent: Elections and Democratic Legitimacy*. New York: Oxford University Press.
Andris, Clio, David Lee, Marcus J. Hamilton, Mauro Martino, Christian E. Gunning, and John Armistead Selden. 2015. "The Rise of Partisanship and Super-Cooperators in the U.S. House of Representatives." *PLOS ONE* 10, no. 4: e0123507.
Arnold, Magna. 1960. *Emotion and Personality*. New York: Columbia University Press.
Azari, Julia. 2017. "What Hillary Clinton's Candidacy Meant for Women." *Vox*, November 6, 2017.
Baker, John P., and Howard Berenbaum. 2007. "Emotional Approach and Problem-Focused Coping: A Comparison of Potentially Adaptive Strategies." *Cognition and Emotion* 21, no. 1: 95–118.

Barber, Brian K, ed. 2009. *Adolescents and War: How Youth Deal with Political Violence*. New York: Oxford University Press.

Barrett, Lisa Feldman. 2017. *How Emotions Are Made: The Secret Life of the Brain*. New York: Harper Collins.

Berona, Johnny, Sarah Whitton, Michael E. Newcomb, Brian Mustanski, and Robert Gibbons. 2021. "Predicting the Transition from Suicidal Ideation to Suicide Attempt among Sexual and Gender Minority Youths." *Psychiatric Services* 72, no. 11: 1261–67.

Blackington, Courtney. 2024. "Angry and Afraid: Emotional Drivers of Protest for Abortion Rights in Poland." *East European Politics* 40, no. 1: 1–20.

Bolger, N., A. DeLongis, R. C. Kessler, and E. A. Schilling. 1989. "Effects of Daily Stress on Negative Mood." *Journal of Personality and Social Psychology* 57, no. 5: 808–18.

Bond, Robert M., Christopher J. Fariss, Jason J. Jones, Adam D. Kramer, Cameron Marlow, Jaime E. Settle, and James Fowler. 2012. "A 61-Million-Person Experiment in Social Influence and Political Mobilization." *Nature* 489: 295–98.

Bowlby, J. 1961. "Processes of Mourning." *International Journal of Psycho-Analysis* 42: 317–40.

———. 1980. *Sadness and Depression*. Vol. 3 of *Attachment and Loss*. New York: Basic Books.

Brazile, Donna. 2008. "Commentary: A letter to the losers." CNN.com, November 7, 2008.

Brouillette, Richard. 2016. "Why Therapists Should Talk Politics." *New York Times*, March 15, 2016.

Brown, Tony N., Alexa Solazzo, and Bridget K. Gorman. 2021. "'Yes We Can!' The Mental Health Significance for U.S. Black Adults of Barack Obama's 2008 Presidential Election." *Sociology of Race and Ethnicity* 7, no. 1: 101–15.

Burgo, Joseph. 2018. *Shame: Free Yourself, Find Joy, and Build True Self-Esteem*. New York: St. Martin's Essentials.

Cassese, Erin C. 2021. "Partisan Dehumanization in American Politics." *Political Behavior* 43, no. 1: 29–50.

Chandler, David. 2014. "Democracy Unbound? Non-Linear Politics and the Politicization of Everyday Life." *European Journal of Social Theory* 17, no. 1: 42–59.

Coburn, Jesse. 2015. "Tearful Moment with Merkel Turns Migrant Girl into a Potent Symbol." *New York Times*, July 20, 2015.

Corr, Charles A., Kenneth J. Doka, and Robert Kastenbaum. 1999. "Dying and Its Interpreters: A Review of Selected Literature and Some Comments on the State of the Field." *OMEGA - Journal of Death and Dying* 39, no. 4: 239–59.

Cramer, Katherine J. 2016. *The Politics of Resentment: Rural Consciousness in Wisconsin and the Rise of Scott Walker*. Chicago: University of Chicago Press.

Crenshaw, Kimberle. 1991. "Mapping the Margins: Intersectionality, Identity Politics, and Violence against Women of Color." *Stanford Law Review* 43, no. 6 :1241–99.

C-SPAN. 2022. "Senate Republican Agenda." www.c-span.org.

Cypel, Yasmin, Paula P. Schnurr, Aaron I. Schneiderman, William J. Culpepper, Fatema Z. Akhtar, Sybil W. Morley, Dennis A. Fried, Erick K. Ishii, and Victoria J. Davey. 2022. "The Mental Health of Vietnam Theater Veterans—The Lasting Effects of the War: 2016–2017 Vietnam Era Health Retrospective Observational Study." *Journal of Traumatic Stress* 35, no. 2: 605–18.

Dadlez, E. M., and William L. Andrews. 2010. "Post-Abortion Syndrome: Creating an Affliction." *Bioethics* 24, no. 9: 445–52.

Daoud, Adel. 2010. "Robbins and Malthus on Scarcity, Abundance, and Sufficiency." *American Journal of Economics and Sociology* 69, no. 4: 1206–29.

Darwin, Charles. 1872. *The Expression of the Emotions in Man and Animals*, 3rd ed. New York: Oxford University Press.

Driscoll, Daniel. 2020. "When Ignoring the News and Going Hiking Can Help You Save the World: Environmental Activist Strategies for Persistence." *Sociological Forum* 35, no. 1: 189–206.

Dunn, Amina. 2020. "Few Trump or Biden Supporters Have Close Friends Who Back the Opposing Candidate." Pew Research Center, September 18, 2020.

Earth.org. 2021. "Greta Thunberg Is 'Open' to Meeting Biden at UN Climate Summit." *Earth.org*, October 21, 2021.

Ekman, Paul. 1992. "An Argument for Basic Emotions." *Cognition and Emotion* 6, no. 3–4: 169–200.

Esping-Andersen, Gøsta. 1990. *The Three Worlds of Welfare Capitalism*. Princeton, NJ: Princeton University Press.

Ferster, Charles B. 1974. "Behavioral Approaches to Depression." In *The Psychology of Depression: Contemporary Theory and Research*, edited by R. J. Friedman and M. M. Katz, 29–45. Oxford, England: Wiley.

*First Draft by Tim Porter: Covering War in a Free Society* (blog). N.d. http://www.timporter.com/firstdraft/archives/000071.html.

Flores, Andrew R., Christy Mallory, and Kerith J. Conron. 2020. *The Impact of Obergefell v. Hodges on the Well-Being of LGBT Adults*. Technical report. Williams Institute.

Folkman, Susan, and Judith Tedlie Moskowitz. 2004. "Coping: Pitfalls and Promise." *Annual Review of Psychology* 55: 745–74.

Folmar, Chloe. 2022. "Sen. Rick Scott Calls 2022 Election a 'Complete Disappointment.'" *The Hill*, November 12, 2022.

Ford, Brett Q., and Matthew Feinberg. 2020. "Coping with Politics: The Benefits and Costs of Emotion Regulation." *Current Opinion in Behavioral Sciences* 34: 123–28.

Ford, Brett Q., Dorainne J. Green, and James J. Gross. 2022. "White Fragility: An Emotion Regulation Perspective." *American Psychologist* 77: 510–24.

Freud, Sigmund. 1917. "Mourning and Melancholia." *International Journal for Medical Psychoanalysis* 4, no. 6: 288–301.

Frijda, Nico H. 1987. "Emotion, Cognitive Structure, and Action Tendency." *Cognition and Emotion* 1, no. 2: 115–43.

Funes, Yessenia. 2022. "The Environmental Movement Faces Burnout: This Woman Wants to Repair That." *Atmos: The Frontline*, August 17, 2022.

Galea, Sandro, Jennifer Ahern, Heidi Resnick, Dean Kilpatrick, Michael Bucuvalas, Joel Gold, and David Vlahov. 2002. "Psychological Sequelae of the September 11 Terrorist Attacks in New York City." *New England Journal of Medicine* 346, no. 13: 982–87.

Gariépy, Geneviève, Helena Honkaniemi, and Amélie Quesnel-Vallée. 2016. "Social Support and Protection from Depression: Systematic Review of Current Findings in Western Countries." *British Journal of Psychiatry* 209, no. 4: 284–93.

Ginzburg, Karni, Tsachi Ein-Dor, and Zahava Solomon. 2010. "Comorbidity of Posttraumatic Stress Disorder, Anxiety and Depression: A 20-Year Longitudinal Study of War Veterans." *Journal of Affective Disorders* 123, no. 1–3: 249–57.

Goldberg, Emma. 2020. "'Do Not Vote for My Dad': When Families Disagree on Politics." *New York Times*, August 27, 2020.

Goldberg, Michelle. 2022. "The Mental Health Toll of Trump-Era Politics." *New York Times*, January 21, 2022.

Gorski, Paul C. 2019. "Racial Battle Fatigue and Activist Burnout in Racial Justice Activists of Color at Predominately White Colleges and Universities." *Race Ethnicity and Education* 22, no. 1: 1–20.

Gorski, Paul C., and Cher Chen. 2015. "'Frayed All Over:' The Causes and Consequences of Activists Burnout among Social Justice Education Activists." *Educational Studies* 51, no. 5: 385–405.

Gorski, Paul, Stacy Lopresti-Goodman, and Dallas Rising. 2019. "'Nobody's Paying Me to Cry': The Causes of Activist Burnout in United States Animal Rights Activists." *Social Movement Studies* 18, no. 3: 364–80.

Gossen, Hermann Heinrich. 1983. *The Laws of Human Relations and the Rules of Human Action Derived Therefrom*. Cambridge, MA: MIT Press.

Gray, Matt J., Brett T. Litz, Julie L. Hsu, and Thomas W. Lombardo. 2004. "Psychometric Properties of the Life Events Checklist." *Assessment* 11, no. 4: 330–41.

Grist, Matt. 2009. *Changing the Subject*. Technical report. Royal Society of Arts United Kingdom.

Gross, James J. 2001. "Emotion Regulation in Adulthood: Timing Is Everything." *Current Directions in Psychological Science* 10, no. 6: 214–19.

Gross, James J., ed. 2015. *Handbook of Emotion Regulation*. New York: Guilford Press.

Gross, James J., and Ricardo F. Muñoz. 1995. "Emotion Regulation and Mental Health." *Clinical Psychology: Science and Practice* 2, no. 2: 151–64.

Haas, Ann P., Mickey Eliason, Vickie M. Mays, Robin M. Mathy, Susan D. Cochran, Anthony R. D'Augelli, Morton M. Silverman, Prudence W. Fisher, Tonda Hughes, Margaret Rosario, Stephen T. Russell, Effie Malley, Jerry Reed, David A. Litts, Ellen Haller, Randall L. Sell, Gary Remafedi, Judith Bradford, Annette L. Beautrais, Gregory K. Brown, Gary M. Diamond, Mark S. Friedman, Robert Garofalo, Mason S. Turner, Amber Hollibaugh, and Paula J. Clay-

ton. 2010. "Suicide and Suicide Risk in Lesbian, Gay, Bisexual, and Transgender Populations: Review and Recommendations." *Journal of Homosexuality* 58, no. 1: 10–51.
Hagen, Edward. 2011. "Evolutionary Theories of Depression: A Critical Review." *Canadian Journal of Psychiatry* 56, no. 12: 716–26.
Halperin, Eran, Roni Porat, Maya Tamir, and James J. Gross. 2013. "Can Emotion Regulation Change Political Attitudes in Intractable Conflicts? From the Laboratory to the Field." *Psychological Science* 24, no. 1: 106–11.
Hammen, Constance. 2005. "Stress and Depression." *Annual Review of Clinical Psychology* 1: 293–319.
———. 2015. "Stress and Depression: Old Questions, New Approaches." *Current Opinion in Psychology* 4: 80–85.
Hancock, Ange-Marie. 2004. *The Politics of Disgust: The Public Identity of the Welfare Queen*. New York: New York University Press.
Hanisch, Carol. 1969. "The Personal Is Political." *Writings by Carol Hanisch* (blog) https://www.carolhanisch.org/CHwritings/PIP.html.
Hari, Johann. 2018. *Lost Connections: Why You're Depressed and How to Find Hope*. New York: Bloomsbury.
Harrington, Michael. 1974. "A Collective Sadness." *Dissent Magazine*.
Harris, William A. 1997. "On "Scope Conditions" in Sociological Theories." *Social and Economic Studies* 46, no. 4: 123–27.
Hatzenbuehler, Mark L., Katherine M. Keyes, and Deborah S. Hasin. 2009. "State-Level Policies and Psychiatric Morbidity in Lesbian, Gay, and Bisexual Populations." *American Journal of Public Health* 99, no. 12: 2275–81.
Hatzenbuehler, Mark L., Katie A. McLaughlin, Katherine M. Keyes, and Deborah S. Hasin. 2010. "The Impact of Institutional Discrimination on Psychiatric Disorders in Lesbian, Gay, and Bisexual Populations: A Prospective Study." *American Journal of Public Health* 100, no. 3: 452–59.
Hickman, Caroline, Elizabeth Marks, Panu Pihkala, Susan Clayton, R. Eric Lewandowski, Elouise E. Mayall, Britt Wray, Catriona Mellor, and Lise van Susteren. 2021. "Climate Anxiety in Children and Young People and Their Beliefs about Government Responses to Climate Change: A Global Survey." *Lancet Planetary Health* 5, no. 12: e863–e873.
Hidaka, Brandon H. 2012. "Depression as a Disease of Modernity: Explanations for Increasing Prevalence." *Journal of Affective Disorders* 140, no. 3: 205–14.
Holmes, T. H., and R. H. Rahe. 1967. "The Social Readjustment Rating Scale." *Journal of Psychosomatic Research* 11, no. 2: 213–18.
Horwitz, Allan V., and Jerome C. Wakefield. 2007. *The Loss of Sadness: How Psychiatry Transformed Normal Sadness into Depressive Disorder*. New York: Oxford University Press.
Hounshell, Blake, and Leah Askarinam. 2022. "Why Senate Republicans Are Feuding over Their Midterm Message." *New York Times*, March 10, 2022.
Huckfeldt, Robert, and John Sprague. 1992. "Political Parties and Electoral

Mobilization: Political Structure, Social Structure, and the Party Canvass." *American Political Science Review* 86, no. 01: 70–86.

Jennings, M. Kent, Laura Stoker, and Jake Bowers. 2009. "Politics across Generations: Family Transmission Reexamined." *Journal of Politics* 71, no. 03: 782–99.

Joseph, Peniel E. 2017. "Barack Obama Forever Changed Black America." *Guardian*, January 7, 2017.

Jost, John T., Chadly Stern, Nicholas O. Rule, and Joanna Sterling. 2017. "The Politics of Fear: Is There an Ideological Asymmetry in Existential Motivation?" *Social Cognition* 35, no. 4: 324–53.

Just, Marion R., Ann N. Crigler, and Todd L. Belt. 2007. "Don't Give Up Hope: Emotions, Candidate Appraisals, and Votes." In *The Affect Effect*, edited by W. Russell Newman, George E. Marcus, Ann N. Crigler, and Michael MacKuen, 231–59. Chicago: University of Chicago Press.

Kahneman, Daniel, and Amos Tversky. 1979. "Prospect Theory: An Analysis of Decision Under Risk." *Econometrica* 47, no. 2: 263–91.

Kalmus, Peter. 2021. "Climate Depression Is Real. And It Is Spreading Fast among Our Youth." *Guardian*, November 4, 2021.

Kaniasty, Krzysztof, and Urszula Jakubowska. 2014. "Can Appraisals of Common Political Life Events Impact Subjective Well-Being?" *Journal of Applied Social Psychology* 44, no. 12: 751–67.

Kantor, Martin. 1992. *The Human Dimensions of Depression: A Practical Guide to Diagnosis, Understanding, and Treatment.* Westport, CT: Praeger.

Karnaze, Melissa M., and Linda J. Levine. 2018. "Sadness: The Architect of Cognitive Change." In *The Function of Emotions: When and Why Emotions Help Us*, edited by Heather C. Lench, 45–58. Springer International/Springer Nature.

Keltner, Dacher, and James J. Gross. 1999. "Functional Accounts of Emotions." *Cognition and Emotion* 13, no. 5: 467–80.

King, Michael, Joanna Semlyen, Sharon See Tai, Helen Killaspy, David Osborn, Dmitri Popelyuk, and Irwin Nazareth. 2008. "A Systematic Review of Mental Disorder, Suicide, and Deliberate Self Harm in Lesbian, Gay and Bisexual People." *BMC Psychiatry* 8, no. 1: 70.

Kübler-Ross, Elisabeth. 1969. *On Death and Dying.* New York: Simon & Schuster.

La Ganga, Maria L. 2000. "For the Loser, a Sudden Lonely Silence." *Los Angeles Times*, November 6, 2000.

Landman, Todd, and Hans-Joachim Lauth. 2019. "Political Trade-Offs: Democracy and Governance in a Changing World." *Politics and Governance* 7, no. 4: 237–42.

Landry, Nicholas, Robert Gifford, Taciano L. Milfont, Andrew Weeks, and Steven Arnocky. 2018. "Learned Helplessness Moderates the Relationship between Environmental Concern and Behavior." *Journal of Environmental Psychology* 55: 18–22.

Landwehr, Claudia, and Christopher Ojeda. 2021. "Democracy and Depression:

A Cross-National Study of Depressive Symptoms and Nonparticipation." *American Political Science Review* 115, no. 1: 323–30.

Landwehr, Claudia, and Nils D Steiner. 2017. "Where Democrats Disagree: Citizens' Normative Conceptions of Democracy." *Political Studies* 65, no. 4: 786–804.

Langford, Catherine Penny Hinson, Juanita Bowsher, Joseph P. Maloney, and Patricia P. Lillis. 1997. "Social Support: A Conceptual Analysis." *Journal of Advanced Nursing* 25, no. 1: 95–100.

Lasswell, Harold D. 1936. *Politics: Who Gets What, When, How*. New York: McGraw-Hill.

Layman, Geoffrey C., Thomas M. Carsey, and Juliana Menasce Horowitz. 2006. "Party Polarization in American Politics: Characteristics, Causes, and Consequences." *Annual Review of Political Science* 9, no. 1: 83–110.

Lazarus, Richard. 1991. "Progress on a Cognitive-Motivational-Relational Theory of Emotion." *American Psychologist* 46, no. 8: 819–34.

Lazarus, Richard S., and Judith Blackfield Cohen. 1977. "Environmental Stress." In *Human Behavior and Environment: Advances in Theory and Research*, Vol. 2, edited by Irwin Altman and Joachim F. Wohlwill, 89–127. Boston: Springer US.

Lazarus, Richard S., and Susan Folkman. 1984. *Stress, Appraisal, and Coping*. New York: Springer.

Lee, Brandy X. 2017. *The Dangerous Case of Donald Trump: 27 Psychiatrists and Mental Health Experts Assess a President*. New York: Thomas Dunne Books.

Lench, Heather C., Thomas P. Tibbett, and Shane W. Bench. 2016. "Exploring the Toolkit of Emotion: What Do Sadness and Anger Do for Us?" *Social and Personality Psychology Compass* 10, no. 1: 11–25.

Lerer, Lisa, and Sydney Ember. 2020. "Kamala Harris Makes History as First Woman and Woman of Color as Vice President." *New York Times*, November 8, 2020.

Levin, Aaron. 2016. "Goldwater Rule's Origins Based on Long-Ago Controversy." *Psychiatrics News*, August 25, 2016.

Levine, Linda J. 1996. "The Anatomy of Disappointment: A Naturalistic Test of Appraisal Models of Sadness, Anger, and Hope." *Cognition and Emotion* 10: 337–59.

Lewinsohn, Peter M. 1986. "A Behavioral Approach to Depression." In *Essential Papers on Depression*, edited by James C. Coyne, 150–80. New York: New York University Press.

Lieberman, Jeffrey. 2017. "The Dangerous Case of Psychiatrists Writing about the POTUS's Mental Health." *Psychiatric News*, November 15, 2017.

Maciejewski, Paul K., Baohui Zhang, Susan D. Block, and Holly G. Prigerson. 2007. "An Empirical Examination of the Stage Theory of Grief." *JAMA* 297, no. 7: 716–23.

Marcus, George E., W. Russell Neuman, and Michael MacKuen. 2000. *Affective Intelligence and Political Judgment*. Chicago: University of Chicago Press.

Marcus, Sara. 2023. *Political Disappointment.* Cambridge, MA: Harvard University Press.

Marczak, Michalina, Małgorzata Wierzba, Dominika Zaremba, Maria Kulesza, Jan Szczypiński, Bartosz Kossowski, Magdalena Budziszewska, Jarosław M. Michałowski, Christian A. Klöckner, and Artur Marchewka. 2023. "Beyond Climate Anxiety: Development and Validation of the Inventory of Climate Emotions (ICE): A Measure of Multiple Emotions Experienced in Relation to Climate Change." *Global Environmental Change* 83: 102764.

Marinovich, Greg, and Joao Silva. 2000. *The Bang-Bang Club: Snapshots from a Hidden War.* New York: Random House.

Martherus, James L., Andres G. Martinez, Paul K. Piff, and Alexander G. Theodoridis. 2021. "Party Animals? Extreme Partisan Polarization and Dehumanization." *Political Behavior* 43, no. 2: 517–40.

Martin, Ryan. 2016. "The Days After: Coping with Election Grief." *Psychology Today*, November 14, 2016.

Masket, Seth E. 2009. *No Middle Ground: How Informal Party Organizations Control Nominations and Polarize Legislatures.* Ann Arbor: University of Michigan Press.

Maxell, Carol J. C. 2002. *Pro-Life Activists in America: Meaning, Motivation, and Direct Action.* New York: Cambridge University Press.

Mazure, Carolyn M. 1998. "Life Stressors as Risk Factors in Depression." *Clinical Psychology: Science and Practice* 5, no. 3: 291–313.

McCarty, Nolan. 2015. "Reducing Polarization: Some Facts for Reformers." *University of Chicago Legal Forum* 9: 243–78.

McClendon, Gwyneth H. 2018. *Envy in Politics.* Princeton, NJ: Princeton University Press.

Mishra, Pankaj. 2017. *Age of Anger: A History of the Present.* New York: Macmillan.

Moagi, Miriam M., Anna E. van Der Wath, Priscilla M. Jiyane, and Richard S. Rikhotso. 2021. "Mental Health Challenges of Lesbian, Gay, Bisexual and Transgender People: An Integrated Literature Review." *Health SA Gesondheid* 26: 1487.

Moll, Clarissa. 2022. "How Shall We Now Grieve Abortion?" *Christianity Today*, May 13, 2022.

Nesse, R. M. 1999. "The Evolution of Hope and Despair." *Social Research* 66, no. 2: 429–69.

Neuman, W. Russell, George E. Marcus, Michael MacKuen, and Ann N. Crigler, eds. 2007. *The Affect Effect: Dynamics of Emotion in Political Thinking and Behavior.* Chicago: University of Chicago Press.

Nolen-Hoeksema, S. 1991. "Responses to Depression and Their Effects on the Duration of Depressive Episodes." *Journal of Abnormal Psychology* 100, no. 4: 569–82.

OECD. 2016. *Society at a Glance 2016: OEDC Social Indicators.* Paris: OECD.

Ojeda, Christopher. 2015. "Depression and Political Participation." *Social Science Quarterly* 96, no. 5: 1226–43.

Ojeda, Christopher, and Peter K Hatemi. 2015. "Accounting for the Child in the Transmission of Party Identification." *American Sociological Review* 80, no. 6: 1150–74.

Ortony, Andrew, Gerald L. Clore, and Allan Collins. 2022. *The Cognitive Structure of Emotions*. New York: Cambridge University Press.

Pacheco, Julianna Sandell, and Eric Plutzer. 2008. "Political Participation and Cumulative Disadvantage: The Impact of Economic and Social Hardship on Young Citizens." *Journal of Social Issues* 64, no. 3: 571–93.

Parker, Kim, Rich Morin, and Juliana Menasce Horowitz. 2019. "Looking to the Future, Public Sees an America in Decline on Many Fronts." Pew Research Center, March 21, 2019.

Parkes, C. 1972. *Bereavement: Studies in Grief in Adult Life*. London: Tavistock.

Patel, Vikram, Jonathan K. Burns, Monisha Dhingra, Leslie Tarver, Brandon A. Kohrt, and Crick Lund. 2018. "Income Inequality and Depression: A Systematic Review and Meta-Analysis of the Association and a Scoping Review of Mechanisms." *World Psychiatry* 17, no. 1: 76–89.

Pearlman, Wendy. 2016. "Narratives of Fear in Syria." *Perspectives on Politics* 14, no. 1: 21–37.

Perry, Tod. 2021. "Teen Kicked Out by Her Parents for Political Activism: Outs Them as Violent Capitol Rioters." *Upworthy*, January 12, 2021.

Petersen, Michael Bang, Joshua M. Tybur, and Patrick A. Stewart. 2020. "Disgust and Political Attitudes: Guest Editors' Introduction to the Special Issue." *Politics and the Life Sciences* 39, no. 2: 129–34.

Pew Research Center. 2012. "Partisan Polarization Surges in Bush, Obama Years." Pewresearch.org, June 4, 2012.

———. 2019. "Partisan Antipathy: More Intense, More Personal." Pewresearch.org, October 10, 2019.

———. 2022. "As Partisan Hostility Grows, Signs of Frustration with the Two-Party System." Pewresearch.org, August 9, 2022.

Phoenix, Davin. 2019. *The Anger Gap: How Race Shapes Emotions in Public*. New York: Cambridge University Press.

Pierce, Lamar, Todd Rogers, and Jason A. Snyder. 2016. "Losing Hurts: The Happiness Impact of Partisan Electoral Loss." *Journal of Experimental Political Science* 3, no. 1: 44–59.

Porat, Roni, Maya Tamir, Michael J. A. Wohl, Tamar Gur, and Eran Halperin. 2019. "Motivated Emotion and the Rally around the Flag Effect: Liberals Are Motivated to Feel Collective Angst (like Conservatives) When Faced with Existential Threat." *Cognition & Emotion* 33, no. 3: 480–91.

Pretorius, Claudette, Derek Chambers, and David Coyle. 2019. "Young People's Online Help-Seeking and Mental Health Difficulties: Systematic Narrative Review." *Journal of Medical Internet Research* 21, no. 11: e13873.

Price, John. 1967. "The Dominance Hierarchy and the Evolution of Mental Illness." *Lancet* 290, no. 7509: 243–46.

Price, John, Leon Sloman, Russell Gardner, Paul Gilbert, and Peter Rohde. 1994. "The Social Competition Hypothesis of Depression." *British Journal of Psychiatry* 164, no. 3: 309–15.

Radcliff, Benjamin. 2013. *The Political Economy of Human Happiness: How Voters' Choices Determine the Quality of Life*. New York: Cambridge University Press.

Radloff, Lenore Sawyer. 1977. "The CES-D Scale: A Self-Report Depression Scale for Research in the General Population." *Applied Psychological Measurement* 1, no. 3: 385–401.

Rae, Nicol C. 2007. "Be Careful What You Wish for: The Rise of Responsible Parties in American National Politics." *Annual Review of Political Science* 10, no. 1: 169–91.

Ridley, Matthew, Gautam Rao, Frank Schilbach, and Vikram Patel. 2020. "Poverty, Depression, and Anxiety: Causal Evidence and Mechanisms." *Science* 370, no. 6522.

Rondón Bernard, José Eduardo. 2018. "Depression: A Review of Its Definition." *MOJ Addiction Medicine & Therapy* 5, no. 1.

Roseman, Ira. 1984. "Cognitive Determinants of Emotion: A Structural Theory." *Review of Personality and Social Psychology* 5: 11–36.

Roseman, Ira J. 1991. "Appraisal Determinants of Discrete Emotions." *Cognition & Emotion* 5, no. 3: 161–200.

Roseman, Ira J., Martin S Spindel, and Paul E. Jose. 1990. "Appraisals of Emotion-Eliciting Events: Testing a Theory of Discrete Emotions." *Journal of Personality and Social Psychology* 59, no. 5: 899–915.

Russell, Glenda. 2000. *Voted Out: The Psychological Consequences of Anti-Gay Politics*. New York: New York University Press.

Satcher, D. S. 2000. "Executive Summary: A Report of the Surgeon General on Mental Health." *Public Health Reports* 115, no. 1: 89–101.

Schattschneider, Elmer Eric. 1960. *The Semisovereign People: A Realist's View of Democracy in America*. New York: Holt, Rinehart, and Winston.

Scherer, Klaus R. 1997. "The Role of Culture in Emotion-Antecedent Appraisal." *Journal of Personality and Social Psychology* 73, no. 5: 902–22.

Schertz, Kathryn E., Sonya Sachdeva, Omid Kardan, Hiroki P. Kotabe, Kathleen L. Wolf, and Marc G. Berman. 2018. "A Thought in the Park: The Influence of Naturalness and Low-Level Visual Features on Expressed Thoughts." *Cognition* 174: 82–93.

Schwartz, Sarah E. O., Laelia Benoit, Susan Clayton, McKenna F. Parnes, Lance Swenson, and Sarah R. Lowe. 2022. "Climate Change Anxiety and Mental Health: Environmental Activism as Buffer." *Current Psychology*, 1–14.

Seligman, M. E. 1972. "Learned Helplessness." *Annual Review of Medicine* 23: 407–12.

Siemer, Matthias, Iris Mauss, and James J. Gross. 2007. "Same Situation–Different Emotions: How Appraisals Shape Our Emotions." *Emotion* 7, no. 3: 592–600.

Skinner, Ellen A., Kathleen Edge, Jeffrey Altman, and Hayley Sherwood. 2003. "Searching for the Structure of Coping: A Review and Critique of Category Systems for Classifying Ways of Coping." *Psychological Bulletin* 129, no. 2: 216–69.

Slone, Michelle, Debra Kaminer, and Kevin Durrheim. 2000. "The Contributions of Political Life Events to Psychological Distress among South African." *Political Psychology* 21, no. 3: 465–87.

Smith, Alex. 2021. "As Climate Worsens, Environmentalists Also Grapple with the Mental Toll of Activism." National Public Radio, November 13, 2021.

Smith, Craig A., and Phoebe C. Ellsworth. 1985. "Patterns of Cognitive Appraisal in Emotion." *Journal of Personality and Social Psychology* 48: 813–38.

Smith, Craig A., and Leslie D. Kirby. 2000. "Consequences Require Antecedents: Toward a Process Model of Emotion Elicitation." In *Feeling and Thinking: The Role of Affect in Social Cognition*, edited by Joseph P. Forgas, 83–106. New York: Cambridge University Press.

Smith, Kevin B., Matthew V. Hibbing, and John R. Hibbing. 2019. "Friends, Relatives, Sanity, and Health: The Costs of Politics." *PLOS ONE* 14, no. 9: e0221870.

Smith, Tiffany Watt. 2015. *The Book of Human Emotions*. London: Profile Books.

Smith, Tovia. 2020. "'Dude, I'm Done': When Politics Tears Families and Friendships Apart." National Public Radio, October, 27, 2020.

Sorkin, Amy Davidson. 2015. "Merkel and the Crying Girl: Five Lessons." *New Yorker*, July 21, 2015.

Spangler, Patricia, Barbara Thompson, Barbara Vivino, and Jacob Wolf. 2017. "Navigating the Minefield of Politics in the Therapy Session." *Psychotherapy Bulletin* 52, no. 4.

Stanley, Samantha K., Teaghan L. Hogg, Zoe Leviston, and Iain Walker. 2021. "From Anger to Action: Differential Impacts of Eco-Anxiety, Eco-Depression, and Eco-Anger on Climate Action and Wellbeing." *Journal of Climate Change and Health* 1: 100003.

Stone, Deborah. 2001. *Policy Paradox: The Art of Political Decision Making*. New York: W. W. Norton.

Taylor, Shelley E., and Annette L. Stanton. 2007. "Coping Resources, Coping Processes, and Mental Health." *Annual Review of Clinical Psychology* 3: 377–401.

Teasdale, John D. 1983. "Negative Thinking in Depression: Cause, Effect, or Reciprocal Relationship?" *Advances in Behaviour Research and Therapy* 5, no. 1: 3–25.

Thoits, Peggy A. 1995. "Stress, Coping, and Social Support Processes: Where Are We? What Next?" *Journal of Health and Social Behavior* 35: 53–79.

Valentino, Nicholas A., Krysha Gregorowicz, and Eric W. Groenendyk. 2009. "Efficacy, Emotions and the Habit of Participation." *Political Behavior* 31, no. 3: 307–30.

van den Bosch, Matilda, and Andreas Meyer-Lindenberg. 2019. "Environmental Exposures and Depression: Biological Mechanisms and Epidemiological Evidence." *Annual Review of Public Health* 40: 239–59.

van Deth, Jan W. 2014. "A Conceptual Map of Political Participation." *Acta Politica* 49, no. 3: 349–67.

Walsh, Katherine Cramer. 2003. *Talking about Politics: Informal Groups and Social Identity in American Life*. Studies in Communication, Media, and Public Opinion. Chicago: University of Chicago Press.

Walter, Amy. 2022. "Can Biden Improve His Grade with Democratic Voters?" *Cook Political Report*, March 4, 2022.

Watt, Douglas F., and Jaak Panksepp. 2009. "Depression: An Evolutionarily Conserved Mechanism to Terminate Separation Distress? A Review of Aminergic, Peptidergic, and Neural Network Perspectives." *Neuropsychoanalysis* 11, no. 1: 7–51.

Webster, Steve W. 2020. *American Rage: How Anger Shapes Our Politics*. New York: Cambridge University Press.

White, Bradley Patrick, Nadia N. Abuelezam, Holly B. Fontenot, and Corrine Y. Jurgens. 2023. "Exploring Relationships Between State-Level LGBTQ Inclusivity and BRFSS Indicators of Mental Health and Risk Behaviors: A Secondary Analysis." *Journal of the American Psychiatric Nurses Association* 29, no. 3: 224–31.

Whitesell, Anne. 2023. "Frame Extension among Pro-Life Groups." In *Annual Meeting of the Midwest Political Science Association*. Chicago: Midwest Political Science Association.

Woods, Michael. 2017. *Emotional and Sectional Conflict in the Antebellum United States*. New York: Cambridge University Press.

World Health Organization. N.d. "Stress." https://www.who.int/news-room/questions-and-answers/item/stress.

Wortman, C. B., and R. C. Silver. 1989. "The Myths of Coping with Loss." *Journal of Consulting and Clinical Psychology* 57, no. 3: 349–57.

Yan, Brandon W., Renee Y. Hsia, Victoria Yeung, and Frank A. Sloan. 2021. "Changes in Mental Health Following the 2016 Presidential Election." *Journal of General Internal Medicine* 36, no. 1: 170–77.

Zaharna, Mia, and Henry I. Miller. 2017. "Politics-Related Depression: Is It Real?" *National Review*, March 3, 2017.

# Index

Page numbers in italics refer to figures and tables.

Aaron, Kevin, 137–38
abortion, 124–29
activism, 137–39
*Affect Effect, The*, 141
*Affective Intelligence and Political Judgment*, 39
Albertson, Bethany, 40
Albrecht, Glenn, 135
Alternative für Deutschland (AfD), 117
Amendment 2 (Colorado), 120, 123
American Political Science Association (APSA), 100
American Psychiatric Association, 4, 71
Anderson, Christopher, 94
Anderson, John, 79
anger (in politics), 32
anxiety, 32
*Anxious Politics* (Albertson & Gadarian), 40
appraisals: appraisal process, 35; appraisal structure of depression, 37–38; appraisal structure of emotions in politics, 39–41, *40*; definition of, 8, 33–34, 144; emotional, 33–34, 195n3; loss and, 36–37, 144; primary appraisal, 34; secondary appraisal, 34; studies about, 35. *See also* irrevocability; stress-appraisal-coping framework
Aristotle, 141
Arnold, Magna, 36–37
"Ascent of Man" (image), 101
Associated Press, 5
*Atlantic*, 32
*Atmos*, 138
Azari, Julia, 89

"Be Careful What You Wish For" (Rae), 101
Behavioral Risk Factor Surveillance Survey (BRFSS), 87–88, 121, 176–81, *178–81*
Bench, Shane, 39
Biden, Joe, 1–2, 59, 84–86, 95
Blackington, Courtney, 124
Blais, Andre, 94
Blitzer, Nate, 77
Boehner, John, 33
*Boston Globe*, 124
Bowlby, John, 20, 196n1
Bowler, Shaun, 94
Brazile, Donna, 79
Breyer, Stephen, 125
British Household Panel Survey (BHPS), 104–7, *106*, 186–90, *187–90*
British party system, 104–5
Brouillette, Richard, 72
Bundestag, 117
Business Insider, 79

capital punishment, 141
Carsey, Thomas, 101
Carter, Kevin, 58–59
CBS, 127
Center for Epidemiologic Studies Depression Scale, 6
Chandler, David, 98
*Christianity Today*, 128
climate change, 134–39
climate distress, 136
Clinton, Hillary, 32, 77–78, 80–81, 89–90

Clore, Gerald, 38
CNN, 77
Cohen, Judith Blackfield, 17
Collins, Allan, 38
competition (in politics), 27
Conway, Claudia, 96
Cook Political Report, 1
Cooperative Election Study, 25, 53–55, 84, 85, 155
coping: coping behaviors, 60; coping strategies, *61*, 61–62, 64–66; definition of, 8, 60, 198n1; democratic citizenship and, 76; depression and, 38, 63–64, *69*, 145; effectiveness of, 62–63; politics and, 9, 64–66, 145, 198n2; reappraisal process as, 65–66, 145–46; strategies recommended for politics, 71–75, *73*, 173–75, *174–76*; withdrawal as, 66, 70, 145. *See also* stress-appraisal-coping framework
Cornell University, 42, 82, 160
Cramer, Katherine J., 99
Crenshaw, Kimberlé, 98
Crigler, Ann, 141

*Daily, The* (*New York Times*), 70
Daily Stress Checklist, 21
*Dangerous Case of Donald Trump, The: 27 Psychiatrists and Mental Health Experts Assess a President* (Lee), 71
Darwin, Charles, 20
death. *See* loss
democracy: avoiding effects of echo chambers on, 116; coping strategies and, 76; depression and, 3, 9–11; elections and, 94–95; personalization of politics and, 97–98, 100; polarization and, 100–101; process preference of, 26
depression: abortion policies and, 124–29; attachment theory of, 20; cataclysmic phenomena and, 17–18; causes of, 6–9; climate change policies and, 134–39; cycle of, 64; definition of, 4–6, 196n5; demobilization effect of, 10–11; democracy and, 9–10; evolutionary theories of, 21; failed activism and, 137–39; generalized depression, 6, 84–86, *85*; LGBTQ policies and, 119–24, *122*, *179*, 179–81, *180–81*; localization of problems and, 38; major depressive disorder, 4–5, 195n1; object-specific depression, 5; other emotions and, 38–39; policies and, 12; political cycle of depression, 3; politics as a cause of, 7–9, 11–12, 17–18, *47*, *55*, 56, 102–3, 149–50; related feelings of, 6; social competition/rank theory of, 20, 197n4; social risk theory of, 20, 197n4; study of politics and, 142–43; therapies for, 12–13; welfare policies and, 129–34, *132–33*, 184–86, *185*. *See also* appraisals; coping; feelings; loss; polarization (of politics); politics; stressors/stress
*Diagnostics and Statistics Manual V* (APA), 4
disappointment, 1–2, 6, 43–48, *47*, 147. *See also* feelings
disposition system, 39
*Dobbs v. Jackson*, 124–29, 144
Donovan, Todd, 94
Douthat, Ross, 1
Driscoll, Daniel, 139

Ekman, Paul, 146, 195n2
elections: British party system, 104–5; depression and, 93–95, *94*; election-depression scope conditions, 80–82; electoral loss, 79–80; electoral loss and generalized depression, 84–86, *85*; Netherlands electoral system for, 91–93, *93*; social identity and, 87–91
Electoral College, 81
emotional regulation, 64, 198n1. *See also* coping
*Emotions*, 34
Esping-Anderson, Gøsta, 9
European Social Survey, 131, 181–86, *182–83*, *185*, 201n1

*Fact Magazine*, 71
fear. *See* anxiety
feelings: family of feelings, 4–6, 36–37, 146–47, 195n2; functions of, 11. *See also* depression
Feinberg, Matthew, 76
"Fighting with a Family Member Over Politics? Try These 4 Steps" (*Time*), 96
*FiveThirtyEight*, 77
Folkman, Susan, 7, 62, 196n6
Ford, Brett, 76
Fox News, 2
fractionalization, 104–7, *106*
Freud, Sigmund, 18–19, 24, 36

Frijda, Nico, 38
Funes, Yessenia, 138

Gadarian, Shana, 40
George Mason University, 136
Goldberg, Michelle, 142
Goldwater, Barry, 71
"Goldwater Rule," 71
Gore, Al, 79
Gossen, Herman, 24–25
grief. *See* loss
Gross, James, 34, 64, 195n3
*Guardian*, 89, 138

Hammen, Constance, 22
Hanisch, Carol, 97–98
Hannity, Sean, 2
Hari, Johann, 134
Harrington, Michael, 149
Harris, Kamala, 89–90
Hatzenbuehler, Mark, 120–21
Hibbing, John, 96
Hibbing, Matthew, 96
Hidaka, Brandon, 7
Horowitz, Allan, 4
Horowitz, Juliana Menasce, 101
*Human Dimension of Depression, The* (Kantor), 23

immigration, 117–18
income inequality, 129–34, *132–33*
*Inside Out* (Pixar), 63
irrevocability: appraisals of irrevocability in politics, 41–42, 144; impact of irrevocable loss and gains on emotions, *51*, 51–52; loss and, 36–39, 53–55, *54*; in politics, 39–42, 54–55, *55*, 145. *See also* loss
*I Think You're Wrong (But I'm Listening)* (podcast), 96

Johnson, Lyndon, 32
Joseph, Penial E., 89

Kagan, Elena, 125
Kahneman, Daniel, 25
Kaiser Family Foundation, 124
Kalmus, Peter, 138
Kamer, Tweede, 91
Kantor, Martin, 23–24
Kirby, Leslie, 35

Klein, Melanie, 36
Kübler-Ross, Elisabeth, 19, 36, 196n1

La Ganga, Maria, 79
*Lancet Planet Health*, 137
Landman, Todd, 26
Landwehr, Claudia, 66, 144
Lauth, Hans-Joachim, 26
Layman, Geoffrey, 101
Lazarus, Richard, 7, 17, 34, 37–38, 196n6
Lee, Brandy X., 71
Lench, Heather, 39
"Letter to the Losers" (Brazile), 79
Levine, Linda, 79
Lieberman, Jeffrey, 71
Life Events Checklist, 21
Lincoln, Abraham, 146
Listhaug, Ola, 94
*Los Angeles Times*, 79
*Loser's Consent, The* (Anderson et al.), 94
loss: aversion, 25; components of, *23*; definition of, 23–24, 143; depression and, 18–22, 36–39, 143–44; failed collection action and, 30–31; goals and, 24, 38; grief as, 18–19, 196n1; impact loss and gains on emotions, *50*; irrevocable loss, 36–37, 39, 48–52, *50–51*, 53–54, *54*, 136–37; lack and, 24, 27; memory and, 29–30; in politics, 7–8, 17–18, 24–31, 143–45, 197n6; public policy and, 28–29, 125–28; social life and, 29; stress and, 21–22; value and, 24–25. *See also* depression; irrevocability; stressors/stress
*Lost Connections* (Hari), 134

MacKuen, Michael, 39, 141
Marcus, George, 39, 141
Marcus, Sara, 145
Mauss, Iris, 34
Mazure, Carolyn, 22
McCain, John, 95
McConnell, Mitch, 1–2
McGovern, George, 79
melancholia, 19. *See also* loss
Merkel, Angela, 117–18
Meyer-Lindenberg, Andreas, 134
Moll, Clarissa, 128
Mondale, Walter, 95
Moskowitz, Judith Tedlie, 62
mourning, 19. *See also* loss

*Mourning and Melancholia* (Freud), 19
Munoz, Ricardo, 64

National Longitudinal Survey of Youth, 107–10, *109*, 190–93, *192*
National Public Radio (NPR), 96, 137
*National Review*, 142
Nesse, Randolph, 21, 63
Netherlands electoral system, 91–93, *93*
Neuman, W. Russell, 39, 141
*New York Times*, 1, 70, 77, 90, 117, 126, 142
Nixon, Richard, 149
Nolen-Hoeksema, Susan, 64

Obama, Barack, 80–81, 89
*Obergefell v. Hodges*, 119–24, *122*, *179*, 179–81, *180–82*
*On Death & Dying* (Kübler-Ross), 19
Ortony, Andrew, 38

Palin, Sarah, 89–90
partisan bonding, 102–3
partisan bridging, 102–3
partisan strength, 104–5
Perot, Ross, 79, 81
"Personal Is Political, The" (Hanisch), 98
Pew Research Center, 80, 82, 101–2, 117
Pierce, Lamar, 80
Pixar, 63
*Planned Parenthood v. Casey*, 126–27
polarization (of politics): background of, 100–101; dehumanization and, 101; democracy and, 100–101; depolarization, 116; depression and, 102–10, *106–7*, *109*, 149–50; partisan animosity and, 101, 115; partisanship and, 101; personalization of politics and, 102–3; social supports for effects on relationships and, 110–16, 201n3. *See also* politics
*Political Disappointment* (Marcus), 145
politics: echo chamber and, 115–16; emotional regulation and, 64; emotions related to, *43*; feelings reported in polls about, 46–48, *47*; importance of loser's consent in, 94–95; irrevocability in, 39–42, 54–55, *55*, 145; loss in, 7–8, 17–18, 24–31, 143–45, 197n6; mental health profession and, 71–72; personal relationships and, 96–100; power in, 97; study of depression and, 141–43; topics in polls about,

44–46. *See also* coping; democracy; depression; polarization (of politics); study design
preferences (in politics), 26–27, 197n4. *See also* loss
Price, John, 20
"Progress on a Cognitive-Motivational-Relational Theory of Emotion" (Lazarus), 34
Proposition 8 (California), 116
*Prozac Nation* (Wertzel), 4
*Psychology Today*, 79, 154, 173
*Psychotherapy Bulletin*, 71
public policies: climate change and, 134–39; *Dobbs v. Jackson*, 124–29; *Obergefell v. Hodges*, 119–24, *122*; redistributive policy, 129–34, *132–33*

Rae, Nicol, 101
Reagan, Stephanie, 96
Resilient Activist, The, 138
*Roe v. Wade*, 124–28
Rogers, Todd, 80
Romney, Mitt, 80–81
Rondón Bernard, José Eduardo, 4
Roseman, Ira, 35, 37–38
Royal Society for the Arts (RSA), 98
ruminative responses (to depression), 64
Russell, Glenda, 120, 123

sadness, 37–38, 63–64
Sahwil, Reem, 118
"Same Situation-Different Emotions: How Appraisals Shape Our Emotions," 34
Satcher, David, 13
scarcity, 26–27, 143, 197n5. *See also* loss
Schattschneider, E. E., 41
Scherer, Klaus, 38
Scott, Rick, 1–2
Seligman, Martin, 19, 139
Siemer, Matthias, 34
Silva, João, 58
Silver, Nate, 77
Skinner, B. F., 19
Smith, Craig, 35
Smith, Kevin, 96
Snyder, Jason, 80
Social Brain Project (RSA), 98
Social Readjustment Rating Scale, 21
solastalgia, 135–37

Sotomayor, Sonia, 125
Standardized World Income Inequality Database, 131
*Stress, Appraisal, and Coping* (Lazarus & Folkman), 7
stress-appraisal-coping framework: overview of, 7, 7–9; political polarization and, 102–3; response of, 146; as scope conditions, 147–49. *See also* appraisals; coping; stressors/stress
stressors/stress: definition of, 8, 196n6, 197n3; depression and, 17, 143; measurements of, 21; terms used in research about, 21–22; types & examples of, 22. *See also* depression; loss; stress-appraisal-coping framework
study design: analysis of BRFSS for social identity and electoral loss, 87–91, 176–78, *178*, 199–200nn2–4; analysis of poll results about politics and depression, 42–48; conclusions drawn from, 142–43; data from CES for electoral loss and depression connection, 84–86, *85*, 158–60; election poll evidence of electoral loss and depression, 82–84, *83*, 160–63, *161*; European Social Survey for electoral-depression connections, 91–93, *93*, 182–84, *183*, 200n5; evidence from BHPS to study impact of polarization on depression, 104–7, *106*, 186–90, *187–90*, 200–201nn1–2; evidence from CES to understand loss and depression, 53–55, *54–55*, 155–58, *157–58*; evidence from surveys of youth to study impact of polarization on depression, 107–10, *109*, 190–93, *192*; Google Trends to study election-depression connection, 86–87, *88*; implications for future research, 144–47; measurement of depression, 5–6; overview of data sources used in, *14*; questions addressed by, 3; for the relationship between depression and political participation, 66–70, *67–69*, 168–73, *170*, *172*, 198n3; for the relationship between politics and depression, 13–15; scope conditions, 147–49; scope of election-depression results, *93*; survey results studying connection between politics and irrevocable loss, 48–52, *50–51*, *161*, 164–68, *166–68*, 198nn1–3. *See also* politics
surveillance system, 39

*Talking about Politics* (Cramer), 99
Teasdale, John, 64
Thunberg, Greta, 137–38
Tibbett, Thomas, 39
*Time*, 96
"Toward a More Responsible Two-Party System" (APSA), 100
Trump, Donald, 1–2, 32, 71, 77–80, 84–86, 90, 95
Tversky, Amos, 25

United States Center for Disease Control, 87, 129
Upworthy, 97
*USA Today*, 96

van den Bosch, Matilda, 134
Vietnam War, 149
*Voted Out: The Psychological Consequences of Anti-Gay Politics* (Russell), 120

Wakefield, Jerome, 4
*Wall Street Journal*, 1
*Washington Post*, 1
Wertzel, Elizabeth, 4
"Why Therapists Should Talk Politics" (Brouillette), 72
Woods, Michael, 146
World Economic Forum, 137

Yale University, 136